The First Session
with Substance Abusers

Nicholas A. Cummings
Janet L. Cummings

Jeanne Albronda Heaton
Series Editor

The First Session with Substance Abusers

A Step-by-Step Guide

JOSSEY-BASS
A Wiley Company
San Francisco

Jossey-Bass books and products are available through most bookstores. To contact Jossey-Bass directly, call (888) 378–2537, fax to (800) 605–2665, or visit our website at www.josseybass.com.

Substantial discounts on bulk quantities of Jossey-Bass books are available to corporations, professional associations, and other organizations. For details and discount information, contact the special sales department at Jossey-Bass.

 Manufactured in the United States of America on Lyons Falls Turin Book. This paper is acid-free and 100 percent totally chlorine-free.

Library of Congress Cataloging-in-Publication Data

Cummings, Nicholas A.
  The first session with substance abusers : a step-by-step guide / Nicholas A. Cummings, Janet L. Cummings.
    p. cm.
  Includes bibliographical references (p.) and index.
  ISBN 0-7879-4933-7 (acid-free paper)
  1. Substance abuse—Treatment. 2. Addicts—Psychology. I. Cummings, Janet L. II. Title.
RC564 .C86 2000
616.86'0651—dc21   00-008844

FIRST EDITION
HB Printing   10 9 8 7 6 5 4 3 2 1

Contents

*To Eldon, disbarred attorney, on the landmark
of your forty-first year of sobriety. Even though you are
now elderly and frail, you will never be forgotten
by the scores of clean and sober persons whom you
sponsored during the past four decades.*

*To Carolynne, surgical nurse, on your twenty-fifth year
of being clean, because you had to beat a severe sexual addiction
before you could maintain your sobriety. You became
a role model for women seeking their freedom.*

*To Willie, twice-incarcerated heroin, alcohol, and
cocaine "speedballer." In the twenty years you have
been clean and out of prison, you created an innovative,
effective program for violent, addicted ex-felons,
who have learned by becoming clean that they were also
freed from their own violent behavior.*

Foreword

Much has changed over the thirty years that I have been a clinician, supervisor, teacher, and student of psychotherapy. Therapy is briefer, more people have access to help, psychotropic medications are more effective, and the stigma associated with psychological help has decreased.

One issue, however, remains constant: therapists have always known that the first session is crucial for both emergency intervention and beginning the process of change. Current mental health practice, moreover, renders the first session even more preeminent, since managed care and insurance benefits are limited and the nature of treatment has focused more on problem solving and short-term goals. In fact, 40 percent of all psychotherapy clients today attend only a single session, and the rest typically have four or five meetings.[1]

As therapists we know that we must use the first session to[2]

- Establish a relationship and working alliance

- Assess the need for crisis intervention

- Evaluate presenting problems and establish a diagnosis

- Explore emotions

- Focus the problem(s)

- Reach mutual agreement on what needs to be done

- Explore options for solution (one of the alternatives may be to continue therapy)

Consequently, the First Session Series has been launched with full appreciation for the magnitude of accomplishing these goals in a single session. Likewise, this series is also intended to demonstrate sensitivity and respect for the diversity of background, culture, and experience of clients we hope to serve.

Much can be said for the generic skills necessary for a successful first session, but most therapists are aware of the necessity of customizing our interventions to the specific needs of our clients. What we need to know for a successful first session with a teenager may be very different from what we need to know for a septuagenarian. Consequently, this series provides students, educators, and practitioners with essential knowledge of how to enrich existing therapeutic skill with specific information fine-tuned to meet the demands of diverse populations.

In denial about what's wrong, substance abusers present with all sorts of issues designed to mask the "real" problem. Nick and Janet Cummings bring clarity and practical experience to bear on unearthing these complex problems during the first session. They provide readers with the background necessary to understand how substance abusers trick not only themselves, their families, their friends, and their employers but also the therapists trying to help them recover. This father-daughter team lifts the fog of misinformation, bringing us the wisdom of years of experience as well as up-to-date information on the complex interplay of social, physiological, and psychological forces influencing addiction. In a down-to-earth and practical way, the authors inform us about the ploys addicts inevitably use during first sessions while at the same time giving us the antidote—thoughtful clinical strategies designed to motivate addicts into successful treatment. Throughout the book, readers are taught to recognize their own enabling behaviors and to replace these misguided techniques with procedures that disarm addicts right from the first encounter.

Discovering how basic therapeutic skills must be adapted to meet the needs of substance abusers is likely to inspire therapists to learn more about enhancing the effectiveness of their first sessions with other populations they serve. Additional titles in this series provide the culturally competent direction necessary to facilitate first sessions with other groups that also require special sensitivity, including older adults, adolescents, and African Americans. With each new book in this series, we hope to provide not only a greater understanding of your clients as a special group but also more compassion for the unique qualities of each individual. And finally, we hope that the wisdom, experience, techniques, and strategies our authors provide will enhance the overall effectiveness of each first session.

April 2000   Jeanne Albronda Heaton
Athens, Ohio

Notes

1. Kleinke, C. L. (1994). *Common principles of psychotherapy*. Pacific Grove, CA: Brooks-Cole.

2. Sue, S., Zane, N., & Young, K. (1994). Research on psychotherapy with culturally diverse populations. In A. Bergin & S. L. Garfield (Eds.), *Handbook of psychotherapy and behavior change* (4th ed., pp. 783–817) New York: Wiley.

The First Session
with Substance Abusers

Introduction

Why devote an entire book to the first interview with the substance abusing patient? Because no other behavioral health problem is less often correctly identified on the first interview than that of substance abuse. Let us look for a moment on the sad facts: substance abusers are in denial, and most behavioral health specialists inadvertently buy into that denial.

Most substance abusers present themselves on the first interview as suffering from marital or job stress. They frequently complain of exhaustion, but fail to mention that the exhaustion comes from having repeatedly to go to work after having done alcohol or drugs for most of the night. They also say they suffer from "frazzled nerves," their own common name for one of the side effects of prolonged chemical abuse. Unfortunately, because psychotherapists are trained to look for and address stressors in the patient's life, the interviewer most often does not challenge the patient's denial and instead begins treatment for everything but the real problem.

The smaller number of chemically dependent patients who admit to such a problem in the first interview are those whose substance abuse has already been identified by spouse, lover, family, employer, friends, police, or the courts. They have either been coerced into coming in or are attempting to delay the world's exasperated, inevitably punitive response to their behavior. Even so, these patients who admit chemical dependency are there to appease and manipulate the environment and are no less in denial than the majority who never mention their alcohol or drug propensities.

The addict's first order of business is to fool the interviewer and enlist her as an ally. Surveys reveal that more often than not the therapist offers treatment other than a direct address of the addiction, much to the delight of the patient, who rewards the therapist with all kinds of "important" psychological morsels to chew on during successive sessions. Patient and therapist are now doing what is most comfortable for both. But even with this unconscious catering to the patient's denial, only 20 percent of patients who have an initial session ever go on to treatment of any kind.[1]

The facts get even more dismal. Of those 20 percent of presenting chemically dependent patients who eventually do enter treatment following the first interview, only one-quarter begin treatment for substance abuse; three-quarters receive treatment for the rationalized problem.[2] It gets worse: only two-fifths of the aforementioned one-quarter (in other words, 2 percent of the total number of people who attended one session) commit to altering their chemically dependent lifestyles as a therapeutic goal, even though these patients admit they are "hooked."[3] The patient's hope that he will become a "social user" is a form of denial that the therapist must constantly counteract, yet most therapists hold out that hope. Is it any wonder that once a patient finally enters a treatment program and seriously grapples with reaching sobriety and maintaining it, we find she has been in unsuccessful treatment several times before?

This book is designed to help you increase your recognition rate and, even more important, your success rate in motivating the substance abuser to become a patient who addresses for the first time the real problem in her life. It is intended for counselors, social workers, pastors, psychologists, and psychiatrists—in short, all who see patients with behavioral problems. Even if you do not think you see chemically dependent patients, you are probably seeing them without knowing it. Today chemical dependency is so ubiquitous in behavioral care that addiction is the primary problem, or alcohol or drugs are exacerbating the primary problem, of 40 to 45 percent of all patients seen.[4]

You save lives by correctly labeling a substance abuse problem during an initial session. The suicide rate among substance abusers is the highest of any group of patients; in addition, many suicides occur following a period of "self-medication" for severe psychiatric problems other than primary substance abuse.[5] As one depressed patient who miraculously survived a serious suicide attempt later noted, "Dying as the solution looks awfully good when you're bombed out of your skull." This truism is especially relevant to adolescents, whose suicide rate is essentially driven by drugs, cult music, and peer pressure, all often converging at a fortuitous moment of group intoxication.

What we have to say is based on over half a century of clinical experience in the trenches with substance abusers. Although we know the research literature and we are solidly grounded in it, we will not bore you with research findings, and we will quote statistics sparingly and only when necessary to make a clinical point. The senior author has written his share of erudite papers on the subject; unfortunately, profound tomes do not one good drug counselor make. Instead, we will walk you through the first session and what precedes it, winding with you through the complex labyrinth that every substance abuser will create for you during the first interview.

Most drug abuse counselors learned their skills and developed their understanding the hard way: as recovering addicts, they have been there! We both have a profound respect and admiration for anyone who is recovering. These individuals have been called on to go through a trying, painful, and engulfing experience that few of us have to go through. But we are not recovering substance abusers and are therefore suspect or second rate in the eyes of some counselors. In our own way, we have been there very vividly with our patients, through all of it, yet our nonaddicted status allowed us to participate with objectivity. Who are we, and how did we learn our skills and achieve our effectiveness with addictive problems?

We are clinical psychologists, father and daughter. We both treat substance abusers, not because we are desperate for clientele, but because we like them and genuinely enjoy working with them. I (Nick) have been treating substance abuse since the late 1940s, but without much success until the late 1950s. At first I hated working with addicts, but practicing in San Francisco, with its then very high alcoholism rate and its subsequent status as the birthplace of America's drug culture, made doing so unavoidable. Addicts' unrelenting deceit and manipulation put me off. When I was forced by career circumstances and my own clinical integrity to properly address issues of substance abuse, I discovered that what I had been calling countertransference was actually the result of my ineptitude. As I became increasingly adept at working with addictive problems, I recognized that substance abusers were not a therapist-frustrating breed of obstinate patients—they could be any one of us.

Anyone can become an addict, and the life of deceit that is so characteristic develops after the addiction. Would you believe that substance abusers are brighter than average (yes, it's true) and present challenges that are far more nimble than those of most patients? I learned the importance of confronting denial without being judgmental. I am challenged by the never-ending games addicts play but am more than compensated by never having to endure a dull moment. Even during their worst of times, addicts have a tremendous sense of humor, and with a therapist who understands them, they can laugh at their own plight when it is cleverly reframed. They are delightfully infuriating patients, but learning this was quite a journey for me.

During that journey, I made many mistakes and was conned innumerable times, but I spent hundreds of hours learning how not to make those same mistakes again. I helped bring back scores of overdosed or suicidal patients from the brink of death. A number of times I rushed an overdosed patient to the hospital in my own car, casting risk of malpractice suits aside, because the ambulance response would have been too late. More than once the patient lay with his head in my lap and, even though unconscious, was vomiting and spitting up blood all over me.

Literally thousands of times I have walked patients through severe withdrawal without the use of alleviating medication, an experience so horrible for them that their recovery is aided by the memory of it. I have been there with my patients in all of the chemical ugliness, and I have heard every excuse. On the rare occasion when a patient presents me with a form of denial I have never heard before, I jump out of my chair with delight, congratulating her on being so clever, and then we both are convulsed with the laughter of knowing. In spite of doing what needed to be done, often resorting to unorthodox methods, I have never had a malpractice suit in fifty years; patients know when we are really on their side. Eventually I was able to sort out all I had learned—both from my patients and from gifted practitioners who worked successfully with substance abusers—and put it into a cohesive approach.

I continued to like my patients and the challenges they presented, and I shared their joy in their recovery. My professional life, however, became painful again when the Haight-Ashbury culture was in full flower. Of course it was sad treating younger and younger patients with full-blown addictions. But my distress came from the realization that many of my colleagues were encouraging drug use among our youth because they themselves were duped into believing this was a newfound freedom and even mind expansion.

I shall never forget one Sunday morning when I went to the hospital emergency room in response to a routine admission late the night before. I had told my family I would be back for 10:00 A.M. brunch. However, there was an anti–Vietnam War protest march from the Ferry Building to Ocean Beach, a distance of about seven miles. As the crowd began to ascend the long, steep climb on that part of Geary Boulevard that passes by the Kaiser Hospital, the combination of LSD and hyperventilation had young people experiencing bad trips. The hospital overflowed with nearly three hundred patients. Fortunately, most could sit on the floor, and every nook and cranny was jammed with bodies. We requisitioned all the Thorazine we could get from surrounding hospitals and the pharmacies that were open on Sundays, as we had run out of our supply by 11:00 A.M. I spent hours talking the most severe patients through their bad trips, and I finally got home at midnight.

Shortly thereafter I wrote an article for one of our professional trade papers warning that Timothy Leary, the so-called high priest of LSD, might be right in predicting that America was to become a drug society.[6] It was scorned or at best ignored by most of my colleagues. One well-meaning but naive psychiatrist took time to reply in a letter to the editor. He asserted that negative drug reactions were not the property of the drug but rather that of unstable or "sick" individuals taking the drug.

The worst was to come when cocaine first became trendy in San Francisco in the late 1960s. Subsequently the National Institute for Drug Abuse (NIDA) stated that cocaine was not addictive, and quoted the American Medical Association as in agreement that it was not medically addictive.[7] I wrote to both NIDA and the AMA that no matter what the medical definition might be, there was a psychological addiction, and that cocaine was potentially our greatest problem to date. I had observed that the euphoria of cocaine was so short lived, the crash so uncomfortable, that the desire to repeat and repeat was compelling.

I received a polite response from the AMA pointing out that because I was not a physician I could not really understand addiction, and that medicine did not recognize psychological addiction. I also received a less polite letter from the director of NIDA stating that I was uninformed and should read the research literature that proved beyond a doubt that cocaine was not addictive. My second letter matched his in directness: I predicted that the day would come when he would lose his job because NIDA would have contributed to the impending epidemic of cocaine abuse. It was after the actor John Belushi overdosed in his dressing room with an eight-inch mound of high-grade cocaine on his coffee table that my prediction came true. I took no joy in it.

In 1977, the membership of the American Psychological Association (APA) elected me their president to take office in 1979. I spent the next three years visiting every state and large county psychological association and confirmed that, except for a few practitioners, neither psychologists nor social workers treated substance abuse. In fact, those practitioners who did were looked down upon as inferior and incapable of treating a more interesting and worthy clientele. I determined then that I would use my presidential address to make the treatment of chemical dependency a respectable therapeutic endeavor. Using the drug vernacular of the time, I played upon a biblical text and called my address "Turning Bread into Stones: Our Modern Anti-Miracle."[8] It was subsequently published in *American Psychologist*. Usually APA presidential addresses receive a few dozen requests for reprints. Mine had to be reprinted three times as the APA answered over seven thousand requests. The address worked. Behavioral health specialists began expanding their practices to address chemical dependency.

My satisfaction was short lived. Over the next two or three years, I watched with dismay as the standard treatment for substance abuse became the twenty-eight-day (hospital) inpatient program; many programs hospitalized the patient for as long as sixty to ninety days. Patients in a hospital haven't quit; they have been just temporarily cut off from their supply and have been given potent substitutes to keep them calm, comfortable, and docile while believing they are in full withdrawal. (Hey, withdrawal isn't so bad. What's all the fuss?)

Probably the most profound, early relevant experience of my (Nick's) life was meeting Bill Wilson, the founder of Alcoholics Anonymous (AA). This was while I was a teenager, long before I had ever considered a career as a psychologist. Bill, as he liked to be called in keeping with the policy of anonymity, founded AA in the 1930s and was largely ignored until *Readers Digest* published its landmark article in 1938. That catapulted the twelve-step movement into the spotlight. My father pointed the article out to me and said, "This man understands alcoholism more than the doctors."

A few weeks later, my father said to me that Bill Wilson was in our area and that he had called Bill and had made an appointment to take him to lunch. Did I wish to join them? I was only fifteen years old, but I jumped at the chance. I was expecting to meet a remarkable man, but I was not prepared for Bill Wilson's intensity and dedication. Even though my father was prominent in the community and I was only a teenager, Bill took time to talk directly with me, making certain I understood what he was saying. I was mesmerized. When I look back, I marvel how his intuitive and pragmatic, albeit crude, understanding of the physiological nature of addiction has stood the test of time, even without an inkling of our current knowledge of cellular biology.

I (Janet) grew up in San Francisco during the 1960s, as drug abuse became glamorous and increasingly touted by ostensibly intelligent psychologists and university professors. As a teenager who abstained from drugs, I found myself out of step with most of my peers and was derided for it. But I had seen and talked with my father's patients. I had sat through his addiction groups, and I had never met a heroin addict who had not first used marijuana in his eventual slide to addiction. So the belief that pot use did not lead to hard-core addictions, popular at the time, seemed naive and non-sensical. I was amazed that people age thirty could have done themselves in so fast that they looked many years older.

Without my father's knowledge and until he caught me, I would eavesdrop as he was on the telephone responding to inebriated and suicidal patients. Even though I was only eight years old, he explained that these conversations were private and very personal. He did allow me to ask questions, which he answered on a level I could understand. No matter how frequently his patients relapsed, he was always there for them. Seldom was he ever able to complete dinner without being called. I was also aware that he would call his heroin addicts every two hours all night long to talk and ease them through the "cold turkey" horror of withdrawal.

I recall one important early experience. Psychedelics ostensibly expanded one's consciousness. This was a generally held belief, yet my own impression in watching people who had dropped acid (LSD) or other hallucinogens was that their consciousness was narrowed. They focused on minutia with the illusion that these were expansive, and all the while they were missing or misinterpreting important stimuli and events. My father indicated that my observation was in agreement with his clinical findings, and both my observations and his findings were later confirmed by research. The earlier research, which had suggested that psychedelics improved mental performance, was measuring the results of the user's increased self-confidence when in a state of euphoria, before the "high" had proceeded to the "I-don't-give-damn" stage. That my observations were confirmed gave me confidence: drug abuse was understandable, but not only that—I could understand it, and this confidence most likely contributed to my decision to learn more by becoming a psychologist.

By the time I completed my doctoral training, I was very comfortable treating substance abuse. I had seen the futility of the drug treatment approach at the Veterans Administration hospital where I took a predoctoral placement. There was a cynicism in the way substance abuse treatment was conducted. The addicted veterans checked into the hospital for specified periods so that they could ensure the continuance of their disability pension. They had no intention of seriously participating in a drug program. Similarly, the staff did not expect to seriously treat them for chemical dependency. There seemed to be a tacit understanding that the system was there to (1) perpetuate the veteran's pension, and (2) fill enough beds to guarantee jobs for the staff.

I was assigned to assist the psychologist who daily conducted the addicts' three-hour group therapy session. Characteristically, the therapist glommed onto Mondays to discuss his own substance abuse problems that had occurred over the weekend. Tuesday through Friday he slept through the group, letting me act as group leader. Looking back I don't know which of his two behaviors I thought to be the most appalling. I took the assignment seriously and began to apply the approach I had learned from my father. Although the cards were stacked against any success, I was able to seriously engage some of the group members, and I was very proud that one made a commitment to a clean life.

I was pleased that on leaving the V.A. I could do my internship and postdoctoral fellowship at American Biodyne, where my father had established a national system treating 14.5 million enrollees in an approach that was abstinence based and effective. Following my internship and postdoctoral fellowship, I remained at American Biodyne in Arizona as a staff psychologist for a few years until the company was sold and the new management instituted a more traditional and far less effective treatment program.

Our approach is decidedly one of abstinence. Refraining from one's chemical is a condition for continuing treatment. Our mantra is that *all insight and understanding are soluble in alcohol or drugs*. In other words, indulging in one's chemical is so powerful a reinforcer that it will wipe out the beneficial effects of weeks and months of psychotherapy. Searching for the so-called psychological causes of one's addiction while continuing in the interim to ingest the addictive chemicals, all in the expectation that the craving will stop once either the proper psychodynamic is uncovered or the appropriate behavioral reconditioning has occurred, is a fantasy bound to disappoint both patient and therapist.

We also insist on a chemical-free withdrawal, as this is an experience the patient will neither forget nor wish to repeat by risking a relapse. There are, of course, exceptions. Some patients and some drugs need to be titrated, and it is necessary to hospitalize some patients to do so. We note these exceptions, but we strictly maintain the criteria for them so that the concept of abstinence for most patients is not undermined or diluted.

We must also explain two points of terminology. Throughout the book we use the term *patient* rather than the currently popular designation *client*. We have found that the latter term lets the substance abuser off the hook ("I am not an addicted patient in serious need of treatment") and helps them rationalize ("I am not addicted and only have psychological problems that need to be discovered and corrected"), thus subtly sabotaging treatment and subsequent recovery.

We also use the term *recovery* rather than *cure* inasmuch as there are cellular changes that render the addiction physiologically permanent, thus leaving the individual always just one step away from being once again enslaved by the offending chemical. The fact that the best treatment is psychological should not detract from the fact that we are dealing with molecular biology.

During the past decades, Nick has taught hundreds of practitioners how to be effective and actually enjoy treating the substance abuser. In more recent years, Janet has helped him in this training. Together we hope that the following pages will help you become more effective in the first session, where most chemically dependent patients are lost. You will note that we constantly interject humor in our treatment because laughter is healing, and in spite of the pain of shedding their denial, our patients have fun along with us. You will see that we laugh with our patients, never at them. In that vein, we ask that you, too, have fun as you read on.

April 2000   Nick and Janet Cummings
Scottsdale, Arizona

Notes

1. Falco, M. (1992). *The making of a drug-free America: Programs that work.* New York: Times Books.

2. Falco, *The making of a drug-free America.*

3. Falco, *The making of a drug-free America.*

4. U.S. Department of Labor. (1998). *Facts and figures about drugs and alcohol in the workplace.* Washington, DC: U.S. Department of Labor.

5. Minkoff, K., & Drake, R. E. (Eds.). (1991). *Dual diagnosis of major mental illness and substance disorder.* San Francisco: Jossey-Bass.

6. Cummings, N. A. (1975). *A survey of addictive characteristics of a random sampling of patients presenting themselves for psychotherapy.* San Francisco: Kaiser Permanente Health Plan News.

7. National Institute for Drug Abuse. (1975). *Nineteen seventy-five statistical report.* Washington, DC: Alcohol, Drug Abuse, and Mental Health Administration Clearinghouse.

8. Cummings, N. A. (1979). Turning bread into stones: Our modern anti-miracle. *American Psychologist, 34*(12), 1119–1129.

1

Who Is the Substance Abuser?

When asked who is the substance abuser, most people, including mental health professionals, readily conjure up stereotypical images:

The raucous middle-aged man with a big belly, bulbous nose, and pasty skin, reeking of alcohol

The furtive young grunge who is rushing the compact disc player he has just stolen to the nearest "shooting gallery" to exchange it for a fix

The streetwalker supporting her habit through prostitution

The inner-city youth who spends most of his time in a "crack house," wherever it might be this week, or "dealing" to the often well-dressed occupants of the cars that pull up to the curb where he stands every evening

The violent felon, twice imprisoned for assault, whose crime-ridden life is liberally laced with all kinds of drugs, as well as alcohol

The hard-core addict is easy to spot. Harder to spot but nevertheless more common is the substance abuser who is a next-door neighbor, a coworker, or even a colleague. Consider the case of Florence, who I (Nick) saw just two years ago.

Florence had a Ph.D. in social psychology and was a full professor at a prestigious university. She also was the principal investigator and project director of a brilliantly conceived and executed program for inner-city adolescent girls. She spent every Saturday morning on-site with her abused adolescents.

Recently, on the way to the center, which was in the heart of the inner city, she was severely beaten and robbed. Once out of the hospital, where she was treated for severe wounds and three broken bones, her doctors referred her for treatment of posttraumatic stress disorder (PTSD). She chose to see me, even though it meant traveling a considerable distance every week for her sessions.

It was obvious that she was a brilliant and compassionate psychologist, well deserving of the reputation she had in the field. I was initially quite taken with the way she spoke of her involvement in the amelioration of the severe abuse to which inner-city girls were subjected. And at first I admired how quickly she had returned to her Saturday work in the inner city. Her doing so was against all medical advice, as her injuries were not yet sufficiently healed.

Then I noted certain inconsistencies that jolted me out of my Mother Teresa countertransference. Her ready return to the inner city was not in keeping with her diagnosis of PTSD. She looked twenty years older than her age of fifty-four. Her skin had a distinct alcoholic pallor along with premature wrinkles. Her hands revealed a tremor in spite of her attempts to hide it by clasping them. Was Florence a substance abuser who already manifested organic signs?

Through a series of interviewing techniques based on the approach that we will discuss in later chapters, I learned that Florence used her weekly trips to the inner city as the opportunity to buy her week's supply of drugs. She lived alone, and every night she smoked crack. Then she would go to bed with a bottle of wine, a behavior known among addicts as sucking on a lemon. Having finished the wine, she would eventually fall asleep. But a stupor is not restful sleep, and the next morning Florence would "crank" herself with uppers (amphetamines) she had also purchased from her corner pusher.

I pointed out that for someone who was trying to improve the lot of people in the inner city, she was participating in one of its most unfortunate aspects. In full denial, Florence reminded me that she was an excellent social psychologist and understood too much about the problems to ever get addicted.

Florence heaped rationalizations upon each other with the intensity of one who must avoid facing the truth. I responded that I had read the story. It was called *Rain,* and it was written by W. Somerset Maugham. It was about a missionary who set about to save the soul of Sadie Thompson, a prostitute. Instead, he found himself partaking of the "sexual depravity" he had been condemning, and he took his own life. I asked if, indeed, she was not taking her own life little by little, the hard way.

Florence determined at that session to enter treatment and go clean. But it was not to be. Three days after our appointment, she was readmitted to the hospital, this time with advanced cirrhosis and pancreatitis, as well as other conditions, all related to her prolonged substance abuse. She died before I could see her again.

We purposely chose to present the case of Florence to demonstrate that the substance abuser not only may be anyone but also may be a person we like, respect, and admire. She may even be one of us.

ERRORS IN POINTS OF VIEW

Before looking extensively at the unlikely array of patients you will certainly see and, we hope, appropriately identify, it is important to see how the inherent biases of those people most involved result in their missing or purposely overlooking the chemical dependency surrounding us. Because of the issues hidden in these points of view, therapists are often thrown off the track and are thus prevented from providing useful help.

The Cultural Point of View: It's All Relative

In addition to differences among families in tolerance or acceptance of substance abuse, there are cultural differences in what is deemed OK. In the inner city, drugs are easier to obtain than bottled water, and children play while their single teenage mothers smoke crack. Children as young as eight are recruited as runners, and gang membership is a matter of survival. But our African American and Hispanic colleagues who work side-by-side with us treating substance abuse have made it very clear that factors stemming from poverty, resignation, or despair do not properly define a culture. They remind us that cultural tolerance in no way lessens the ravages of substance abuse on children and adults. We have relied on these colleagues to help us sift acceptable from unacceptable behavior in the light of cultural variables. But they have hammered into us over and over that when we are confronted by the denial of an addict, our need to confront that denial is necessarily ubiquitous—it knows no cultural boundaries. A therapist who holds the point of view that drug addiction differs according to culture or skin color can dilute and hamper the work he has to do.

True, there are cultural differences as to the definition of social use, but the patients who come to us have already slipped far down the slope of addiction, or they would not be seeing us. You must be cognizant that an addict will attempt to excuse his addiction by proffering the claim that his behavior is considered socially acceptable by his ethnic or cultural group. Our job is to treat addicts, not to engage in philosophical discussion of what is culturally or ethnically acceptable social behavior.

These considerations are integral to establishing a therapeutic alliance with the chemically dependent patient, and we will be discussing them in detail. In addition to the biases developed from our families and culture, there are other points of view that obscure what is happening in the first session.

The Patient's Point of View: It Ain't Me

To the patient, the addict is always the other guy. It is very interesting that when patients identify the other guy, they can be amazingly accurate. This is because those who are chemically dependent read a great deal on the subject (some are even reading this book) and understand it as only one who has been there can; but then they do two things, both of which they do well: (1) they project their knowledge onto those around them who are abusers, and (2) they bolster their own denial by comparing themselves to those exhibiting levels of addiction more advanced than their own. They thus succeed in avoiding even a modicum of self-understanding.

Friends, including behavioral health practitioners, are often startled when someone ostensibly close to them enters a drug rehabilitation program after years of chemical dependency unnoticed by anyone. They are even more startled when one or two in their circle enumerate accurately the telltale signs that had been present for months or years. Persons who had noticed may be skilled practitioners who understand addiction, or they are recovering addicts, but more often they are persons who are living in denial of their own addictive problem.

After Florence died, a member of her psychology faculty was outspoken in deriding his colleagues for having overlooked the signs that Florence had been exhibiting. Actually, Florence had kept her chemical abuse successfully hidden; nonetheless, he loudly proclaimed that had her colleagues been more vigilant, she might still be alive. Not quite a year later he was admitted to a drug rehab program for his own abuse of many years' standing. In having concentrated for years on Florence's subtle symptoms he had avoided looking at himself, and in deriding the faculty he may have been uttering his own unconscious plea for help.

When a substance abuser gets into trouble, she can always find another addict who is in even greater trouble, implying that it is the other person who is the addict, not she. If arrested for driving under the influence (DUI), there is the excuse, "I am not like the other people appearing before the court today who are here for the second or third DUI." When the second or third DUI arrest occurs, the excuse is, "I'm not the drunk who caused an accident or ran over a pedestrian." So pervasive is denial that every arresting officer jokes that all drunk driving can be explained by the universal lament, "Honest, offisher, I only had two beersh." (The person's blood alcohol level tells the true level of alcohol consumption, contradicting the legendary two beers.) Similarly, the person fired for being drunk or stoned on the job or for frequent absenteeism rationalizes, "At least I got another job right away, so I don't have a problem like the unemployed guy. I just had a boss who had it in for me." The "boss who had it in for me" excuse is good for a succession of job losses, up to and including the final one, after which the drunk or stoner is too far gone to get another job. Thereafter, he repeats over and over to anyone who will listen (usually his own inebriated friends) the story of the unfairness of that terrible last boss. Even now he is denying the problem!

In explaining how facile this denial can be, we can use the analogy of a person whose calorie craving has resulted in his being overweight, a very common phenomenon in American society. The woman who is obese will make certain there are no full-length mirrors in the house. By seeing only the reflection of her face, she can pretend she is only a little overweight. If when going by a large plate-glass window she inadvertently catches the reflection of her full body, she will experience initial shock at seeing her true girth. Then denial will resume, and she will remind herself that plate glass always distorts. A fat man sitting in a room when another obese man walks in will smirk to himself, "My belly isn't as big as that guy's." Actually, his is probably a lot bigger, and that is why he desperately needs the denial.

The Family's Point of View: Blame the Addict for All Trouble

Because a spouse or other family members are clamoring for treat-ment of the chemically dependent relative does not mean that they want the effective or appropriate treatment for that person. There are many exceptions, of course, but practitioners are amazed how often a family that is demanding treatment turns around and sabo-tages it when arrangements are made. A family member—especially the spouse, lover, or parent—is more often than not the patient's *enabler*, defined as the person who makes possible the continuation of the offender's addictive behavior. It is not uncommon for more than one member of the family, or even the entire family as a unit, to behave as enabler. Examples of enabling behavior abound.

An alcoholic in our program had been dry for six weeks when his spouse, who never drank, joined the Wine of the Month Club and received a case of fine wine early each month. She would open each case and array the bottles on a counter in the laundry room. By the third month, the patient, who had then been dry for over four months, unable to resist any longer, opened the first bottle and was within one day back to his previous binging behavior. The wife was furious; she complained to the therapist that treatment was not working and informed him she had no intention of paying the overdue bill for his services.

We were consulted by the juvenile court when a frequent school problem got out of control. A group of high school students were caught smoking pot a block from the school during the noon recess. They were suspended from school, and the matter was remanded to the juvenile authorities, as the inhabitants of the apartment building where this took place had called the police.

Along with their lawyers, the parents stormed the school and the officers, charging the authorities with everything from false arrest to brutality (one girl had tried to scratch the arresting officer's eyes and had to be restrained).

Schools and police know this scenario well in all of its variations, and they refer to it as the "everyone else but not *my* darling" syndrome. No wonder that Carroll O'Connor, the actor who lost a son to heroin, admonishes unequivocally, "Get between your child and drugs any way you can." There are certainly parents who do this, but the enabling parent is all too common today. Those parents who really want to respond appropriately may find it difficult in the current "blame the schools" climate. Psychotherapists need to be cognizant of the parents' plight and be prepared to assist sincere parents, especially when their tough love may be required.

There are principally two reasons for enabling behavior. The first is that the enabler has issues that require the continuation of the substance abuse on the part of the spouse, lover, parent, or child. These issues may range from a need for a feeling of safety—"he won't be able to leave me"—to a need to be in charge, which the addict's debility accords. When the situation gets out of control, the enabler seeks help for the addict but aborts that help just as soon as the status quo has been restored. The "Wine of the Month" case is such an example. The wife insisted her husband seek treatment when the alcoholic behavior resulted in his losing his job. After he had been sober long enough to obtain a new job, she sabotaged the treatment.

The need to maintain a family mythology is the second reason for enabling. Although the foregoing case of the outraged parents would fit into that definition, the family mythology is usually more pervasive, as the case of Megan illustrates.

Megan, a beautiful, classic blonde in her late twenties, was the second wife of a handsome, successful, and debonair middle-aged man,

Bob. There were two young children as beautiful as their parents, and the home was perfect and worthy of being featured in *House Beautiful*. Bob liked cocaine and had the income to indulge in it frequently. On occasion, and especially on weekends, he would mix cocaine (an upper) with alcohol (a downer), a form of "speedballing" that would result in abusive behavior; sometimes he would beat the children, but mostly he would batter his spouse.

Megan had a need to present an idyllic picture to her parents and to the world, and indeed, "perfect" was the word used by friends and others to describe this family. Megan created a family mythology to sustain the illusion. The children were indoctrinated with the excuse that Daddy worked hard and could not help "blowing off steam," and they were never, never to mention to anyone that Daddy hit them or their mother.

On one occasion, when Bob had battered her to the extent that make-up would not cover the bruises, Megan crashed the car into an abutment so that she could attribute the bruises to the automobile accident. The children dutifully maintained the family mythology, even after Bob overdosed and had to be hospitalized. Megan whisked him off to an expensive private rehab program in a distant city so that all could be hushed up.

Megan was an enabler, and she taught her children to be enablers. It was only after Bob died of an overdose that Megan was finally distraught enough to tell her therapist the truth. She had to grapple with the guilt that, perhaps, without her enabling behavior Bob might have had to get help before he eventually died of his abuse.

Whether family members are sincere or are enablers, they need to be involved in the substance abuser's treatment. We are often asked how one can tell the sincere family member from the enabler. This is difficult, because all family members are *sincerely in denial,* even the ones who are not the primary enablers. The primary enabler needs treatment to understand and change that behavior, and family members who are not enablers need help in addressing the guilt feelings stemming from their mistaken belief that they are causing the addictive behavior. The latter issue is very common for children of all ages (even after adulthood) who have been taught by an enabling parent to take responsibility for mom or dad's chemical dependency.

It is important that the enabler not be misdiagnosed as sincere, and vice versa, a differentiation that you cannot easily render without meticulous clinical consideration. A rule of thumb is to regard the family member or members who are making the most noise and avidly blaming the addict for everything as the most likely to emerge as primary enablers. The nonenablers are more circumspect and are likely to be as weary of the enablers as they are of the addict. The nonenablers do not need the addict in order to validate themselves, whereas this is the presenting issue with the noisy, complaining enablers. The enablers clamor, "I would be happier and more successful and would have no troubles," without the addict. These same enabling family members will be the first to "rescue" the addict from the therapy by sabotaging the treatment just as it begins to produce results. Without family involvement, few addicts succeed in treatment. So important is this consideration that we have devoted all of Chapter Eight to the enabler.

Probably the most frequently encountered family problem is that of spouses who have finally left their addict and have decided to rebuild their lives without him. There is a tendency to respond to the patient's plea and return to the marriage after too short a period of sobriety. The enabler will do so out of need to return to the halcyon days of a false but safe relationship; the sincere spouse will feel guilty that not to do so would jeopardize the spouse's recovery. Without counseling, both types of spouses will invariably make the wrong decision.

The second most frequently encountered family problem involves the exasperated parent or parents who have finally thrown out the adult child who is abusing drugs. The temptation to let the son or daughter prematurely return to the home with the first sign of recovery is intense. Probably these parents have been enablers all along, but in any case, the parents must be counseled that an important part of any person's recovery is for her to become self-supporting.

The Medical Point of View

To satisfy the medical definition of addiction there must be "physical cravings" on withdrawal, as manifested by an array of physical symptoms; withdrawal from opioids (for example, opium, its derivatives, and its synthetic variations: morphine, dilaudid, percodan, heroin, and so on) has always served as the model. This definition has proven not only inadequate but also unfortunate, in that it does not explain the severity of many addictions. It has led the medical profession and the public to believe that any substance that has not been declared medically addictive is not a matter of concern. As noted previously, the assurances by both the government and the medical profession lulled many into believing cocaine was not an addictive substance. History and clinical experience have demonstrated that faulty assurances coming from ostensible authorities served as an inadvertent and tragic impetus to the cocaine epidemic.

Historically, it would seem that under the medical definition, every substance is presumed nonaddictive until proven otherwise. Innocent until proven guilty is important in criminal justice; it is nonsensical in the physical world. This is not mere rhetoric, for every new sedative, pain reliever, or mind-altering drug that has become part of our pharmacopoeia was initially heralded as being nonaddictive and without side effects. In the absence of any evidence, it may be impossible to predict that something will be addictive, but there is also an overriding responsibility not to prematurely declare that something is nonaddictive. Time reveals the fallacy of such declarations as one by one, everything from benzodiazepines (for example, Valium) to methadone shows up on the street for sale to addicts who clamor for them. Even Ritalin, a stimulant prescribed and perhaps overprescribed for attention deficit disorder (ADD) and attention deficit hyperactivity disorder (ADHD), has a street value, and it is often peddled to middle schoolers by the very children for whom it is prescribed. These boys often manage to build up a stash that allows them to sell the surplus for as much as two and three dollars a tablet. Only time is necessary to reveal the consequences of continuing to assure the public that each new mind-altering drug is not addictive.

Of importance to you in the first session is to be mindful that a prescription drug, dispensed legally and responsibly, may have become an addictive substance with prolonged use. Too many therapists erroneously believe that prescription drugs are safe, when in fact there are far more people in the United States addicted to medically prescribed "safe" drugs than there are addicted to heroin, cocaine, and other illegal drugs combined.[1] Be wary of the patient who complains that only a certain drug is helpful; she may be addicted to that drug.

We have prepared Chapter Three to alert you in the first session to the kind of person most likely to become addicted to particular drugs. In addition, we have grouped drugs according to class; we do this because once a person is addicted to a drug, he is addicted to all drugs in that class. The medical profession is too often oblivious to this transfer to an addictive equivalent; physicians often use drugs of the same class as substitutes for another drug to which the patient was obviously addicted.

The Psychological Point of View

The psychological point of view that regards all addictions as being learned behaviors would seem to stand in direct contradiction to the medical point of view that insists in all cases that there be a physiological basis. To the behaviorist there are no "addictions" in the strict sense, as the behaviors so labeled are really habituations that can be unlearned. Treatment, therefore, is reconditioning, deconditioning, negative response extinction, or whatever term might be applicable to explain the unlearning.

Under discussion here are not the excellent behavioral techniques being used in rehab programs that respect the physiological aspects of substance abuse, but rather those approaches that deny cellular changes in addiction and offer the patient the hope of becoming a "controlled" drinker. This term seems in itself to be an oxymoron, for the only persons who count drinks and are obsessed with controlling their ingestion of alcohol are the alcoholics, who invariably lose count and, therefore, control.

Most of us were trained in the context of the psychological definition of addiction, and as such are prey even before the first session to the patient's insistence and belief that she can, with a little help from us, succeed in restoring chemical equilibrium. Throughout this book we caution you against espousing a purely psychological model of substance abuse. It is as seductive to the psychologist as the solely medical model is to the physician.

It is the ubiquitous fantasy of substance abusers that they can become "social" users, and they really do not need a misleading psychological theory to bolster their denial of the importance of abstinence. We recall a patient who had been through three unsuccessful controlled drinking programs before entering our program. He was doing well, and he had been abstinent for over seven weeks. Then he missed the evening group in the eighth week. He telephoned two days later, stating he had been practicing his controlled drinking when somehow he seemed to have forgotten a lesson or two and found himself "unexpectedly drunk" for several days.

A PRAGMATIC POINT OF VIEW

Both the medical and psychological models are important in the treatment of substance abuse, but only in combination with each other, not singly. In this section we look at such a combined model, pragmatic and effective, that we have developed and employed successfully for more than thirty years.

The Substance Abuse Practitioner's Point of View: A Synthesis

There are life experiences and cultural influences that provide the learned aspects of substance abuse, and, as will be shown in the next chapter, there are cellular changes in the body of the substance abuser over time that are the physiological basis for the insatiable craving and the pain on withdrawal. Pragmatically, it is often impossible to separate the two components of addiction. Which is the most important? One might as well ask, What is more important when measuring area, length or width? Clearly it is impossible to answer the question as posited, but one can look at individual rectangles and discern that some are long on length and short on width, making the answer for that particular rectangle apparent. There are all manner of rectangles, with varying degrees of length in relation to width, just as there are variations among addicts: some are more influenced by physiology, others more influenced by learning. But let us make no mistake: in every rectangle there is both length and width, and in every addict there are both biological and psychological determinants.

One needs only to stay up one night with a heroin addict who is withdrawing and who is doing it "cold turkey," observing the suffering from both profuse diarrhea and vomiting as well as severely alternating chills and sweat, to be convinced of the physical aspects of withdrawal. Yet denial, which is the most universal and pervasive feature of all addictions, is a psychological phenomenon, as are the effective therapeutic interventions that lead to recovery. Further, the ongoing determination to stay clean (abstinent), known among recovering addicts as surrender, is also a psychological process.

What Do the Numbers Say?

In Chapter Two, we will look at the specifics of drug addiction, including drug preferences, as well as genetic, in utero (prenatal), and environmental-cultural contributors, and finally look at special populations. First, it might be helpful to look at the statistics, enabling the reader to appreciate the specifics of abuse and their extent in the total population.

According to NIDA and the National Institute on Alcoholism and Alcohol Abuse (NIAA), substance abuse is all around us and in a variety of forms. Thirty-five million Americans abuse alcohol, and approximately half that, seventeen million, abuse marijuana. A startling forty million abuse legal drugs, both prescription and over-the-counter varieties. There are three million heroin addicts, and, following a period when heroin addiction was declining, it is once again on the increase. There are four million persons regularly abusing cocaine or crack cocaine, and five million regularly abuse amphetamines (methamphetamines, crystal meth, and so on). Eleven million regularly abuse barbiturates.[2]

Do not attempt to add these up, as there is considerable overlap. Polydrug abuse is the order of the day. Exact numbers are hard to come by, but estimates place chemical dependency in America at a low figure of 15 percent of the total population and a high figure of 20 percent. This means that one in six or one in five Americans is a substance abuser. It bears repeating that 40 to 45 percent of all persons seen by behavioral health specialists have substance abuse problems: either they are addicted, or substance abuse is exacerbating a primary psychological condition.[3] In either case, the substance abuse needs to be addressed as part of treatment. Yet most practitioners rarely address chemical dependency problems, or they take the approach that with continued psychotherapy the chemical dependency will evaporate. Look over your treatment load. In how many cases might you have failed to identify substance abuse? Can you do better?

Perhaps the most significant statistic from NIDA and NIAA is that 71 percent of substance abusers are employed. This means that most will have health insurance, and almost all are potentially in your treatment room, now or in the future. Only 21 percent of substance abusers are unemployed, marginally employed, homeless, or in prison.[4] Under Medicaid even many of these are potentially your patients.

Think for a moment of the implications for your practice. If approximately thirty-five to forty million Americans are addicted, and 71 percent of these are employed and have health insurance, approximately one in three of the patients who walk into your office are likely to be addicted if you only see patients with employer health insurance, or almost one in two if you see persons covered by Medicaid, Social Security Disability, and Medicare. Are you identifying a number even close to that figure? How many addicts are you failing to even suspect, much less identify?

Who Is the Pusher?

No discussion of the addict would be complete without looking at the question of who is the pusher. For the most part the pusher and the user are one and the same. This means that both the addict and the pusher are sitting unidentified in your office. You will never see the drug lord or the mafioso, the ultimate supplier, who is far removed from the grubby level of hard-core addiction. It is the addict sitting unidentified in your office who, in order to pay for his habit, is forced to become a dealer in drugs. Each addict-dealer obtains a supply, takes out what he needs for personal use, then "steps on" (dilutes) the remainder, which he then sells. The purity or potency of the chemical depends on how often it has been stepped on before the present buyer acquires it. Those far down on the chain are getting low-grade drugs, and when they are lucky enough to get their hands on high-grade heroin, for example, merely taking the usual dosage results in an overdose because of the difference in potency.

It is not unusual that a patient referred to you has been charged with "possession with the intent to sell." The individual may be a stockbroker in an Armani suit, so unlikely to be a pusher that you accept the patient's protestations that this is a mistake. Yet every brokerage house, large law office, and factory—and every other conceivable employment setting—has its addict pusher. You will be referred a twelve-year-old boy who has been accused of selling Ritalin on the school grounds. The parents are outraged, the boy looks angelic, and in your mind you dismiss the allegations as a mistake. Be reminded that nearly a third of the Ritalin prescribed to school children is being resold by these same children.[5] Many of our schools are awash in recycled Ritalin, and the parents are the last to know it.

The images of the crack dealer standing on the corner in the inner city, the "needle man" (heroin dispenser) in the shooting gallery, the "clerk" in the crack house, the outlaw motorcycle gang peddling speed (amphetamines), the furtive grunge lurking near the school, and the "pizza man" who makes the rounds in an unmarked, nondescript old van are the ones that most persons associate with the pusher. If these are the people you are looking for, you are unlikely to see them in your office.

Most large workplaces have at least one employee from whom drugs are readily available, and these are often trusted employers or even members of the executive suite. We have treated a number of highly successful executives and professionals who had introduced cocaine into their law firm, advertising agency, or brokerage house as a way of supporting their own several-hundred-dollars-a-day addiction. One beautiful and hard-driving account executive confessed after her fall to poverty and disgrace that while she was on top, her money went for cocaine, fast cars, and fast men, in that order, all of which had to be supported by peddling cocaine to her coworkers. But even simpler than that, everyone has an acquaintance who is known for being able to obtain for his friends "whatever candy you want."

With all due respect to the medical profession, the pusher is sometimes as close as the kindly physician who has the reputation among users as a "script doctor." These script doctors, although in the minority, are still all too common, and they are well known to addicts through their underground. There are three types. The first is the well-meaning physician who wants to alleviate all pain and discomfort. This physician overly prescribes pain killers, sleeping pills, and other mind-altering drugs; he is too naive to realize that the addict is the one who always comes in requesting a specific drug and is obtaining prescriptions from a number of other physicians so that no one physician is aware of the extent of the medications the patient is receiving.

The second type of script doctor is the "impaired" (addicted) physician, who because of her own chemical dependency cannot stand to see someone "strung out" (in withdrawal). Addicts present themselves feigning far greater discomfort than they actually feel, easily obtaining a legal prescription to carry them until they can obtain their illegal drug of choice.

The third type is the unscrupulous physician who is actually illegally trafficking in legal drugs. Because he is issuing an enormous number of prescriptions, this physician needs a "cover," such as a specialization in weight reduction, thus ostensibly explaining the large number of daily prescriptions issued for amphetamines. A variation on this unscrupulous type is the physician who purposely addicts the patient so that thereafter this patient is a source of a steady income stream.

In your first session with a patient, be alert when you find out that the person is the patient of any of the foregoing types of physicians. These doctors are well known in the medical community but characteristically ignored by a profession that is reluctant to report a colleague who is suspect.

I (Nick) was the psychologist who was impaneled to treat most impaired physicians in my community. In that role, I saw the unfortunate and the cynical, but I knew when my physician patients were truly in recovery: they no longer overly prescribed to their own patients. My worst experience was the demise of a close friend, a prominent psychiatrist and a past president of the American Psychiatric Association. He was accused by a number of women of having addicted them with weekly intravenous injections of barbiturates (for example, sodium amytal), thus tying them to his expensive practice in perpetuity. They further accused him of raping them while they were under the "twilight sleep" of the drug, which caused me to wonder if he suffered from his own drug-impaired judgment.

I will never know the full story because my friend and colleague denied the charges, but rather than sustaining a hearing by the medical board, he forfeited his license. He was not able to stem the tide of notorious publicity, casting embarrassment on all of us in the behavioral health professions. Of the unfortunately too many times that drug addiction or drug pushing among colleagues has come to my attention, this case is among the saddest for me because of the respect I had for this man's contributions and stature in the field. It remains a constant reminder of how easy it is to miss the problem of substance abuse, especially in the first session.

Notes

1. Schuckit, M. A. (1989). *Drug and alcohol abuse: A clinical guide to diagnosis and treatment.* (3rd ed.). New York: Plenum Medical Book Company.

2. National Institute on Drug Abuse and National Institute on Alcohol and Alcohol Abuse (1999). *NIDA and NIAA 1998 statistics.* Rockville, MD: NIDA and NIAA Publication and Distribution Centers; also see the following websites: http://www.nia.nih.gov and http://www.nida.nih.gov.

3. Falco, M. (1992). *The making of a drug-free America: Programs that work.* New York: Times Books.

4. U.S. Department of Labor (1998). *Facts and figures about drugs and alcohol in the workplace.* Washington, DC: U.S. Department of Labor.

5. Moore, T. J. (1998). *Prescription for disaster.* New York: Simon & Schuster.

2

Presenting Problems
Different Tugs from Different Drugs

M ost psychotherapists, particularly clinicians trained in the behavioral treatment of chemical dependency, know little or nothing about the properties of specific drugs and how they affect different individuals. This lack of information leaves therapists vulnerable to the patient's denial, resulting in a psychological diagnosis that completely overlooks the addiction. There are telltale signs of addiction that are present in the first session but are missed because the psychotherapist does not know what to look for and what to ask about. Which of the following statements are true, and which are false?

It is impossible to hide drug abuse from a knowledgeable clinician.

Addiction results in permanent physiological changes that are forever discernible.

Drug preference varies according to gender, ethnicity, and socioeconomic status.

Drug addiction can include the medication the doctor gives as a substitute.

It is possible to reveal the addiction on the first session in spite of the patient's denial.

Addiction is always to the same family or class of drugs.

Addicts can have a preference for a drug even before they have tried it.

Children can be born addicted.

If you answered that each of these statements is true, you are correct. But do you know why each is true, and what to look for in your patients that would reveal what you need to know about that patient within the first session? As we have discussed, substance abuse is widespread in American society. However, when it comes to chemical dependency, one size does not fit all. People have individual, gender-based, cultural, and age-related preferences, tolerances, and susceptibilities. These are so varied, yet so understandable, that knowledge of them gives you a road map to your patients' addictions; these addictions will be glaringly obvious during the first session if you have this knowledge.

Behavioral health practitioners are startled when they realize what a broad scope of chemicals is available for someone to abuse, but this large smorgasbord does not seem to be enough for many abusers. There are "cookers" (underground chemists) busily turning out designer drugs; these drugs are constantly altered in different ways by each cooker, so that the person ingesting designer drugs has no way of knowing what might be the effects of the latest chemical alteration. Yet designer drugs have no end of buyers, in spite of the buyers' awareness that they may be the first to try this new batch. It is interesting that the users of designer drugs are often young people who are otherwise fanatic regarding what they put in their mouths—living as vegetarians who eat only organic foods and are so strict about this that they drink only bottled water. The paradoxes of substance abuse are remarkable!

A BRIEF PSYCHOPHYSIOLOGY
OF ADDICTION

Before getting into the specifics of substance abuse, we think it is important for you to have some understanding of the interplay between the physiology and psychology of chemical dependency. This understanding will alert you to what you can expect to see in the first session, but even more important, what these observations mean for treatment. Understanding the road to addiction, or specifically how people get hooked, gives you the key to how to begin unhooking them.

As a knowledgeable clinician, you can be of far more help to your patients. Simply explaining the addictive craving, its permanency, and what can be done about it gives the patient courage in the first session to go ahead with treatment. Explaining to the patient that he became addicted during his mother's pregnancy because she was ingesting that particular drug makes the remarkable specificity of that addiction understandable and the need for abstinence from the drug acceptable. Being able to give the physiological reason why switching from alcohol to Xanax will not help someone's addiction may be just the precise information the addict needs in the first session for her to decide in favor of psychotherapy instead of medication.

As we will discuss in the following sections, there are specifically three bases of addiction, even though most often they can be separated only theoretically: (1) genetic, (2) in utero (prenatal), and (3) environmental.

Genetic Influences

The genetic mapping of addictions is in its infancy (alcoholism having received most of the initial attention by molecular biologists). It is a difficult process inasmuch as there is not simply one gene marker or even a series of gene markers, but rather a complex array of genetic factors interacting with each other as well as with the environment. The determination of genetic factors in your patient will craft what information you give. It is not only incompetent but also cruel to promise social use to a patient whose addiction is genetically influenced.

One genetic factor is well known and can serve as an example. In metabolizing alcohol, the first step is the transformation of the alcohol molecule into acetaldehyde. This is accomplished by the body's alcohol dehydrogenase enzyme. Interestingly, acetaldehyde is even more intoxicating than alcohol. Most individuals transform the alcohol into acetaldehyde at a steady and timely rate, so they feel the intoxication early on. For them there is an early perception of the effects of the alcohol (blurred vision, unsteady gait, slurring), which results in the signal "I have had enough." Some individuals, however, have a genetically determined slower-acting variety of the alcohol dehydrogenase enzyme. These individuals drink and drink without feeling the effects, only to have large quantities of alcohol suddenly converted to acetaldehyde, with the result that they are now very drunk. We have all known this type of person without knowing there is a genetic basis.

The important consideration for you is that such individuals have a ten times greater chance of becoming alcoholics. This genetic predisposition is found most commonly among Native Americans, where one out of every seven individuals has the slower-acting variety of the alcohol dehydrogenase enzyme, the highest proportion yet discovered among any group. But looking at the predisposition alone does not take into account the influences of environment. What if such a person were born into a home where the family is Seventh-day Adventist or Mormon, religions that forbid alcohol? No matter what a person's genetic background, if she has never tasted alcohol, she is less likely to become alcoholic. However, teetotalers with the genetic predisposition will rapidly manifest addiction if they abandon their religious prohibition.

Prenatal Influences

It has long been known that children born of heroin- or crack-addicted mothers are heavily addicted at birth and have to undergo withdrawal. This addiction is in addition to other physical and mental consequences and even abnormalities. One of the earliest findings of the methadone programs created by the federal government in the 1970s for heroin addicts was that not only were the babies of women in these programs born addicted to methadone, but the physical and mental ravages they suffered were worse than those seen with heroin babies.

All addictive drugs are addictive to the fetus. The fetus is unable to metabolize chemicals on its own; the substance must eventually leave the fetus and be metabolized by the mother. In addition, even small amounts are relatively enormous to the tiny fetus. These two factors together result in rapid, deep-seated fetal addiction. This is true of all addictive chemicals, many of which have been extensively studied in their prenatal effects.

The best known of these effects is fetal alcohol syndrome (FAS), the most common chemically induced birth anomaly, which surprisingly continues to be missed in its less flagrant form (known as fetal alcohol effects, or FAE) in many child guidance clinics. The number of FAS and FAE children continues to grow because most mothers and many physicians believe that small amounts of alcohol ingested by the pregnant woman are harmless to the fetus. This is not only untrue, but the younger the fetus, the more significant the resulting FAS. Even in cases where prenatal exposure to alcohol has produced no other discernible anomalies, the individual so exposed will nonetheless be at increased risk for alcoholism.

Armed with this knowledge, you will develop sensitive antenna that will look for substance abuse when the first-time patient is pregnant. The misinformation that the placenta and amniotic sack protect the fetus from chemicals ingested by the mother is just that—misinformation. Even more alarming is how widely believed this falsehood is among women and—more amazing—many professionals. But even those who know better seldom ask a pregnant patient about substance abuse.

Once you have determined that your pregnant patient is chemically dependent, immediate referral for prenatal care is mandatory. The care must include immediate detoxification and withdrawal. You may, and even should, work with the prenatal program during the duration of the pregnancy and even beyond.

You must remember that even after the newborn is withdrawn from the chemical to which it was addicted prenatally, it is latently addicted to that chemical for life. Thus, a child born of a heroin-addicted mother, once he ingests heroin again, be it at age eleven or thirty, is instantly readdicted. The physiological reason for this will be described later in this chapter.

Environmental Influences

Environmental influences on both physiology and psychology are ever-present, but not always apparent. For example, a chronic depression may have its roots in genetics, such as unipolar depressive disorder, but the psychological solution chosen by such an individual may be to seek euphoria. This is often accomplished in childhood through thrill-seeking behavior until the individual in adolescence discovers the euphoria produced by cocaine. The type of cocaine to which such an individual may become addicted will vary with the environment in which the person lives. The inner-city youth will most likely prefer crack cocaine because of its relatively low price and easy availability, whereas the suburban professional will choose powdered cocaine in spite of higher cost because of its purity and stronger effect. In this illustration physiology (genetic depression) has led to a psychological behavior (thrill seeking) which, in turn, is replaced by a chemical addiction whose type is influenced by environment. Similarly, environment can interplay with physiology and psychology, with the result that a class of drugs (uppers, downers, and so on) may become the specific addiction for an individual.

The earlier in life that a person is exposed to an addictive substance, the stronger the likelihood of addiction. This is true not only because peer pressure is greater in youth but also because psychological reinforcement has a more pronounced influence in the growing organism.[2] Furthermore, the individual does not become addicted to just the drug to which she has been exposed but to the entire class of which the drug is a member. For example, the alcoholic is not merely addicted to alcohol but to an entire class of substances known as central nervous system (CNS) depressants. When an alcoholic is exposed to another CNS depressant (for example, benzodiazepines, barbiturates), he is already addicted to that substance. This phenomenon explains why it is a fallacy that chemical dependency can be cured by substituting a substance that is interchangeable in the addictive process. The chemical dependency in such instances is continuous and uninterrupted.

Psychological reinforcement is well known to behavioral health professionals, who tend to focus more on psychological and environmental factors than on genetic and prenatal factors. The peer pressure in adolescence to experiment with alcohol and drugs is alarming, but augmenting this are parental indifference and cultural influences. Parents who in the 1970s were highly involved in the drug culture of the time are ambivalent about confronting the problem with their children. Also potent factors are the ubiquitous drug abuse found amid the poverty and unemployment of the inner city, and the example offered by families in which the parents do drugs in front of the children. In the Irish culture, the son is not regarded as a man until he can drink heavily. The Jewish culture, in contrast, regards heavy drinking as disgusting. (Years ago, when one of the authors diagnosed the alcoholism of the president of a local Jewish congregation, the rabbi telephoned, chastising the psychologist with the pronouncement, "There are no Jewish alcoholics!") More recently, the university has developed a culture wherein 44 percent of college students don't just drink but binge drink.[3] Examples of environmental reinforcement abound.

In assessing the relative importance of biology versus psychology, we must recall our analogy of the rectangle, which is always dependent on both length and width for its area. With particular individuals, we can often discern the relative importance of either biology or psychology, but in most instances, making such a determination is never as simple as calculating area. What is critical for you is to appreciate the importance of both factors, to understand how each is addressed differently in the first session and in subsequent treatment, and to ensure that neither is allowed to become part of the patient's incessant denial.

Physical Alterations

Very few counselors or psychotherapists are aware that brain cells experience permanent changes in response to physiologically addictive substances. Three essentially irreversible changes take place in the body:

1. The body ceases to produce naturally occurring antianxiety and antidepressant chemicals.
2. Brain cells are permanently altered to respond to the same substance in the future.
3. The liver is altered and may be damaged permanently.

Let us look at each of these changes in more detail, as they will determine much of the course of the first and subsequent sessions.

1. *The body gradually ceases production of antianxiety and antidepressant substances.* In the same way that a healthy thyroid will cease to excrete thyroxin if oral thyroid medication is taken over time, the brain behaves as though there is no longer a reason to produce

enkephalins, endorphins, and dynorphans, because the drugs are replicating these substances and thus rendering them redundant. This is especially true for narcotics, and the effect is in a sense permanent. It may be six months to a year after withdrawal that a patient's natural substances are again produced in normal amounts, and this is a trying time, as the patient is without both these natural enzymes and her ingested chemical.

Those working with addicts know that heroin addicts are not to be trusted until after a year of being clean, and alcoholics in Alcoholics Anonymous (AA) are called "babies" until the second year. The risk of relapse is greatest during this period when the abstinent patient is without any buffer. Finally the body begins to produce the natural substances, but any subsequent use of the addictive chemical results in an immediate (rather than gradual) decrease and halt in their production. The sooner the reexposure to the addictive substance after withdrawal, the more dramatic the immediate decrease and halt in the production of the body's (and especially the brain's) natural chemicals. Furthermore, the younger the addict, the more dramatic the halt in production. The tragedy is especially severe for children, whose natural chemical production has not yet matured. It takes a considerable overcoming of the turbulence of adolescence before the body's own mechanisms, both physiological and psychological, have matured. Unfortunately, teenage drug users are skipping their adolescence, with lifelong consequences.

2. *Brain cells affected by addictive substances are designated to respond to the same substance in the future.* This is nature's way of neutralizing an exogenous or poisonous substance: converting it to a necessity. The committed cells do their job well, and for life will crave the substance to which they were designated to respond. As the individual continues abusing, he requires more and more of the substance to produce the "high" (euphoria), because the responding cells are doing their job of neutralizing the chemical. Eventually the increasing number of cells involved will require the addict

to ingest quantities of the drug that originally would have resulted in an overdose. This all-important phenomenon is known as drug *tolerance;* once established, it never diminishes. An addict can be chemical free for ten years, but if he resumes the substance abuse, within days his body's level of tolerance will return to the level that was originally achieved over a period of years. Alcoholics who had built up to a quart of whisky a day are surprised to find that even after fifteen years of abstinence, if they start drinking again they require that quart a day within a week or two. Heroin addicts who undergo detox to bring their habit down to a manageable cost are disappointed. Their $300-a-day habit returns within days.

People trying to lose weight experience what also could be called tolerance. Once an adipose (fat) cell has been formed in the body, it never goes away. The cell deprived of calories will lose its mass but will never lose its cellular structure, including its nucleus. This cell remains empty. (Picture a box of one hundred sandwich bags. That box can be held in the palm of one's hand. But fill each bag with a sandwich, and it will require the entire kitchen floor to display the result. Removing the sandwich is like the adipose cell losing its fat; the now flat bag remains.) Demonstrating the propensity of all cells to survive, the fat cell thereafter craves calories and will usurp calories out of the usual assimilation sequence in order to restore itself. This is why obese persons who have lost weight complain that it takes fewer calories for them to get fat again than it takes thin persons to gain weight in the first place. Eventually, if the person has changed eating and exercise habits for the better, the craving abates, but it never completely disappears. Given one extensive calorie binge, the cells seem to come alive with a full-blown craving.

3. *The liver is altered and often permanently damaged.* The process of converting a chemical from a poisonous to a neutral or useful substance occurs in the liver. In these metabolic processes, many addictive drugs are converted from physiologically damaging chemicals with few or no psychoactive properties into psychoactive substances that are less damaging to bodily organs. It must be emphasized again

that the cells designated to do this job will forever want to do their job, and they crave the opportunity to metabolize a particular drug. Furthermore, with continuing abuse, the liver is overworked, rendering the addict susceptible to cirrhosis and other forms of liver disease.

Can There Be Nondrug Addiction?

A controversy rages among the experts over whether "compulsions" for something other than a chemical can be addictive. In recent years there has been a proliferation of activities labeled by therapists as being addictive. These range from compulsive gambling and compulsive shopping to compulsive sexual activity. More recently the public has been bombarded by articles in the popular media that have heralded video game addiction and even Internet addiction. Recently a woman arrested for credit card fraud claimed the defense of Beanie Baby addiction. She claimed she was so compelled to acquire all Beanie Baby dolls, including the rare and expensive ones, that she was driven to fraudulently use other people's credit card numbers to satisfy her craving.

There is no question but that the concept of addiction can be expanded to ridiculous proportions. However, there is now evidence that there can be nondrug addictions that have a previously unrecognized strong physiological component.[4] During the "rush" (excitement of anticipating and then engaging in the behavior), epinephrine, also known as adrenalin, and norepinephrine are at high levels, and endorphins and enkephalins are released. It is likely that serotonin levels are also elevated at this time. Much of the "addiction" is to the chemicals that the body itself generates. The obvious psychological reinforcers, such as a big win for the compulsive gambler, are also pertinent. Clearly these addictions are in some measure truly chemical; however, the self-generated chemicals may in considerable measure be a triggered response to habituated psychological factors that preceded the eventual chemical reinforcement.

Compulsive gambling and compulsive eating can not only invoke certain physiological effects (the rush of epinephrine for the former, anxiety-sedating effects for the latter) that are addictive, but they can be substituted for the primary addiction in an individual who has become abstinent. Recovering alcoholics are highly susceptible to gambling as a replacement, whereas recovering barbiturate addicts readily replace their drug with food. These two nondrug addictions can also serve as addictions without any other form of addiction preceding or accompanying them. They demonstrate the compelling physiological and psychological cravings that accompany drug addictions. Furthermore, they are treatable through the same approaches that are effective with alcohol and drug addictions, with abstinence being the key for successful recovery. However, many so-called addictions in the popular press (for example, to sex, shopping, video, and the Internet) that have also gained acceptance by some professionals still lack evidence of a strong physiological base. The criterion that cellular change accompanies psychological reinforcement in a true addiction is a credible threshold that so far only compulsive gambling and compulsive eating have convincingly demonstrated. The more fanciful addictions (shopping, video, Internet) seem to be avoidance mechanisms, whereas sex addiction is found in individuals who demonstrate a wide variety of psychological problems.

From the treatment perspective, the "chicken-or-egg" question has yet to be answered, if, indeed, there is an answer. From your standpoint, the important consideration is that of treatment. There is overwhelming evidence that there are lifelong cellular changes that render the abstinent addict just one step away from relapsing into the highest level of tolerance achieved. This seems to be true for compulsive gambling as well as alcoholism, for in time all addictions respond to abstinence with a reduction of the craving that compels the addict to swallow, inject, smoke, inhale, or snort whatever is his or her "bag" (preferred substance).

LET'S LOOK AT THE BAGS

In this section we will discuss the substances that are frequently abused; some of these are legal, others illegal, but all are readily found on the street. The drugs are presented by class, for as we have already mentioned, addiction to one drug easily generalizes to the drugs belonging to the same class. We only briefly address the mechanism by which each drug acts in the body, so as to give you a thumbnail sketch. There are ethnic, cultural, class, gender, and age differences in the choice of drugs (an individual's bag), and although there are distinct trends, you also must remember that there are many surprising exceptions to these modal choices.

It is important to always remember that there is not a single premorbid addictive personality, so do not look for one. The ubiquitous lying, cheating, rationalizing, and conning are manifestations of the addiction. Valuable information can be derived from understanding the bags, so along with typical users, we will describe typical presentations on the first interview.

Uppers (Stimulants)

Drugs used as stimulants primarily affect users by heightening their sensitivity to all forms of stimulation. Consequently users experience grandiose expectations of themselves and others, they overreact to minor events, and they experience intense preoccupation with irrelevant details. We will look at both cocaine and amphetamines.

The primary mechanism of *cocaine (crack, snow, snort, nose candy, powder)* is a short-acting but powerful inhibitor of dopamine and of norepinephrine reuptake. Because cocaine is short acting, users need to frequently readminister the drug, which can be snorted, injected, or smoked (freebased). The euphoria likely results from the norepinephrine (NE) system, inasmuch as reuptake blocking causes increased active levels of NE. The "crash" results from the exhaustion of the NE system, which results in drastically reduced levels of active NE. The combination of relatively brief euphoria followed by a severe crash makes repetition compelling and exacerbates the addictive process.

The typical users of crack cocaine are persons of lower socioeconomic status (often minorities) because it is inexpensive and easily available in the inner city. Its low cost per "hit" is deceptive because users require multiple hits to sustain the high and avoid the crash. Consequently, a crack habit is ultimately a very expensive one.

When an addict becomes successful and leaves the inner city, as is the case of high-paid athletes, for example, the drug of choice almost overnight becomes the more expensive higher-grade cocaine. It is also a common drug of choice for hard-driving, successful (at least until cocaine takes its toll) yuppies who need to always be at their peak of energy and performance. Cocaine is also the drug of choice for those suffering from chronic depression that began in childhood and results in an adult who consistently feels "wooden." These individuals state in treatment that cocaine made them feel alive. Finally, it may come as a surprise to you that cocaine is a common drug of choice for adults who in childhood were erroneously given Ritalin or other stimulant medications for misdiagnosed ADD or ADHD.

When you see a cocaine addict for the first time, you will find his talkativeness striking. In spite of their running chatter, coke addicts do not say much of importance. If pressed for the presenting problem, they readily blame the other guy for their troubles. The addicts who are snorting rather than shooting will have the telltale runny nose. But the primary thing to look for is the patient's sheer and absolute grandiosity. The expansiveness and bragging rolls off the patient's tongue without much restraint.

The opposite will be true if the patient is crashing. There will be a profound depression in which all the vegetative signs are of recent origin. It is as if the patient woke up one or two days ago, suddenly feeling depressed and suicidal. Real depression does not hit that suddenly; when you are confronted with lack of a genuine presenting problem, coupled with either grandiosity or sudden depression, cocaine addiction is likely.

The primary mechanism of *amphetamines (speed, uppers, meth, crystal, crank;* archaic: *reds, black beauties)* is to release newly synthesized monoamines (norepinephrine, dopamine, and serotonin) and then block their reuptake. The increase in NE enhances alertness and motor activity while decreasing fatigue. The increased dopamine (DA) in the system causes stereotypical behavior and is likely responsible for the psychosis and paranoia associated with amphetamine use. The increased serotonin (5-HT) in the system causes some stereotypical behavior and may also contribute to the psychosis and euphoria. Amphetamines are usually taken orally, but advanced users inject the drug, hastening the psychosis and paranoia. Some kind of paranoia, often leading to violent behavior, is the result of heavy, prolonged use.

Recently in Phoenix a man who had been on a methamphetamine binge for several weeks poured gasoline over his two-year-old daughter and burned her alive. He did not flee from the police, reporting that he had purged his daughter's soul of the bad spirits that had invaded her. He offered as proof of the evil spirits that the burning little girl crawled more than ten feet before she died, a fact confirmed by the police in their assessment of the physical evidence. The drug-induced paranoia told him that the malevolence was attempting to escape the burning body and accompany his daughter's soul to heaven. In jail awaiting trial for murder, the speed-induced paranoia cleared up; this father is not only remorseful but also aghast at his behavior. His remorse, however, did not constrain him from using drug-induced insanity as a defense.

Typical users of amphetamines are adolescent girls and young women who wish to lose weight; they readily obtain prescriptions for amphetamines from so-called diet doctors and even from their primary care physicians. It is easy to abuse this prescription drug, using it as an upper and going beyond the intended goal of losing weight. Many of these dieters graduate to street versions. As with cocaine, many chronic depressives self-medicate with the cheaper amphetamines. Ritalin, Cylert, and Dextroamphetamine are stimulants used to treat ADD and ADHD, and are also found on the street. Most of the street versions are found in our schools, as are Ritalin and Cylert, which, as mentioned earlier, are resold by the children for whom they were originally prescribed. A surprising number of children receiving these stimulants, and especially those who received them because of misdiagnosis, graduate to street versions of these drugs or even the stronger and cheaper crystal meth and other forms of speed that are "cooked" in underground laboratories throughout the nation. (These "cooking kitchens" are everywhere, but the neighbors seldom realize their proximity until one of the kitchens blows up. Unfortunately, the cookers too often partake heavily of their own products and become careless.)

Methamphetamine (crystal meth) is available only rarely by prescription, so almost all of this drug is obtained on the street. It is very popular among teens and even younger children, with the average age of first use being fourteen. Many working-class persons see this as the drug of choice because it is cheaper than cocaine, and the euphoria lasts much longer. Many accidents in plants and other blue-collar employment centers have been traced to amphetamine use and its accompanying carelessness. Amphetamines are frighteningly popular with truck drivers who need to stay up on long hauls.

Because of the euphoria and her decreased appetite for food, the amphetamine addict is quite thin, eventually to the point of emaciation, especially if she is injecting the drug. This kind of physique, in the absence of compulsive exercise or anorexia, should alert you to explore for other signs of amphetamine addiction. The mainliner will have needle marks, but most addicts use the drugs orally. Nervousness, inability to sleep, irritability, and eventually fleeting paranoia are all signs of speed use. Because of the often intense insomnia, many addicts will resort to alcohol or other downers at bedtime, and, interestingly, the patient is more likely to report this secondary use rather than the primary use of speed. It is important, therefore, to inquire about speed when the patient is thin, irritable, and insomniac. Girls and young women will manifest tweaking behavior—the picking of their face or the pulling of their hair.

Downers: Depressants and Opiates

There are two very distinct types of downers, and although they both have a sedating effect, they are so different in their action that we have listed them together only because they are lumped together in common parlance among addicts and, surprisingly, by some physicians.

The first group are the depressants, such as alcohol and benzodiazepines, that work on the gamma-aminobutyric acid (GABA) system; the second group are the opiates (narcotics), whose action is on the endorphin (and enkephalin) system. Although alcohol is the far most common drug in use, it is listed after the benzodiazepines and barbiturates for two reasons: (1) these are the drugs most commonly and regularly mixed with or substituted for alcohol, and (2) the pharmacological actions on the GABA system are very similar.

Central Nervous System (CNS) Depressants

Known in the medical profession as minor tranquilizers, almost all *benzodiazepines (benzos, downers, ropies; Valium, Librium, Xanax, and many others)* are obtained legally because physicians freely and sometimes too liberally prescribe them. Consequently, the street name of benzos (as differentiated from bennies, for the once very popular Benzedrine) is rare, as is the term "downer." The only common street name in this class is "ropy" for Rohypnol, a benzodiazepine that is known as the date-rape drug and is available only on the street. It is banned in the United States because it has been used by young men on dates in the very kind of sexual assault on women that its tag line suggests. However, it is legally available in Mexico, and because of demand it is smuggled into the United States.

The primary mechanism for benzodiazepines is the facilitation of GABA neurotransmission. GABA is the primary inhibitory neurotransmitter, and when it is stimulated, nerve transmission is reduced, and CNS depression results. This depression further blocks nervous system stimulation that originates in the reticular formation in the brain stem, and thus diminishes activity in the area of the brain associated with emotion (that is, the amygdala, hippocampus, and hypothalamus). The person is seeking a drug-induced "cool" with an absence of troubling emotions.

Typical users of benzodiazepines are the various kinds of patients to whom physicians freely hand out prescriptions. These include anyone complaining to the doctor of depression, anxiety, or even bereavement. Middle-class "nervous housewives" who would never think of taking a street drug can and do obtain large quantities of Valium; they abuse the drug but rationalize their behavior because it is a doctor's prescription. They overlook the fact that they may have five different physicians prescribing, each unknown to the others.

Individuals with underlying phobias or mitral valve prolapse (MVP) who are prescribed Valium can overly rely on them to dissolve their phobias, and they thus rapidly become dependent. Alcoholics are often given Librium as part of their treatment for alcoholism, and a large number learn to prefer it to alcohol because it is longer lasting and does not show the telltale signs of inebriation. Even more frequently, alcoholics learn to use Librium in combination with alcohol to potentiate the effects.

Xanax has replaced both Librium and Valium as the benzodiazepine most prescribed by doctors. Librium was first introduced as a minor tranquilizer that was supposedly nonaddictive. When this proved to be wrong, Valium was heralded as a benzodiazepine that was more effective and not addictive. Because the half-life (the period in which the drug remains partially active after the initial effect) of Valium is nine to ten times that of Librium, it is no wonder that Valium was found to be far more addictive than Librium, as the user typically ingests more Valium long before the previous dose has reached its half-life. When heroin dries up on the street, hopheads (heroin addicts, also known as junkies) buy and swallow, and even shoot, large quantities of Valium to see them through.

The benzodiazepine abuser will present with a calmness that belies any need for the patient to be seen at all. The affect can be flat, or it will be displaced so that important problems are minimized, while trivial problems are exaggerated. There may be a history of traffic accidents but with no DUI charges because the benzo addict escapes the Breathalyzer test. The patient will complain that he just can't get it together. A housewife may not quite get to the grocery store or begin other errands. There may be sleeplessness at night accompanied by the patient's sleeping a good part of the day. The most telltale sign is a peculiar forgetfulness, such as forgetting to pick up the kids at school or the day-care center. If the patient has been off the drug, she will feel an incredible nervousness, often described as "jumping out of my skin."

The mechanism of *barbiturates (downers, barbs;* archaic: *yellow jackets, dolls)* is similar to that of the benzodiazepines in that they act on GABA, except that there are increased effects on the reticular system, with the greater likelihood of coma or death. Before the advent of benzodiazepines, these drugs were in widespread use, both legally and illegally. One of the most frequent reasons a mental health professional was called to the emergency room was for barbiturate overdose. The tolerance level between the sought-after "warm fuzzy" feeling and coma can be very small, and it may change from time to time.

Typical barbiturate abusers were exactly the same people who are now described as typical users of benzodiazepines; they have now been moved on to the use and abuse of the latest CNS depressant drug. At one time, physicians prescribed barbiturates as freely as they now give benzodiazepines. From the best-selling novel and subsequent movie *Valley of the Dolls,* which glamorized barbiturate use among middle-class housewives, through several other movies, to the recent movie *Copycat* in which Sigourney Weaver washed down pills with copious quantities of alcohol, the TV and motion picture industries do much to popularize the housewife's prescription drug abuse. There were a number of problems with barbiturates, and physicians were relieved to move on to benzodiazepines without having to change their prescribing patterns. Short-duration barbiturates are still used as anesthesia, and some of long duration are used as anticonvulsants. And there are still barbiturates on the street, but they are sought after by longtime users who never switched to the newer CNS depressants or by addicts who cannot obtain an immediate prescription for their preferred benzodiazepine because they are ingesting it much faster than the rate at which it is prescribed to them. To hide their addiction to benzodiazepines and not jeopardize a continued source from their physicians, these addicts supplement their prescriptions with illegally obtained barbiturates, as both drugs belong to the same class and are interchangeable.

The barbiturate abuser will present with a calmness, flat and displaced affect, and other symptoms and behaviors typical of the benzodiazepine addict. Do not be surprised to see the same history of sleep reversal, traffic accidents, and forgetfulness, along with the jumping-out-of-my-skin nervousness without the drug.

A number of CNS depressants once in wide use have fallen out of favor, because of either the problems associated with them or their propensity to be widely abused by patients who were prescribed these drugs. Again, most have been replaced by benzodiazepines, but they still linger, and you may have a patient who has remained addicted to the older medication. Again, with the exception that this will be an older addict, the symptoms and behaviors resemble those associated with benzodiazepine addiction.

Meprobamate (Miltown, MB-TAB, PMB, Equagesic, Equinil, Meprospan) was among the first of the new genre of "tranquilizers" to appear after World War II. It was freely prescribed because it was believed to be both safe and nonaddictive. Quickly it became the most widely abused drug in history, and frequently it was combined with alcohol. The "M&M" (Miltown and martini) was the rage, and it was chic to have a bowl of Miltowns on the coffee table during a party. In time it became apparent not only that the meprobamates were highly addictive but that withdrawal could result in grand mal seizures and death. Consequently, these drugs are rarely seen today.

Methaqualone (Quaalude, sopors, ludes) is a barbiturate-like drug that became popular as a sexual facilitator, especially for women who would take it at "swinger" parties or even with their boyfriends. It has a very high abuse potential, and the withdrawal is worse than that from barbiturates. It is characterized by delirium, convulsions, and even death. Its uses as an anticonvulsant, local anesthetic, or antitussive are better met by other medications, and the drug was banned in the 1980s. It continues to be sought after because of its reputation as a sexual facilitator, and it is available on the street as "ludes" or "soaps."

Before the advent of neuroleptic and antipsychotic medications, chloral hydrate was widely used in mental hospitals to quiet patients. It has many barbiturate-like effects. It is a short-term sleep aid, suitable for one to three nights for patients with agitation, but it causes respiratory depression thereafter, and from the outset causes severe gastrointestinal (GI) upset. For these reasons it is rarely seen today.

Paraldehyde is a barbiturate-like liquid that was used in the past to supposedly facilitate alcohol withdrawal. It was discontinued because patients quickly began to prefer it to alcohol in spite of the fact that it causes GI irritation and very bad breath. If alcoholics can get their hands on it, they will use it for a grand party, often ending up in the emergency room. Diagnosis of severe paraldehyde overdose is easily established from the pungently bad breath.

Finally, glutethimide (Doriden) and methyprylon (Noludar) are barbiturate-like in their action but are still prescribed for motion sickness. If these are abused it is because some kid has found it in the medicine cabinet at home and discovered that she can get high on it.

The symptoms and behaviors of users of these various "outmoded" CNS depressants will closely resemble those seen in benzodiazepine abusers. The difference will be that this is an older addict who has been addicted for a long time or who has recently resumed a previous addiction to barbiturates or these other less common drugs, thus accounting for the preference. Because physicians no longer prescribe these substances, the patient has learned to purchase them on the street. It is surprising how many of these addicts are still being seen and misdiagnosed in the first session with a psychotherapist.

The mechanisms of *alcohol* are essentially the same as those for benzodiazepines and barbiturates, so we will not repeat them. Measure for measure, however, alcohol is less potent and requires greater quantities to obtain the level known in the drug and alcohol world as "stoned." (For a person to seek that state is a certain sign of alcoholism, which raises alarms about binge drinking among college students.) More than with other substances, there is an early interference with certain motor functions such as walking and talking, making the ingestion of too much alcohol apparent to others, while the drinker is unaware of the reduction in motor function. Chronic alcoholics at some point reach the stage of the blackout, in which they walk and talk almost normally but recall none of the things they did or that happened during that period. These episodes can last from minutes to days, but mostly their duration is a matter of six to twelve hours.

Alcohol remains the most widely used and abused substance in the United States, as well as in most countries throughout the non-Islamic world. (Although it is forbidden by Islamic law in a number of countries, alcohol ingestion exists, but alcoholism is rare.) Within any culture are superimposed familial influences; sometimes family attitudes are counter to the culture in which the family is living. This can be especially true for immigrants whose mores of origin may clash with their new environment. Individuals raised in alcoholic families are predisposed to becoming alcoholics. But surprisingly, there is a similar predisposition for individuals who are raised in families that are strongly against any alcohol use. When the familial influences coincide with cultural and ethnic factors, there is less conflict leading to alcoholism. Many families of Italian or French descent would not think of eating dinner without wine, and many fathers of Irish extraction are proud of sons who can "hold their liquor" (engage in heavy drinking without losing control, although brawling seems to be an admired exception).

We have already discussed the slower-acting dehydrogenase enzyme as a well-known example of genetic predisposition to the overuse of alcohol. In contrast, the so-called Asian flush found among many Asians is an allergy to alcohol that mitigates against heavy drinking; for some individuals, the severity of the allergy makes any drinking whatsoever too unpleasant.

As we mentioned earlier, individuals who sustained prenatal exposure are especially predisposed to alcoholism, sometimes beginning at an early age. This is true of prenatal exposure to all drugs, but physicians are much more likely to address the pregnant woman's use of drugs other than alcohol, believing that small amounts of alcohol are harmless. In addition, the earlier in life (childhood, adolescence) alcohol use begins, the more likely the addiction will occur. Those children and adolescents who reveal the early signs of future Axis II disorders frequently become alcoholics in adulthood. Axis II children include those who, as children, are overly indulged, as well as those whose needs are inconsistently met by their parents.

As might be expected, those who are predisposed to anxiety or depression often begin to self-medicate with alcohol. One drink relieves the depression or dissolves the anxiety, but in time it takes more and more drinks, resulting in dependency. Furthermore, as a CNS depressant, alcohol only aggravates depression in the long run, and the rebound anxiety after drinking only aggravates the person's anxiety. Yet many depressives or anxiety neurotics self-medicate with alcohol and find themselves having to increase both frequency and amount because the temporary relief is followed by exacerbation. A dependency is created that escalates to addiction. It can be said that the more a person drinks medicinally, the more likely the addiction. Lifelong social drinkers have been shown to be those who use alcohol only convivially. College students under the stress of being away from home the first time and who lack the coping skills necessary for self-motivation are especially susceptible to seeking relief from homesickness through drinking. Of these individuals, the ones most likely to fall prey to alcoholism are those who seek popularity over academic success. Such persons, unfortunately, are the ones likely to become officers in the fraternity or sorority houses and set the pattern of initiation and other rites that involve binge drinking.

It surprises counselors and therapists when they learn that the most common alcoholic in the United States is the "beeraholic." There is a myth that a person cannot become an alcoholic on beer, yet people who drink one to two six-packs every night, or who are never without a beer can in hand all weekend long, abound. These are mostly men, but women are catching up, often preferring wine but more and more taking to the familiar beer can in the hand.

Let us look at the potencies. Whisky is generally eighty proof, or 40 percent alcohol. Beer is 4 percent alcohol, so ten ounces of beer (less than one can) is equivalent to a shot of whisky. Thus two six-packs (at twelve ounces per can or bottle) is equivalent to fourteen shots of whisky, a hefty amount for one night. At 12 to 14 percent alcohol (by volume), a thirty-two-ounce bottle of wine is also the equivalent of twelve to fourteen shots of whisky; "wine people" characteristically drink most or all of one bottle each night after work.

Pure alcoholics (that is, those who abuse solely alcohol) are patients forty-five and older. We have not seen a patient in years who is under forty-five and an old-fashioned alcoholic. The current chemical dependency scene is one of polydrug abuse, with alcohol being the most common ingredient in cross-addiction. Your patient under forty-five will mix alcohol with uppers, downers, marijuana, and cocaine, at least occasionally; most prefer alcohol with just one of these other substances.

Alcohol is known among many addicts as "mother's milk." Heroin addicts who abandon heroin and are still alive after fifty are often very heavy drinkers, as are former heavy LSD users. Amusingly, Timothy Leary, known as the High Priest of LSD, in the few years preceding his death made the following pronouncement: "After that long journey through psychedelics, I have found that Ripple Wine is the best high."[5] Further, alcohol in combination with almost any drug will potentiate that drug's effects. Addicts mix it principally with cocaine, barbiturates, and benzodiazepines, but addicts may combine any drug with booze. Former heroin addicts being treated with methadone have found that mixing methadone with alcohol produces a high rivaling heroin yet yields a drug-free urine test.

The alcoholic of long standing will have pasty skin, and those of very long standing will manifest some shakiness of the hands. There will be a history of blackouts. Most alcoholics will not be so advanced as to have developed a bulbous nose and large bags under the eyes, but it is surprising how often those are still seen in older patients. If the patient is mixing alcohol with other drugs, especially CNS depressants, the debilitating effects will be accelerated. Further, the patient can present any of the symptoms and behaviors listed for the drugs involved in the cross-addiction.

Alcoholics will present for problems other than their drinking. The most frequent will be marital stress, job stress, or both; if the patient has been referred by the court, it most likely will be for DUI, and sometimes for disorderly conduct.

Opiates (Narcotics)

Opiates and *opioids, including morphine (morph), codeine, demerol, methadone,* and *heroin (horse, smack, H, shit),* are known as *narcotic analgesics* because their action mimics the endogenous (that is, the brain's own) opioid system, which includes enkephalins, endorphins, and dynorphans.

Patients who are placed on self-administering doses of opiates—especially morphine, codeine, and demerol—for pain are likely to become addicted. Patients who are given these pain killers on a predetermined regimen or schedule are far less likely to become chemically dependent. The tendency to go beyond the pain-killing aspects and into euphoria is compelling and leads to addiction, whereas a schedule is constructed to keep the use of the opiate within treatment bounds.

About half of all heroin addicts in the United States reside in New York City, probably because of the availability of smack, but also probably because of the comfort that derives from being a part of a group so large as to be a subculture. Typical heroin users are graduates of lesser analgesics. For several years heroin use was declining, but in recent years there has been a significant resurgence. This has been attributed to the entertainment and fashion industries that have made the drug chic; in fact, the fashion magazines have gone so far as to tout "heroin chic." Their influence on teenagers and young adults who consequently took up the drug was so alarming that President Clinton invoked the powers of his office to warn both the fashion industry and Hollywood of possible sanctions if they continued to make heroin glamorous.

Nurses who have easy access to hospital supplies prefer morphine, and often falsify records to support their habit. Recently Demerol has become the abused drug of choice among health professionals in general, especially if they have access to the narcotics cabinet.

Long-time stimulant users (of cocaine, crystal meth) use heroin either to speedball or to calm the side effects of long-term stimulant abuse. These include insomnia, anxiety, and paranoia, all relieved by heroin, which then often ascends to becoming the primary addiction. Stimulant addiction is increasing; so is the trend to relieve its negative effects with heroin.

Narcotic addiction is severe addiction and involves the most consistent denial and deceit. Heroin addicts especially do not present for psychotherapy; if they do, there are compelling reasons. One would be because heroin has temporarily dried up on the street, which occurs whenever the police have made a very large supplier drug bust. In such instances the psychotherapist will see a patient who is fidgety and even tremulous. He will tend to pace, complaining of an "anxiety attack" and requesting a prescription for lesser narcotics. Or finding that not forthcoming, for Valium or other benzodiazapines. If denied a prescription the patient may erupt in anger, berating the psychotherapist. This can alternate with an inappropriate breeziness, most often of the "Who needs you?" variety. As withdrawal progresses, the heroin addict is severely strung out, suffering from painful abdominal cramps, along with vomiting and diarrhea. At that moment, the addict will do anything for a fix, rendering late-night convenience stores and gas stations sitting targets. These are desperation robberies, for the patient is so strung out that caution is impossible. The strung-out narcotics addict will reveal the same desperation in your office. They will beg for a fix. Often they have been sent to you because they previously were begging the emergency-room physician or on-call doctor for the same fix they want from you. They know they cannot be prescribed heroin, but they name the lesser narcotics they know and want: percodan and dilaudid. These addicts resent codeine and darvon because these yield less of a high.

More likely you will see a patient because he or she is a health professional whose license is on the line for pilfering from the narcotics cabinet, a lawyer who is about to be disbarred, or some other professional who wants to escape the consequences of the opiate addiction. We have seen a number of athletes who had been suspended, and even more musicians who got caught. These patients will minimize the degree of addiction, but you can discern the severity from the needle marks, known as spider tracks. Do not just look in the usual places such as arm and leg veins: look between the toes. Long-standing heroin addicts have burned out most of their veins, leaving permanent spider tracks. Clever mainliners will begin early to shoot in obscure places so as to hide their addiction. In the beginning, narcotics addicts snort the drug or take it orally, but they soon find that the quantities they need are too great without graduating to the needle.

An exception to this pattern of progression to the needle is the middle- or upper-class housewife who disdains the idea of using the needle. Instead, she ingests larger and larger quantities of pills, often mixing them with alcohol.

It is difficult, if not impossible, to truly engage a heroin addict who is well fixed, or high. They are the cleverest of liars and the most convincing of con artists, even when they are hip-deep in trouble. The drug makes them feel confident and invulnerable. The longer they are on the jitters, however, the more productive will be the interchange. For the most part, your task will be to motivate and refer the patient for the difficult detoxification and withdrawal ahead. However, if in the first session you completely miss the narcotics addiction, the subsequent treatment will be a nightmare of patient deceit: you will be drawn into a number of discrepancies, contradictions, and even traps.

Hallucinogens

The mechanisms of *psychedelic drugs (LSD, lysergic acid, acid; mescaline, mesc, peyote; psilocybin, sacred mushrooms, shrooms)* have not been sufficiently studied and therefore are not understood. It is believed that these chemicals involve stimulation of 5-HT2 (serotonin, type 2) receptors.

There are four types of typical users. The first of these includes those in college who are not great students, or the converse: bright individuals who should be in college but instead are going nowhere. Both of these types of young persons believe they are expanding their minds and have discovered internal truths that no one else knows. The second group is composed of persons who wish to drop out of society. For such individuals the psychedelic facilitates the illusion that the world is wrong or corrupt and that she is justified in not participating in society. The third group is an often transitory one. It is composed of prepsychotic individuals who want to blame drugs for their frightening and impending psychosis. Their involvement with psychedelics understandably terminates with their hospitalization, but for some who remain in the prepsychotic state for years, these drugs maintain the rationalization that "I am not really going crazy." The fourth group is almost quaint in today's drug scene. These are the army of "deadheads" who veritably worship the late Jerry Garcia and who follow the Grateful Dead from concert to concert. Hallucinogens are still readily available on the street, but their use and abuse is far below the level of the "psychedelic era" of the 1960s and 1970s.

At the first session, the user is likely to talk about anything except his hallucinogens. If he comes in because he has begun having bad trips, his expectation is that you will help him have only good trips. The deadheads are obvious in their appearance; in contrast, users who are in college but going nowhere do not always fit a stereotype. Occasionally they exhibit bizarre behavior in public while they are tripping out and, depending on the community and the level of tolerance, get picked up by the police.

Although *marijuana (cannabis, Mary Jane, pot, grass, weed)* may have mild hallucinogenic properties, it is not classified pharmacologically as a hallucinogenic drug. Actually, the exact nature of how this drug works remains unknown, because the federal government put a halt to all research with marijuana. We have included it in this section for the convenience of referring back to this material, because popularly it is usually lumped into this category.

Marijuana is second only to alcohol as the most abused drug in the United States. It is the entry point into drugs for almost everyone who progresses up the ladder of addiction, discrediting the once widely held notion that smoking pot does not lead to hard drugs. However, not everyone moves on to hard drugs, and there are many "potheads," many of whom are employed or marginally employed. There are also individuals who use marijuana only occasionally and never progress to extensive use.

Marijuana is used by persons of all socioeconomic levels and of almost all ages: children, adolescents, young adults, and middle-aged adults. However, most middle-aged users began in childhood, their teens, or as young adults. Marijuana is occasionally used by successful adults at parties, especially by those who had experimented with the drug in the "hippie era." But the majority of users are young persons, sometimes as young as eight years old. The younger the onset of usage of marijuana, the more likely it is that the individual will move on to harder drugs.

The chronic user, or pothead, is typically a person of low motivation who is attracted to a drug that allows her to lay back. However, the drug is known to produce amotivational syndrome, raising the chicken-or-egg question. Many potheads are found in small counterculture colonies in remote areas. Favorites are the coast and the deep forests of Northern California, but remote areas in New Mexico, Idaho, and Montana are also in vogue. Many potheads continue to live in the city and engage in some semblance of employment. Such jobs as gardening (yard work) are favorites because no one bothers the individual, who can remain stoned while working.

The most striking characteristic of the first session with pot users is that the interview does not seem to go in any productive direction. This is a reflection of the amotivational syndrome, in which the patient expresses a vague dissatisfaction, but with nothing specific. He may complain that he cannot keep a job, but is unable to explain why. These are generally easygoing patients who are affable and do not blame anyone. There is the general impression of a nice person, but one who is empty. She demonstrates a nominal interest in certain activities (music, movies, sports, literature), but the intensity or commitment is lacking. If you are not aware of the ramifications of the amotivational syndrome, the interview can be perplexing.

Mixes of Other Drugs

There are numerous *designer drugs* (*Ecstasy, XTC, white China, synthetic heroin, nexus, eros*) with slight alterations of chemical structure, making it nonproductive to study their effects, as the chemical under study will disappear before the study is even undertaken. Cookers (underground chemists) work independently, so the product of one chemist is different than that of all others. This, too, makes study impossible. Nonetheless, the general mechanisms of these drugs are essentially known.

MDA (Ecstasy, XTC) is now really a class of drugs, each with a slight variation in structure. These act on a small percentage of specialized serotonin neurons in the brain. The drug kills these cells in about twenty doses, thus requiring the cookers to come up with a slight variation that will act on a different small number of neurons. As the user switches from one variation to another, eventually there are none of these specialized neurons left. The immediate result is that this class of drugs no longer produces the desired effect and the user finds himself more and more abusing alcohol. This brain damage is permanent and the neuron deficit reveals itself as "a quart short" as the user reaches his older years. At present, it's almost exclusively young users.

Gamma-hydroxybutyrate (GHB) has a structure similar to GABA (see the discussion of the CNS depressants). The drug suppresses dopamine release, with a subsequent rebound and increase in dopamine as well as natural endogenous opioids. Relaxation and euphoria are the result. In 1990, GHB was widely distributed as a health food supplement that would promote weight loss and muscle development. It was banned the same year because of widespread reports of poisonings resulting in seizures and deaths.

Alpha methyl fentanyl (white China, synthetic heroin) is the most common of a group of fentanyl analogs deriving from a powerful synthetic opioid. It has an action very similar to real opioids, but tends to be more powerful than morphine and is sold on the street as white China or synthetic heroin.

A drug of deception, *2 C-B (4-bromo-2, 5-dimethoxyphenethylamine, Nexus, eros)* is sold as Ecstasy, but it actually has a far more intense hallucinogenic effect than Ecstasy. Users expecting the effects of Ecstasy are often terrified, and some suicides have resulted.

Although widely sold on the street, designer drugs have remained legal because cookers stay one step ahead of the authorities.

By creating a new drug that has not yet been chemically identified and listed under the Controlled Substances Act, they avoid prosecution. Users are smug that they too can escape charges for possession of an illegal substance, inasmuch as the latest version has not yet been catalogued as such. The jeopardy, of course, is that the individual is risking unknown consequences by being the first to ingest the latest variation. If the local anonymous cooker is inept and the user becomes ill and even dies, there is no recourse under product liability laws. A frequent contaminant of designer drugs is MPTP, which causes Parkinsonism. Yet there is no end to those who volunteer to be the first. Who are these persons? As might be expected, many are underachievers doing little in life; others are seeking to go all the way and drop out of society. The surprising users are the yuppies who are bored with their lives, are pushing themselves beyond their limits in order to succeed, and perceive a need to "crash" periodically. These crashes tend to take the form of a monthly three-day weekend on designer drugs.

The most typical presentation will be the rather successful yuppies who will talk about being bored with life in spite of pushing themselves. They will not reveal the periodic crash into designer drugs unless you ask. When confronted with a patient in this age group who is ostensibly succeeding but is insecure about whether she can keep it up, you should be alerted to possible use of designer drugs. The patient is well into the successful world and cannot risk arrest for use of illicit drugs. The fact that designer drugs are elusive and "legal" makes them attractive to this person. Typically the use is occasional or periodic and does not present addictive features. Those who become addicted have moved on to other drugs, mixing designer drugs with other drugs for a bigger kick.

Although the mechanisms are not entirely known, it is believed that *dissociative anesthetics (phencyclidine, PCP, angel dust; ketamine, Special K, Vitamin K)* bind to sigma receptors, which are possibly related to schizophrenia, or to glutamate (an excitatory amino acid neurotransmitter) receptors, or to both.

Developed mostly as anesthetics for animals, these substances are used in veterinary medicine and provide a cheap high. Therefore, the primary user is a younger person in the inner city or of lower socioeconomic status. It is also used by prepsychotic individuals who want to blame the drug for their psychotic symptoms. At times such persons are pushed over the edge into full-blown psychosis, with alarming results, such as attempts to fly off a tall building, or violent behavior toward others. Some individuals mix these drugs with other drugs to increase the high. With the emergence of designer drugs, which are also inexpensive, the use of dissociative anesthetics has greatly diminished.

You are unlikely to see these individuals unless the drug has resulted in bizarre behavior that led to their admission to the county hospital. This is most likely with angel dust. You may be asked to help with a differential diagnosis of a prepsychotic individual who was pushed into a full-blown psychosis. A history of indulging in cheap drugs and the sudden onset of the bizarre behavior are important clues in establishing the diagnosis.

Inhalants are legal substances that were never intended for ingestion. They include gasoline, airplane glue, organic solvents, antistick cooking spray (such as Pam), some marking pens, correction fluid and correction fluid thinner, nail polish remover, paints, industrial solutions, adhesives, butane in cigarette lighters, and aerosol propellants. It is estimated that the average household will have between fifty and one hundred commonly used substances that can be inhaled to attain a high.

Inhalants produce an intoxication in the brain but also result in damage to brain cells. With continued use, more and more brain cells are affected. It is difficult to assess to what extent the neuropsychological problems seen by behavioral care practitioners were preceded by abuse of inhalants. Before you diagnose ADD, ADHD, or other similar conditions, it is important to gain the child's or adolescent's confidence and obtain an accurate history in this regard.

Inhalant abuse is widespread among children, adolescents, and young adults of lower socioeconomic status. It is cheap, universally available, and legal. Use usually begins with one child in grammar or high school learning about it from an older sibling or friend and introducing it to his classmates. Because most inhalant abusers are boys, it seriously raises the question of how many of the problems seen in boys are due to brain damage from repeated inhalant abuse. In addition, it is surprising how many children, adolescents, and young adults who were placed on Ritalin or other stimulant medications following the misdiagnosis of ADD or ADHD become inhalant abusers once they achieve young adulthood. Some children start earlier, selling their Ritalin to their friends and classmates while substituting the free and plentiful inhalants.

Typically the child or adolescent has been brought in by the parents or has been referred by the school, because of poor grades and even worse attendance. The patient does not want to be there but may feign cooperation to get the matter over with. There are times when the child or adolescent has been caught in the act of inhaling, so the purpose of the visit is out in the open. Most of the time, however, the patient has been brought in because of the consequences of the abuse. When confronted with this age group and with a report of poor school performance and attendance, you should look for tremulousness, reports of severe mood swings, and soiled spots on clothing. More advanced abusers show severe motor problems due to the permanent damage to the motor cortex that inhalants eventually cause.

Inhalant abuse has gone beyond the former airplane glue–sniffing level. It is now the most frequent form of substance abuse among children and adolescents, with some schools reporting as many as 20 percent of their students involved. The complete availability of these inhalants makes them impossible to control, and latchkey kids have plenty of time to get high on the endless array. You should not be dissuaded by the youth of the patient, as the practice has become common among third graders.

The Ultimate Mix: Speedballing

It is important to give special attention to the growing practice of speedballing, the taking of an upper and a downer at the same time. This produces a virtual roller-coaster ride, inasmuch as the body does not shut down one system in favor of the other but attempts to accommodate both at the same time. The strain on the nervous and cardiovascular systems is enormous, and death is not infrequent. Although hundreds have died, the public hears about speedballing only when such celebrities as John Belushi or Kurt Cobain succumb.

Speedballing differs from the practice of taking a downer to relax after partaking of cocaine or another upper. It is a deliberate simultaneous intake for those who have become jaded or bored with the more usual high and who can afford to buy the costly cocaine and heroin. There is also lesser speedballing, and although it is not as disastrous to the body in the immediate term, with prolonged use it can be physically debilitating. Those with less money mix amphetamines with benzodiazepines, and the person who would never think of buying an illicit drug can experience low-grade speedballing all day long by taking large quantities of over-the-counter cold medications and reducing the sleepiness of the antihistamines (downers) with corresponding amounts of amphetamines (uppers). This person is a potential menace on the highway and can experience severe reactions in the evening when she joins spouse or friends in convivial before-dinner cocktails. This lesser form of speedballing is one of the most frequent reasons someone is inexplicably carried to the emergency room.

I'LL GET HIGH ON ANYTHING:
A THERAPIST'S SUMMARY

The historical reassurance by NIDA that cocaine is not addictive is unfortunately matched by the Food and Drug Administration (FDA) in its repeated assurances that the latest mind-altering drug was not addictive. We saw how the first of these, Miltown, quickly became the largest-selling drug in America. Within a few years it was seen as having high addiction potential; it is almost never prescribed today. Librium followed, and was thought to be nonaddictive. When this was found to be untrue, Valium was heralded with assurances that it had none of the drawbacks of Librium and was nonaddictive. Soon Valium became the most prescribed drug in America.

We have already discussed the tendency of NIDA, the FDA, and other relevant agencies to presume the "innocence" of the latest mind-altering drug, only to discover later that the substance was addictive. When reports begin to come in regarding the drug's negative characteristics (for example, that it is addictive, potentially lethal when mixed with alcohol, hazardous for drivers), drug manufacturers tend to ignore them as long as they can. It sometimes is literally a matter of years before the information is distributed to physicians in "drug alerts." To us there was no reason to believe that Xanax, initially heralded as a nonaddictive benzodiazepine, would not now be regarded as addictive.

Since Xanax came on the market, more recent benzodiazepines such as Atavan and Serak are being regarded as "less addictive." Our prediction, because of the cellular changes and behavioral reinforcement that accompany benzodiazepines generally, these newer drugs will one day have their own physician drug alerts.

One of the problems is with the FDA approval system: once a drug is approved, there are no follow-up clinical trials. It takes time and considerable usage before the problems surface, and by that time the FDA is long gone. Meanwhile, the manufacturer is attempting to delay the dissemination of information until after the patents have expired on its "best-seller."

Practitioners who treat substance abuse must pragmatically accept the fact that someone who is determined to get high will find a chemical with which to do it. We saw a man who was consuming three boxes of Bromo-Seltzer a day just to get enough bromine from the small amounts found in that over-the-counter medication. We saw another a man who remained sober following his successful completion of a drug rehab program. However, his physicians were worried because his potassium level was low enough to endanger his metabolism. It was eventually discovered by an intern who pursued the cause of the patient's black mouth that this man was consuming two pounds of licorice per day. During his drinking days he used licorice to mask his alcohol breath; he apparently became addicted to licorice and quadrupled his intake after giving up alcohol. The large amounts of licorice were leeching his potassium. Impotent men will obtain Trazadone (Desyrel) in the hopes of getting the drug's infrequent but rather painful side effect of priapism. They take the drug in such large doses as to almost guarantee this result.

Two rather startling examples are illustrative of the abuser's determination.

Water, Water Everywhere

In the past, when the so-called chronic inebriate was subject to involuntary hospitalization, I (Nick) discovered emphatically what later became the truism that an addict can and will find something to get high on. In the state hospital where I was working, suddenly all the patients were behaving as if they were very drunk. They had moved their cots into the large men's and women's bathrooms that were characteristic of the state-run institutions of the time. We concluded that some kind of still had been hidden in the bathrooms and was churning out alcohol. Our maintenance crews all but tore apart the relevant parts of the building, but found nothing.

In a matter of two more days, during which time our patients were very, very drunk, we discovered that they were doing this on water. A recent admission was a biochemist who taught his fellow patients that if you drink eight gallons of water per day, the pH level of the blood is altered and you feel drunk. The patients tried it out and were delighted. For efficiency's sake, they moved their cots into the bathrooms so as to be near the water, as eight gallons is an enormous amount to drink in one day. Further, this put them

near the toilets, an imperative brought on by their huge water intake. It was fortunate that we discovered the cause of their inebriation and put an end to it, for if the pH imbalance had continued for
a couple more days, severe medical consequences and even death
would have resulted.

Everything's Up-to-Date in Addict City

Within weeks following the introduction of Viagra, the drug was
found on the street. Substance abusers incorporate it into their
chemically dependent behavior in two ways. The first is to use Viagra in combination with nitroglycerin or other nitrate medications,
which are used medically to lower blood pressure in patients suffering from angina or other forms of heart disease. Abusers mixing the
two insist that there is an increase in both sexual performance and
accompanying euphoria. This combination can drastically lower
blood pressure and can prove fatal. Warnings have been issued by
the FDA not to mix Viagra with blood pressure medication, but substance abusers are not known for their attention to such warnings.

The second method is to take Viagra in combination with amyl
nitrate and amphetamine. This odd combination is thought to
increase stamina on intercourse. However, the practice can lead to
cardiac arrest. The combination speeds heart rate and respiration
while decreasing blood pressure, creating extreme physical distress.
In spite of these hazards, the combination is very tempting to men
who are impotent as a result of prolonged substance abuse and seek
yet another chemical solution, or to those who are "sex addicts" and
wish to perform beyond normal physical limitations.

SPECIAL CONSIDERATIONS

No discussion of the specific properties of drugs and their effects on
various populations can be complete without paying special attention to two exceptional instances: (1) substance abuse among older
adults and (2) so-called foodaholism.

The first is of importance because more Americans are living longer, and psychotherapy under Medicare is the fastest-growing sector of our practice. Yet most psychotherapists know little about the treatment of older patients, and the prescribing physician forgets that medication trials did not include the elderly. Much of this oversight is in the process of being rectified, and the field of geropsychology is new, exciting, and growing. Yet even geropsychologists know little about chemical dependency among older adults and are unaware that it is largely iatrogenic—that is, induced by doctors. For these and other compelling reasons, we have added this section.

Foodaholism is important to addictionology because the physiology, cravings, and treatment of food addiction not only closely parallel what occurs in substance abuse but also may well be the prototype for it. This provocative notion encompasses the fact that overeating can both excite and sedate. To many physiologists, the original addiction in childhood is to sugar, and this addiction is carried forward into adulthood in forms that predispose many to substance abuse.[6] The increasing use of sugar among infants and young children may be an overlooked factor in subsequent chemical dependency. To the small child, sugar is the ultimate high.

Substance Abuse Among Older Adults

Most active substance abusers do not carry their behavior into old age, as the health consequences of drug addiction mitigate against longevity, although a few substance abusers do make it to their sixties and even beyond. Most chemical dependency among older adults is iatrogenic, however. This is a growing and important area for counselors and therapists inasmuch as the federal government is including us in Medicare networks. We shall be seeing more of the elderly. It is important to realize that the confusion and befuddlement of an older adult who is suspected of Alzheimer's or other dementia often clear up in a few days to two weeks when the chemical reason for the patient's mental state is discovered and corrected. The following are considerations all practitioners should note.

- Physicians do not consistently warn patients not to use alcohol in combination with their prescription medications. Many persons who have been moderate, social drinkers all of their lives suddenly find that their usual one drink before dinner or wine with dinner is potentiated by another CNS depressant (such as a benzodiazepine). Unfortunately, the older person may not be aware of the effect.

- As a person grows older, she has less tolerance for alcohol. The moderate degree of social drinking she has engaged in all her life may now result in intoxication. Again, the older person is not likely to be aware of the change in effect. Again, physicians do not warn the patient, often reassuring her that her amount of alcohol consumption is reasonable.

- The elderly forget they have taken a medication and frequently take extra doses unknowingly. Practitioners need to involve a family member as monitor and make use of the easily available mnemonic devices that dispense the pills on a schedule.

- The elderly are a very overly medicated group. Physicians characteristically dismiss the elderly with a patronizing "You're not as young as you used to be" and send them out with yet another pill. Some of these medications are antagonistic to each other, or they overly potentiate each other; still others should be prescribed with care. The National Institute for Aging publishes a list of over seventy common medications that should not be prescribed for older adults or should be dispensed with great care and extreme caution.[7] Although this list is readily available and widely acknowledged, most physicians have never seen it. These include CNS depressants, antidepressants, and narcotic analgesics, all of which should be prescribed with caution and in smaller doses.

- More than for younger patients, physicians are too quick to inappropriately medicate the elderly for grief or other psychological conditions. The pervasive attitude is that "I can't really do very much for this old person."

• Pharmokinetic changes in older adults may cause them to react differently to medications. Briefly, these reactions include the following:

The rate of absorption of drugs is slowed down, so there may be an unexpected delayed reaction.

All psychotropic medications (other than lithium carbonate) bind with proteins; because the levels of these proteins decrease with age, older patients are susceptible to toxic responses and require lower dosages.

Hepatic (liver) metabolism declines with age, increasing the amount of unmetabolized medications, thus enhancing the potential for toxicity.

Most drugs are excreted primarily through the kidneys; because older adults have decreased kidney function, excretion may be delayed, leading to toxicity.

The drugs with the highest abuse potential are CNS depressants, such as benzodiazepines and barbiturates. Given for their sedating effect, they can often cause oversedation and even coma in the elderly. This oversedation is often accompanied by a sense of helplessness, withdrawal, and disordered behavior, and can be misdiagnosed as depression. Other drugs that can produce oversedation in older adults are sedating tricyclics, sedating antipsychotics, and inappropriate combinations of common medications.

Confusion is a common reaction to medication in the elderly and can result from oversedation, anticholinergic side effects, or the toxic effects of lithium carbonate. Older adults with early or subclinical brain dysfunction or dementia are especially susceptible to confusion, which may appear as disorientation, irritability, agitation, sundowner's syndrome, assaultive behavior, hallucinations, or a combination of these. Their condition is then most often misdiagnosed as full-blown dementia.

Tremors and shaking can be severe in older adults, probably because of lowered dopamine levels. Patients who have been prescribed phenothiazines and other drugs over many years may develop uncontrollable shaking when they are older, which can be treated only by increased dosages of the offending drug. This sets up the next level of uncontrolled shaking, with the need to once again increase the dosage. Eventually there is a point where nothing will work.

The Foodaholic: Special Comments on Food Addiction

Although definitely demonstrating many of the physical and psychological characteristics of substance abuse, calorie dependency differs in a number of ways and requires special consideration. The foodaholic is not everyone or even most of those who overeat and are obese. Genetic factors, such as "slow metabolism" and general body structure, contribute to obesity; they do not necessarily contribute to food addiction, however. But the persons born with unlucky genetics make up only a small percentage of the existing obese population. Most obese persons have developed poor nutritional and exercise habits, but they do not use food addictively. The food addict is specifically defined as that person who eats because he is depressed, lonely, or anxious, or experiences a combination of these. Compulsive eating relieves or dulls these emotions; if the person does not resort to overeating, his anxiety mounts to an intolerable level. In addition, the foodaholic is fearful of commitment in relationships, uses scarfing as a way of blunting the loneliness that results, and then feels safe because seldom is a potential lover attracted by obesity.

Every foodaholic has a list of "nemesis foods." These can include ice cream (by the quart), peanut butter (by the jar), chocolate (by the box), and the surprisingly ubiquitous white bread (by the loaf), usually with copious amounts of butter. The nemesis varies, but whatever it is (defined as the food of which one taste triggers scarfing), it is always high in calories. Quantity is important, but no amount of carrots, spinach, or other such healthful food can quell the craving for fats and sugars.

Satiety helps shift the nervous system from sympathetic activity to parasympathetic activity, which is most involved in digestion. This shift also signals to the person, "I have had enough." Overeating makes the shift even more dramatic, with an abrupt reduction of the hormones and neurotransmitters associated with stress. Therefore, scarfing has a direct effect on the limbic system, reducing its ability to generate strong emotions. The foodaholic experiences freedom from anxiety, loneliness, and depression, and if not, will continue to overeat until that relief is forthcoming. It is possible that enkephalins and endorphins, and perhaps even serotonin, are associated with oversatiation. Thus, along with the psychological reinforcement of relief from nervous tension, the foodaholic may also become dependent on the chemicals her body produces when she overeats.

Women are more likely to become foodaholics than are men, who have fewer inhibitions with regard to using alcohol and illicit drugs. Individuals who were "sugar addicts" in childhood are at high risk for any addictive behavior in adulthood, but the link is most clear with food addiction. Individuals raised in families where food was the medium of communication are particularly susceptible. These families are of two types. In the first, food is used as both reward and punishment. (For example, "You had a great report card; have a cookie," or "Your report card is bad; go to bed without supper.") In the second, the parents purvey food rather than convey affection. Food becomes the primary means of comforting the child, who in turn fails to learn other means of comforting herself. Individuals who were raised in substance abusing families and were hurt by it often vow never to abuse drugs when they attain their own adulthood. However, they have been indoctrinated with addictive behavior by their parents, and not surprisingly, food addiction is the compromise. It is addictive behavior that can be rationalized by telling oneself, "I am not abusing drugs or alcohol." Finally, individuals whose early dependency needs were never met or were inconsistently met often learn to depend on food for their solace.

It must be emphasized that foodaholics are no less adept at denial than those with outright chemical dependencies. However, the foodaholic's denial understandably differs in content and often in form, so this will be specifically addressed in our discussion of the denial expected from addicts in general on the first interview. The foodaholic's denials are often exceptionally adept, as body weight of three hundred to four hundred pounds is not easily hidden or dismissed.

The concept of *abstinence* for the compulsive eater poses a dilemma inasmuch as the person still has to eat. But this is a contradiction only for the normal eater. The foodaholic, when not in denial, knows and understands that abstinence means refraining from scarfing, nemesis foods, and eating when lonely, anxious, or depressed.

Notes

1. Murray, R. M., & Stabenau, J. R. (1992). Genetic factors in alcoholism predisposition. In E. O. Pattison & E. Kaupman (Eds.), *Encyclopedic handbook of alcoholism*. New York: Gardner.

2. Wallace, J. (1982). Alcoholism from the inside out: A phenomenological analysis. In N. Estes & M. Heineman (Eds.), *Alcoholism: Development, consequences, and interventions*. New York: Mosby.

3. Brokaw, T. (1999). "NBC Nightly News" (January 21).

4. Carlson, N. R. (1986). *Physiology of behavior* (3rd ed.). Boston: Allyn & Bacon; Bloom, F. E., Lazerson, A., & Hofstadter, L. (1985). *Brain, mind, and behavior*. New York: W. H. Freeman; Carnes, P. (1992). *Out of the shadows* (2nd ed.). Center City, MN: Hazelden.

5. Personal communication, October 1985.

6. Cummings, N. A. (1982). *Biodyne training manual* (2nd ed.). South San Francisco: Foundation for Behavioral Health; Feingold, B. F. (1974). *Why your child is hyperactive*. New York: Random House.

7. Hartman-Stein, P. E. (1998). *Innovative behavioral healthcare for older adults*. San Francisco: Jossey-Bass.

3

Identifying the Problem
in the First Session

The treatment of substance abusers is discouraging at best: if there is any abstinence at all, most often there is only a brief period of recovery before patients resume their addictive behavior. In our experience, the lack of success with psychotherapy begins with the first session. Far too often, the therapist fails to discern and address the addictive problem as primary and pursues instead derivative or collateral problems. The patient has thrown out these latter problems as bait, often in ostensible sincerity if he is in denial. The patient is consciously or unconsciously all too happy to accommodate the derailed psychotherapeutic endeavor and gladly cooperates in the avid pursuit of the irrelevant. For reasons we shall discuss in the chapter on countertransference, the therapist in this case has inadvertently bought into the denial. The most common type of first session conducted with these patients is one in which the therapist misses the addictive problem totally or partially.

Over a period of eighteen years, the senior author and his colleagues, as part of a research project, tracked 3,726 patients who were identified in the first session by skilled addiction therapists as being chemically dependent. In subsequently verifying the diagnoses, the researchers found that of these 3,726, only 4 turned out to be false positives—that is, patients not actually chemically dependent. This is a negligible error rate, indicating that if the signs and symptoms of addiction are strongly present, the diagnosis of addiction is very likely to be accurate. Compare this to the error rate in identifying chemical dependency by therapists unskilled in addictionology: in a random sampling of 205 of these 3,726 patients, only 11 percent were identified as chemically dependent, whereas the actual rate was 100 percent. This suggests that most therapists are able to identify roughly one in ten of patients who have a significant substance abuse problem.

The four patients who were false positives had manifested such unusual behavior that it might be worthwhile to describe them and to understand the reasons for the false-positive evaluation.

Thelma was a twenty-eight-year-old single woman who was self-referred because of what she called "my alcohol problem." In the first session it was determined that the patient was upset because whenever she got drunk, perhaps ten or twelve times a year, she would always have sex with another woman in spite of her subsequent revulsion. She would vow this would never happen again, only to repeat the drunken sexual behavior a few weeks later. It became apparent that Thelma was a repressed lesbian who professed to be heterosexual. She fought against her repressed sexual desires until frustration drove her to get drunk again. Then, losing her inhibitions, she was able to indulge her sexual orientation, all the while blaming her behavior on the alcohol. In subsequent sessions, she was helped to accept her true sexual orientation, whereupon the heavy drinking disappeared as no longer necessary.

Although Thelma was not an alcoholic, a note of caution is indicated. Substance abuse, and particularly alcoholism, is higher among lesbians and gay men than in the corresponding heterosexual population. In part this is because so much of homosexual social interaction takes place in lesbian and gay bars. Others in the gay community have suggested that lesbians and gay men seek chemical relief from the tension associated with societal disapproval and with having to remain in the closet in many job and social situations. Also, it must not be overlooked that gay men have commonly used such drugs as "poppers" (amyl nitrate) to enhance sexual performance and endurance, thus opening the door to possible wider drug abuse.

Rick was a policeman referred by the metropolitan police department for alcohol rehabilitation as part of standard procedure after the third time he reported for duty while intoxicated. He readily but erroneously admitted to being an alcoholic. Actually, Rick was scared to death of being a policeman. He was certain that on his next shift he would either be killed or kill someone else, the latter being even less preferable than the former. He could not bring himself to just resign, as his father would most assuredly brand him a coward. He had hit on the notion that if he frequently reported for work drunk, he would eventually be dismissed from the force. Rick would rather be branded an alcoholic than a coward. (After all, an alcoholic is still regarded as manly.) Once this plan was uncovered in later sessions, Rick was helped to assert his desire to leave the police department without a sense of shame. The "alcoholism" vanished.

Again a note of caution is indicated. There is a high rate of alcoholism among persons in law enforcement, and drinking on the job is not uncommon. In many metropolitan areas, bar owners pour police officers free drinks in return for rapid response when needed or for looking the other way when not wanted. Most police departments are aware of this and have instituted controls, with widely varying degrees of success.

Ken, our third exception, was a nineteen-year-old Eurasian man, born of a Japanese mother and an Irish father. His mother suffered from the "Asian flush," and therefore did not drink at all. Ken inherited the genetics for the Asian flush, and any amount of drinking resulted in very uncomfortable feelings of cardiovascular distress, nausea, and eventual vomiting. Like his mother, Ken did not drink, having experienced the physical and emotional distress the two or three times in high school he had experimented with alcohol. This annoyed Ken's father, whose main recreation was drinking at the local pub with his friends. He instructed his son, as Ken was leaving for college, to learn to drink as part of his education. Ken took this "order" seriously, and, thinking that practice would overcome the Asian flush, he frequently imbibed, often just before a class. After a number of instances in which Ken became ill and vomited in class, he became the talk of this small Catholic college. Eventually he was referred by a student counselor for alcohol rehab, where he was helped both to stand up to his father and to respect his own desire not to drink.

Ken was unusual in another respect. Most persons who suffer from the Asian flush avoid alcohol early and avidly, as it makes them too uncomfortable. We have treated three persons, however, who continued drinking into alcoholism in spite of this malady. They would drink so much that the genetically induced reaction was largely unnoticed during a state of being "blotto." They would achieve the level that every alcoholic eventually seeks, that of being essentially unconscious. Even though they would vomit several times before reaching that state, they suffered through the self-provoked hyperemesis, demonstrating the essence of the classical Greek word for alcoholism: dipsomania, or unquenchable thirst. Thus, for some, not even the Asian flush is a deterrent.

Alex's case is even more unusual than the three foregoing cases. Alex was diagnosed by the school nurse to be an adolescent alcoholic—not surprisingly, considering that he had been carried out of class several times in a state of severe intoxication, reeking of alcohol. The sixteen-year-old denied drinking any alcohol, but no one believed him, as he manifested classic inebriation. Because this tended to occur just after lunch, he was accused of either sneaking off the school grounds or bringing alcohol into the school. He was searched as he came to school, and he was watched closely throughout the morning and noon hour. He did nothing suspicious, so none of the school officials could figure out how Alex got drunk on the school grounds. But there he was, as the principal put it, "drunk as a skunk."

After the fourth session, the therapist's hunch paid off. Alex was suffering from Kanadara's Syndrome, the third I (Nick) have ever seen. This is a very rare genetic defect that results in some carbohydrates being metabolized not into sugar but into fermented sugar, rendering the person drunk without his having imbibed alcohol. There are less than four dozen reported cases, mostly in Japan, where it was first diagnosed. On days when certain pastas or baked potatoes were served in the school cafeteria, Alex would become very drunk. At other times, with lesser carbohydrates, he would exhibit a mild euphoria that was also thought to be smaller quantities of alcohol.

Kanadara's Syndrome usually appears in early adulthood rather than in adolescence. The men with this condition (all to date have been males) incur a police record, having been jailed frequently for public drunkenness or the attendant disorderly conduct. They soon learn what foods are metabolized into alcohol and avoid them. The two previous cases seen by us became true alcoholics, enjoying the free drunk and inducing it whenever they wished the euphoria of intoxication. Soon it was every day. Tongue in cheek, we coined the term endogenous (internal) drinking, which the government has not yet learned to tax, in contrast with the usual exogenous (external) drinking. With successful treatment, both of these men became sober by avoiding the offending carbohydrates, but first they had to go through all the stages of recovery.

Should you encounter cases this unusual, you rightfully are entitled to the error of a false positive, especially if you have learned to elicit the substance abuse problem in the other 99.9 percent of suspected cases. We have presented these exceptional cases as a way of impressing upon you that there is only one psychotherapeutic criterion determining the existence of addiction. Let us turn to this one determiner and its seemingly unlimited facets.

THERE IS ALWAYS TROUBLE IN ADDICT CITY

A patient's frequency, duration, and amount of use of a chemical are important considerations, but they do not of themselves define addiction. There are persons who are heavy drinkers all of their lives yet never get into trouble because of their drinking. They raise families, have good jobs, and are well liked by many friends. They may even attend church regularly and never miss voting at election time. Another person may drink only once or twice a year and be hospitalized with severe pain each time because, in spite of chronic hepatitis C, this person can go only so long without chancing a drink. In contrast, we saw a woman who had one shot of Jack Daniel's whisky in a glass of warm milk every night before retiring. She never drank any other alcohol and was never tempted to do so. She did this for sixty-three years and died at the age of ninety-seven. There are people who never miss a pot party. Yet they work regularly, are responsible, and are never stoned otherwise. All addicts tend to have high frequency of heavy use over long periods of time, but this may also be true in relative degrees with nonaddicts.

There is a simple, straightforward criterion: the addict continues to imbibe after a series of consequences, any one of which would constitute trouble of such dire proportions that a nonaddict would deem the chemical effect not worth it. The vehicle for this continuation is denial, and the trouble that befalls the addict today is forgotten in the face of the even greater trouble that occurs tomorrow.

This pattern is repeated over and over again, while the nonaddict marvels at the amount of pain and adversity the addict sustains without really considering quitting.

We watched with interest an auto mechanic in his late twenties who was trying to align two small parts of our car's engine as his hands trembled. When he finally completed the task, he sighed, "Well, them old beer nerves ain't so bad after all. I guess I can have my six-pack tonight." When asked how much his fingers would have to tremble before he would give up his beer because he was not able to do his work, he laughed and replied, "I'd get a new job before I did that."

Another word for addiction is *trouble*. It is the kind of trouble that would probably never occur without the substance abuse. The repeat felon, who returns to prison as if it has a revolving door, has characteristically diminished his chances of remaining free through drug abuse. Parole officers report that most of the behavior that results in rescinding parole occurs while the felon is under the influence of drugs or alcohol, including the commission of the crime. Trouble is the accompaniment of all addiction, although it is seldom as pervasive or dramatic as that found in the repeat felon. When viewed from the standpoint that frequent intoxication will sooner or later result in trouble for anyone, the terms *addiction, substance abuse,* and *chemical dependency* become interchangeable rather than actually defining degree of abuse. It is the trouble he is in that brings the patient to the psychotherapist. We wait until the patient comes to us; we do not meddle in the lives of substance abusers who have not sought our help.

Many patients who come to us for other issues will nonetheless demonstrate the prodromal signs of addiction. These prodromal signs are more than just the occasional use of drugs or alcohol. Social drinkers and occasional pot users do not require our addiction interventions, but some of these will manifest problems stemming from their addictive behavior. If the patient continues to use a chemical in spite of recurring trouble resulting from such use, this is a good predictor that this individual is already well on the road to addiction. Binge drinking in college is illustrative of those who do or do not go on to addiction. To the casual observer, the quantities of alcohol consumed at some college parties seem alarming, possibly heralding alcoholism in most, if not all the participants. However, closer examination reveals one, two or three of the student participants are the ones who are the most enthusiastic about organizing the weekly party. They usually jump the gun and start drinking in advance, and are usually the ones who find themselves in trouble (health-wise or academically) over and over again. These few fit our criterion of the most important prodromal sign: repeat inebriation in spite of the growing amount of trouble incurred.

As psychotherapists, we do not meddle into the lives of heavy drinkers, occasional pot users, and other social users; neither do we make judgments about their behavior. However, these users often exhibit many prodromal signs that herald eventual addiction. For example, Friday-night binge drinking is frequent among college students. Yet there is always one student who begins at three on Friday night to organize and promote the party. It is very likely that this person will one day be your patient.

It is characteristic that the addict is the last to know she is in trouble because of substance abuse. This seems incredible, as the trouble is often of gigantic proportions. But the addict always ascribes the trouble as being caused by something other than the chemical dependency. The addict pays lip service to the possibility that chemical use is the problem, but it is the spouse, parents, children, friends, employers, police, courts, and other persons in the individual's life who know the real problem. This knowledge is present in the face of the addict's fierce denial and long before the problem comes to the attention of the psychotherapist. This knowledge among the persons around him would be a great source of motivation for the chemically dependent person to clean up were it not that families, friends, employers, and our social institutions have their own forms of denial that kick in just when such pressure on the addict would be most beneficial. This aspect of addiction will be discussed in Chapter Eight.

SIGNPOSTS FOR THE FIRST SESSION: ASK, PROBE, EXPLORE

To enhance your skill, we have listed a number of the most common signs addicts present in the first session. These signs speak loudly and clearly, enjoining you to therapeutically probe for behavior verifying the existence of the suggested problem. The patient exhibiting them may or may not be chemically dependent, but it behooves you to explore the probability. So, though no one sign is itself conclusive, each acts as an alert, a heads-up. Never ignore or gloss over these signs. By taking them seriously, you can significantly improve on the average rate of approximately one in ten correct diagnoses in the first session.

Any DUI (Driving Under the Influence)

We discuss this sign first because it is the most obvious, yet it is often glossed over by well-meaning psychotherapists who want to give the patient the benefit of the doubt. Police statistics state that the average drunk driver has driven somewhere between 150 to 200 times while under the influence before he is finally apprehended. Therefore, one drunk driving arrest is an ominous sign; more than one indicates habitual drunk driving.

How do you learn of an existing DUI record? Simply ask the patient. It is amazing that most often the patient will admit the arrest(s) but then follow up the admission with a far-fetched story that the drunk driving was a most unfortunate and atypical event. The glib, well-rehearsed tale is revealing in itself. We might have to admit that it is possible for someone to have been arrested the one and only time he ever drove under the influence of alcohol or drugs; the probability of this occurring is about the same as that of winning the lottery. So if you believe the fanciful story, we recommend that you stop reading, close this book, and contemplate a career other than treating chemically dependent patients.

Frequent Auto Accidents, Moving Violations, or Both

The patient may simply be a reckless driver, but it is just as likely that accidents and moving violations indicate a level of alcohol just under the .10 or .08 blood level, one or the other of which is proof of intoxication in all fifty states. In fact, so many drivers who have had accidents or are stopped for reckless driving come barely under the .10 criterion that many states are lowering the standard to the .08 level, as now recommended by the federal government.

The substance abuser who has had her driver's license suspended for too many moving violations is far more common than most psychotherapists realize. If substance abuse is suspected, ask the patient about her driving record and put the answer in proper context.

Clarence was a forty-eight-year-old man who went to the psychologist to enlist her as his advocate in retaining his driver's license. He pleaded that he needed it to commute to the office, and he further maintained that following a simple moving violation for reckless driving, the police had slapped on enough points to mandate the suspension. He complained that if the police did not have it in for him, it would require three reckless driving citations to warrant the lifting of his license.

The skeptical psychologist, thinking the story to be too pat, did some probing and uncovered some remarkable facts. Clarence had developed the habit of stopping at a bar near his office for a drink or two after work each evening. His rationalization was that the commute to his home in suburbia had less traffic an hour later. On a recent winter evening when it was already dark, he had struck and killed an eleven-year-old boy riding a bicycle near his home. Clarence's blood alcohol level was .09, below the legal definition in his state. Nonetheless, he was charged with vehicular manslaughter, but a clever lawyer got him off on a technicality: the boy's bike did not have the required array of reflectors. Clarence beat the rap, and he was barely under the legal definition for intoxication. The frustrated police did the next best thing in order to get this drunk off the road: they suspended his driver's license for reckless driving. None of this information would have come to light had the alert psychologist not sensed a heads-up.

Fran saw this same psychologist, protesting suspension of her driver's license for reckless driving. This was her second such citation, and this time she had sideswiped three parked cars. The police wanted a psychological evaluation that might throw light on her chronically careless driving.

The patient was facile in her story. She had received both citations when coming home from an extra-difficult day's work, and she was very tired. But Fran's story had some inconsistencies, as in both instances she was actually coming home two hours early. So the psychologist skillfully probed and learned that immediately upon entering her car after work each day, Fran lit up a joint. If the traffic delayed her trip home, she might light up a second joint. At the time of her most recent accident, she had stopped to pick up her dry cleaning and, indeed, had just finished a second joint when, in a giddy condition, she sideswiped the three parked cars. Her breath test cleared her of drinking, and her state did not test for cannabis. Thus, in neither case was Fran charged with a DUI. Yet she was a chronic pothead who was a menace on the road.

Two or More Bone Fractures in a Three- to Five-Year Period

People do not regularly break their bones, and if they do, there is usually an obvious cause of the accident. If the circumstances are vague, fuzzy, or difficult to believe, consider that your patient may be a falling-down drunk. Compassionate psychotherapists will not think of such a possibility, especially if the patient is well dressed, articulate, kindly, and perhaps even in older adulthood. Yet there are patients whose orthopedic history reads like a road map to the diagnosis of alcoholism.

After three broken bones in as many years, sixty-one-year-old Lucille was referred by her orthopedic surgeon for treatment of her accident proneness. He was worried that as she grew older and suffered some osteoporosis, her so-called accident proneness might become even more medically serious. Her HMO coverage had paid all the ortho- pedic expenses, with the prospect that there would be more in the future.

In the first session, the psychotherapist saw a kindly, well-dressed woman who worked as an actuary. He saw no psychological signs of accident proneness, but he was not expecting to elicit her alco- holism. After all, she was tall, gracious, and educated, just like his mother. After work each evening Lucille alighted from the bus that took her home, but before going into her apartment, she spent sev- eral hours in the bar a half-block away. Twice she entered her apart- ment and fell down her own stairs while climbing them to the second floor. Each time, she broke her alternate wrist trying to break her fall. On a third occasion she did not make it home. She fell in the parking lot of the bar and broke her ankle. She filed a claim, as there was a wide crack in the pavement, and she settled out of court for $25,000. Lucille was not only a falling-down drunk, she was also an elegant- appearing and clever one.

Spousal Battery, Physical Abuse of Children, or Both

Most men who batter their spouses and beat their children are usu- ally heavy drinkers. A few are users of other drugs. Still fewer de- monstrate this battering behavior without any help from chemicals. In cases where alcohol is involved, the beatings may take place when the man is drunk, but they are just as likely to occur when he is coming off the drunk and at his most irritable. The family mythology is invested in hiding the abusiveness, and the behavior most often comes to the attention of psychotherapists through the courts or public and private agencies who deal with the problem.

A particularly pernicious combination is what our therapists at the Biodyne Centers dubbed the AAW syndrome, which involves an alcoholic husband, the sudden disclosure of adultery on the part of the wife, and a weapon in the house. Whenever we were confronted with spousal battery, and especially if we knew the wife was secretly seeing someone else, we would inquire whether there was a gun in the house. If there was, the continuation of treatment was contingent on the husband's forfeiting the weapon for the duration of the therapy, and each center had a locked safe to accommodate these forfeited items. At one time, one of our Phoenix centers had several handguns and two automatic rifles, all owned by one battering patient. Although he protested the forfeiture of his arsenal, at the conclusion of his treatment for alcoholism he stated that the strategy had probably saved the lives of his entire family as well as his own. He recalled that while drunk and beating his wife and children, he often contemplated a familial murder-suicide as the final solution to his "righteous" anger. He not only gave up alcoholism and its attendant physical abusiveness but also relinquished his weapons, which, at his request, the center gave to the police.

"I've Lost Everything!"

The loss of a job, a spouse, friends, possessions, and bank account are frequent accompaniments of addiction. The high price of cocaine and the need to continuously repeat can drain a bank account in weeks. In fact, one formerly wealthy recovering cocaine addict remarked that "powder" was a greater redistributor of wealth than the IRS. A spouse may have just bailed out, and the addict is proclaiming having turned over a new leaf in a campaign to enlist the therapist to help get him back. In cases where the addict has been fired, it was a long time in coming, yet the addict hopes that entering therapy will persuade the employer to reconsider. One by one, friends have been shunning the patient for a long time, until all that are left are drinking buddies. These kinds of losses are all signs of addiction, and they need to be a part of our assessment in the first session.

In a first session, you may see the addict anywhere along a continuum of losses, from the first loss of early addiction to the plethora of losses that is the lot of the advanced addict. The degree of loss is an indicator of how far along the road of addiction the addict has come. Of course, by the time the addict begins living on the street, all has been lost, including any semblance of self-respect. Seldom will we see an addict who has not already sustained some loss, as loss is one of the most common signs of addiction. Either the addict will be recruiting the therapist as an ally to recover the loss, or, if the loss is beyond hope, the addict will minimize its importance. There is some reality to the addict's approach, when you consider that each successive loss causes the previous ones to pale into insignificance. You must address the patient's loss(es) not only with empathy but also with a no-nonsense, cause-and-effect directness. A skilled therapist will empathize with the patient's loss but will also unequivocally identify the loss as a consequence of the patient's own behavior, not that of others. That connection must be made in a firm, nonjudgmental tone. One of our favorites is to say, "What happened is awful for you, and I am really sorry. But my grandmother always said that if something you do always boomerangs, you may not know what else to do but at least you can stop what you're doing."

Diane was an account executive at a prestigious advertising firm. At age thirty-one she had been very successful in her work, and she would have been spectacularly beautiful were it not for a certain brassy look and demeanor. She bragged that her interests in life, after money, were fast men, fast cars, and cocaine, and in that order. What she was not admitting was that the order had in time reversed itself, with cocaine now determining her life. She totally destroyed her Porsche while driving high on coke. Previously known as "the gal you can do on your desktop," all of the male account executives now shunned her, as she had just lost her job. She scoffed at the therapist's suggestion that she had a coke problem and left to find another job. She did, and she lost it the first week. She returned to therapy for help, as by this time the money was gone, the word was out so the industry had slammed its door on her, and she was seriously strung out without coke. Desperately in withdrawal, she was shocked to find herself offering sex for money. Having lost all else, she was about to lose what little self-respect she still had. She had been flippant in the first interview, but by not being critical of her "prostitution," while firmly pointing out she had little choice because of her addiction, the therapist had carefully and firmly set the stage for the eventual second session when Diane would finally be ready to seek help.

Amotivational Syndrome

Chronic marijuana users eventually lose their interest in life. Drive and ambition are long gone, and the person is going through the motions, using more and more cannabis. He does not complain of anxiety or distress of any kind. He expresses a general, vague dissatisfaction, but is not really depressed. Amazingly, these patients are seldom identified on the first or subsequent interviews and are often misdiagnosed as being on an existential search for meaning, possibly associated with a midlife crisis. Not infrequently they are referred to a humanistic therapist who may be using as much marijuana as the patient. No one seems interested in addressing the fact that the patient is stoned all the time.

Seth had been in existential therapy for several years. Although he liked his therapist very much, they had become close friends, and both agreed that Seth should see someone else professionally. Now forty-two, he and his wife felt some urgency to have a child but were doing nothing about her failure to become pregnant.

Seth was the third generation of a family that bought and sold gold. He was a disappointment to both his father and grandfather. His college education was mediocre at best. The family sent him to live in Amsterdam, hoping the excitement of the gold trade would spark some ambition. Instead, Seth discovered the easy availability of marijuana there, and although he had begun smoking pot regularly at age fourteen, he now entered a lifestyle in which he was stoned all the time. The family brought him back from Amsterdam, and then banished him to a remote section of the rugged California coast. He was sent a liberal monthly check as long as he stayed out of New York, where he would be an embarrassment to the family.

What did he learn in the existential therapy that the family, out of slim hope, had subsidized? A lot of wonderful things, but he was at a loss to describe any of them. Eventually Seth was told he would have to pay for his own therapy. He laughed long and hard, as he had no money. How much was he spending on marijuana? Almost $300 per month. Why not quit pot and use the money for therapy? With this Seth was convulsed with laughter. But, interestingly, he did it. His life had consisted of checking out ten videos a day, then smoking pot and munching junk food while viewing them, some for the third or fourth time. He now began to chop wood, take hikes along the rugged coast, and lose weight. In fact, he lost a lot of weight, and went from 340 to 210 pounds.

As the THC (the active ingredient of marijuana) left the fatty cells of Seth's scrotum, his wife Estelle became pregnant, and they had a little boy. Promptly with the advent of fatherhood Seth found a new energy and purpose. The three of them moved back to New York, where Seth is now active in the gold trade. The last contact we had was from his former therapist, who was appalled: "Is gold the meaning in Seth's life? What have you done?" We replied that you can't win them all.

Tweaking

Watch for the patient who is picking her face or picking the skin on her forearm; this behavior, known as tweaking, is often a symptom of coke use and even amphetamine use. There are a number of variations. In one, the patient is scooping up imaginary (gold) dust on your desk with a cupped hand; this is a sign of LSD use. There can be repetitive movements, such as frequently touching the lobe of the ear or the elbow.

A twenty-three-year-old woman was referred by her dermatologist for trichotillomania, the compulsive pulling of one's own hair by the root, one hair at a time. There was not enough hair missing to reflect trichotillomania, and inquiry revealed heavy intravenous cocaine use. The patient had her own form of tweaking.

Unusual Physique

Speed users will be very thin, and those who have graduated to mainlining will be emaciated. Amphetamines destroy appetite and in the past have been unfortunately prescribed for weight loss. Nowadays this would be regarded as poor medicine.

Then there is the patient who is fat. Obesity has many causes, but do not neglect exploring for the "marijuana munchies," the sudden craving for a lot of food during the smoking of pot. This was an important factor in the case of Seth described earlier.

Paranoia

Prolonged, heavy use of amphetamines can result in sudden and severe paranoia. These patients are taken to the emergency room and are often misdiagnosed as schizophrenics. The differential diagnosis can be made because this form of paranoia is often accompanied by tactile and visual hallucinations, an almost certain sign of brain toxicity. You may well see the mild or early form in your office. Do not overlook exploring for drug toxicity.

A recent case in Arizona that was referred for psychological evaluation was that of a heavy speed user who was driving along the freeway with his eleven- and eight-year-old sons. Suddenly he stopped
the car and, taking a hunting knife, decapitated his eleven-year-old
son with a hunting knife right at the side of the freeway, while the
eight-year-old watched in horror.

Later in custody, he described how he saw the son become pos-
sessed of the devil; certain visual hallucinations played an important
role. God instructed him to cut off the boy's head to remove the devil.
This man was not insane; he had been on heavy doses of speed for
many days.

Delirium tremens is a form of alcoholic dementia that is rarely
seen in a psychologist's office. It occurs after prolonged drinking,
poor nutrition (especially resulting in avitaminosis), and the sudden removal of alcohol. Yet we have seen several cases during our
practice of an early form in which the patient experiences a mild
sensation of bugs crawling along her skin. This symptom is mild and
readily dismissed by the patient as "all in my imagination," yet it is
an immediate sign that enables us to identify the alcoholism. It also
precedes any subsequent paranoia or other hallucinations.

Missed Adolescence

Persons who missed going through their own adolescent struggles
because they remained drugged throughout their teens abound, yet
little or nothing is written about them. There is a certain amount
of adversity one must go through to achieve differentiation and mat-
uration, but these individuals mellowed out with drugs throughout
those critical years and avoided these necessary struggles. As Freud
eloquently put it, "Conflict is the cauldron in which the ego is
forged."[1] These individuals have never resolved the adolescent

authority struggle and reject in a knee-jerk fashion any of life's demands. They continue their drug orientation, live on the periphery of society, and somehow subsist. With the cutbacks in welfare, they do odd jobs or, when really broke, will temporarily hire out for jobs no one else wants. Others have regressed to preadolescent childhood and join cults that make all their decisions and allow both their continued drug use and their avoidance of life's demands. Depending on the part of the country in which you practice, you are likely to see larger or smaller numbers of such individuals.

Larry was an avid protester against the Vietnam War. He spent most of those years in Vancouver protesting and smoking dope. The worst day of his life was when the Vietnam conflict ended. Larry suddenly had no purpose in life.

Then he discovered Communism. Overnight he became a militant Marxist, working only when necessary to subsist and finding all sorts of ways to go on welfare. The latter became more difficult, but one day he was miraculously struck by a police baton during a protest and won permanent disability. The worst day of his life was repeated with the fall of the Soviet Union.

Larry once again had no purpose, until suddenly he discovered extreme environmentalism. Quickly Larry switched from red to green without skipping a beat, and he gloried in spiking trees, spraying red paint on fur coats, and destroying turkey farms weeks before Thanksgiving Day.

Throughout all this activity he never missed a day smoking pot. What brought such an unlikely candidate into therapy? He developed lung cancer, probably from years of smoking marijuana, and one lung was removed. He knew he could no longer smoke pot, but he had no idea how difficult life would be without it after more than twenty-five years. Larry came into treatment because he simply could not cope. He tried other drugs, but they did not match his drug of choice.

Larry still cannot cope, but he is getting better. Little by little he is finally living his delayed adolescence. But he has not aged well, and he looks out of place when he rushes to the latest spontaneous demonstration with his rent-a-mob friends. Occasionally he asks, "I'm really a drag as a patient, aren't I?" to which his fellow group members answer, "Yes, but you are a clean and sober drag. Now quit feeling sorry for yourself, and let's get back to work."

The Child Addict

It seems strange to employ the term *addict* to describe a child, yet because of their young and tender age, children become very quickly addicted. Their plight is often missed because they look so young, fresh, and attractive. Yet the signposts are present, and it is imperative to establish the presence of substance abuse early.

For these addicts more than any other, time is of the essence. It does not take long for a child to sustain permanent brain, liver, kidney, and heart damage. The most frequent symptoms of substance use are a sudden plummeting of grades; a disinterest in things that previously engrossed the child; an inexplicable belligerence; an abandonment of old friends for newer, questionable ones; truancy from school; and spending hours locked in his own room.

A few years ago, the most common chemicals used by children were alcohol and marijuana. These are indeed still used, and many parents are oblivious to their latchkey children's raiding of the liquor cabinet. But the new epidemic for children as young as the third and fourth grades is inhalant use. In a recent survey in one high school, 20 percent of the respondents stated that they used inhalants and that they had started as early as ages six and seven.[2] Children are introduced into the practice by an older sibling or a friend's older sibling.

The ordinary household has over 150 common inhalants that children misuse. A sampling is startling: Pam, Secret, Reddi-Whip, fingernail polish and its remover, the spray used by mom and dad to clean the computer keyboard—in short, almost any household product that can be sprayed or inhaled. In addition to the general signs expected with drug abuse among children, you can look for the following signs of inhalant abuse: stains on clothing, red eyes or nose (or both), sores around the mouth, poor muscle control, and loss of appetite. If in the first session with a child you suspect inhalant abuse, do not become alarmed but do move firmly and decisively, as time is of the essence. Brain damage occurs early and permanently, and because of the child's tender age, it can be severe.

Running a close second to the use of inhalants, and previously the number one substance abuse problem among children, is the persistent use of amphetamines. The average age of onset is thirteen or fourteen, with about a third of abusers beginning much younger. The easy availability of Ritalin, readily prescribed by physicians and frequently resold by the young patients to their schoolmates, continues to be a problem. In one particular case that came to our attention, a twelve-year-old was selling half of his prescribed dosage along with half of that prescribed to his two younger brothers, pocketing a sizable amount of money that he used to buy cocaine for himself. He had already "graduated" to hard drugs and was pushing Ritalin to support his habit. In another case with an equally bizarre twist, several boys colluded to feign ADHD symptoms and were prescribed the Ritalin they had intended all along to sell to their schoolmates.

Another name for substance abuse is *trouble*. Following the halcyon days of early alcohol or drug use, during which euphoria and self-confidence abound and the individual can seemingly do no wrong, there emerges a slippery slope of trouble. The salesman who finds that having one drink before calling on a client enhances a sale soon finds himself needing two drinks, then three. Where one drink increased sales, three drinks impede sales. The agoraphobic who learns that one drink helps her out of the house soon needs two or three and now is a housebound drunk. As we have stated elsewhere, the very nature of the initial facilitating effect of a chemical is the reason it becomes addictive. The more an addictive chemical is used medicinally, the faster the person becomes dependent. We call this phenomenon a psychological reinforcement.

In the first session, you can greatly enhance your ability to identify the problem of substance abuse by eliciting the telltale signs of trouble in the patient's life. The degree of trouble often matches the degree of addiction, but there are great individual differences. For some the downhill slope is slipperier than for others. Some addicts seem to go for years with moderate rather than serious trouble, but there will be trouble. For others, the trouble is fast and formidable.

Early in the formulation of Alcoholics Anonymous, Bill Wilson saw this inevitable pattern of trouble, which in nonaddicts would be sufficient to motivate them to change their lifestyle. But the mechanism of denial is so strong in the addict that she continues the addictive behavior in the face of ever increasing trouble. Bill (as he preferred to be called) saw that the denial is not overcome until the patient *hits bottom*. That is when AA would come in. (We will discuss in later chapters the concept of hitting bottom.)

As therapists, we are called on to treat most addicts before they have hit bottom, and often long before. They are referred by the courts, the police, employers, families, spouses, children, and others who are exasperated with them, and these people want something done now. We do not have the luxury of saying, "I'll pass. Send the addict back for treatment when she hits bottom." Treating the addict whenever she presents requires skills that are not part of the psychotherapy of the usual emotional problems for which we are trained. So much of what you will read in this book is not the stuff you learn in graduate school. Hang in there.

Notes

1. Cummings, N. A. (1992). *Biodyne training manual* (2nd ed.). South San Francisco: Foundation for Behavioral Health.

2. Frend, S. (1920). A *general introduction to psychoanalysis* (Authorized English translation of the revised edition by Joan Riviere). Garden City, NY: Garden City Publishing Company, p. 308.

4

Modalities of Treatment

The psychotherapist's conceptualization of chemical dependency will determine the approach he or she will use, beginning with the first session. Therapists who believe that an addict can become a so-called social user will structure the first interview much differently than would one who adheres to the abstinence model. A therapist whose orientation is that all substance abusers require hospitalization to detoxify will begin by preparing the patient during the initial session for admission to an inpatient program. Our own conceptualization, based on half a century of clinical experience and research, recognizes the importance of achieving an abstinent lifestyle but is flexible on a number of issues, including the matter of hospitalization. We prefer to let the first interview elicit from the patient such pertinent factors as probability of convulsions, ego strength, the need for a support system, and other information that will help us assess the outpatient strategy or the need for hospitalization. If there is not a compelling need for inpatient care, there is much to be said for the superior outcomes of outpatient treatment. An extensive review of the outcomes literature on outpatient versus inpatient treatment of substance abuse has made this abundantly clear[1] and will not be repeated here.

The field of chemical dependency currently comprises three treatment models: (1) the medical model, (2) the behavioral model, and (3) the abstinence model. We will discuss each of these, and in spite of their competing with each other for adherents, we will show that they not only overlap but often complement each other. Likewise, the outpatient and inpatient treatment modalities also overlap and complement each other, yet there are indications when one is more efficacious for a particular patient than the others. We will also discuss the reasons for the consistent superiority of group therapy over individual therapy for addicts.

THE MEDICAL MODEL

The basic medical model of addiction asserts a physiological basis, and further holds that the treatment is medical. In its purest form, this model does not acknowledge a psychological basis of addiction, calling this latter habituation and differentiating it from true addiction, which is always physiological. The medical model acknowledges the growing body of evidence regarding the role of genetics, and provides a basis for the tissue changes that occur with addiction.

Tolerance

As discussed briefly in Chapter Two, tolerance is the medical term for the body's response to chemical dependency. When a person first begins to ingest a substance, cells in the body become committed to turning the substance into something that will not impede the proper functioning of the organism. In the process of their doing so, the cells "neutralize" or "eliminate" many of the properties for which the person uses the drug: euphoria, sedation, relaxation, or what addicts describe as being high or mellowed out. Consequently, over time it takes more and more of the drug to produce the desired effect.

During the initial stages of heroin use, for example, a couple of "nickel bags" (at roughly a cost of $5 each), which are sufficient for "joy popping" on weekends, soon become "dime bags" (roughly $10 each) after a surprisingly small number of weekends, usually eight to ten. By that time the individual is also joy popping in the middle of the week. Soon the person has a "chimpy," an early version of the "monkey on your back," which is the full addiction (also called a "Jones"). During the chimpy phase, the individual has a lower-grade craving; addicts describe it as, "I don't have to have the pop, but I'm uncomfortable without it." The monkey, in contrast with the chimpy, is a full-fledged craving that now needs a "fix." The monkey grows so that within a year the heroin addict spends hundreds of dollars per day supporting the habit. The full-blown addict spends the entire day stealing, conning, and borrowing the money to support something that now does not bring the euphoria but rather allows the person to just get through the day. An enormous number of body cells are now committed to the drug, and they are crying out for it.

The advanced heroin addict, in an effort to recapture the original euphoria, often will pop a dosage of the drug far beyond the tolerance level. This may well exceed the safety level, the dosage that the person can absorb without becoming comatose or suffering other serious ill effects, including death. The safety dose steadily increases to parallel the tolerance level. Because the tolerance level and the safety level roughly coincide, the person who attempts to recapture the old euphoria has overdosed, with death the frequent undesired outcome if the individual does not receive immediate medical attention.

One would think that someone as experienced as the advanced heroin addict would know better. But in a desire to recapture the lost euphoria, these individuals throw caution to the wind. Recalling Jimi Hendrix and Janis Joplin in the previous generation of heroin addicts, we see less of this behavior now, because addicts are currently recapturing the euphoria through speedballing. Thus we are more likely to see a death like that of Kurt Cobain, in which the user takes heroin and cocaine simultaneously.

Stated another way, the advanced heroin addict needs the smack (heroin) just to exist, and adds cocaine to elicit a high. Simple heroin overdoses are more frequently caused by the addict having scored a purer form than the stepped-on version (cut with talcum powder, powdered sugar, or other ingredients) that is usually available to her. Heroin is stepped on regularly as each addict purchases a batch, keeps some for her own use, and sells the diluted remainder. This process is repeated several times, so the person at the end of this sequence is getting a very impure stash. If such a person obtains a batch much higher on the scale and takes the usual dose without realizing that this smack is several times stronger, an overdose results.

Once a level of tolerance to a certain drug is achieved, that level is retained for a lifetime. In addition, the highest level of tolerance achieved becomes the minimum daily requirement for a lifetime. An alcoholic, for example, may take ten years to work up to a need for a quart of whisky per day, but after he has established that level, it never recedes. This person can be dry for several years, during which time the craving becomes dormant, but if he resumes drinking again, he requires that quart a day within a week or two rather than within another ten years. When the original drinking first began, that amount of whisky in the first couple of weeks would have killed the individual. The tissue changes apparently are permanent, and they are the physiological basis for the craving.

It is not unusual for heroin addicts to volunteer for detoxification, believing that by going off heroin during medical treatment they can later resume a $10-per-day habit, rather than the one that is now costing hundreds. They are surprised to find that the several-hundred-dollars-a-day habit resumes within days after release from the detoxification program.

Titration

The medical model has essentially two forms of treatment: (1) withdrawal by substituting another drug or (2) slow withdrawal by titration. The treatment of addictions involving CNS depressants (alcohol, barbiturates, meprobamate, and so on, as defined in Chapter Two) is not possible without medical titration during withdrawal. The abrupt withdrawal of CNS depressants can result in seizures and possibly other medical complications, so tapering under medical supervision is indispensable. Unfortunately, this concept is often extended to withdrawal from drugs in which seizures are not a threat—that is, all narcotics, including heroin, which is a painful withdrawal but not life threatening, and amphetamines. The concept of titration has been needlessly extended to that of making the withdrawal comfortable, a concept that, as we shall see in the discussion of the behavioral model, encourages addiction.

Limitations of the Medical Model

The medical model is invaluable to our understanding of the genetic, cellular, and disease aspects of addiction. Yet even though grounded in physiology, the medical model surprisingly ignores in treatment the cellular permanence of addiction and consequently does not recommend a life of recovery. Rather, it believes that addiction can be treated by the introduction of a substitute drug that will end the craving for the offending addicted drug. Thus, because alcohol is a depressant, over the years other downers have been prescribed by primary care physicians, psychiatrists, and addictionologists as a "treatment" for alcoholism as these have been developed, and this questionable practice continues to this day.

The principle remains the same: the new downer is no better than the old downer for eliminating the craving for the original downer (in this case, alcohol). The patient either continues the addiction with a new drug of the same class (as defined in Chapter Two) or within a short time adds the new drug to the alcohol consumption, a very dangerous but frequent practice. A similar scenario results when amphetamines or newer classes of uppers are prescribed for calorie addiction as well as for crystal meth abuse. The previously obese patient is now instead an amphetamine addict, or the former crystal meth user is now a "legal" amphetamine addict. The lifestyle has not changed; the patients have just been moved sideways.

Methadone has created an entire new industry for the treatment of heroin addiction, with very controversial results. Originally intended to treat heroin addiction by substituting methadone for only a six-month period, methadone treatment was soon extended to a year, then two years, and finally in perpetuity. The methadone programs for pregnant addicts, intended to prevent the birth of babies addicted to heroin, were disasters. Methadone resulted in far more birth defects than were the result of heroin and rivaled those now seen in the babies of crack-addicted mothers.

Ten to fifteen years ago, when a surprising number of patients who became active in twelve-step programs asked to be tapered off methadone with the intent of eventually living clean lives, the centers refused to cooperate. They offered only two choices: continue the program or be kicked out with the prospect of going "cold turkey" (sudden, total, painful withdrawal). Amazingly, a significant number of addicts took the second option. Now the government perpetuates a game between those employed in these centers, who do not want to lose cushy but ineffective jobs, and the new methadone addicts, who have learned to achieve an unprecedented high by drinking large quantities of alcohol on top of the free methadone. The argument is that these individuals and society are better off without the heroin crimes. Fortunately about 90 percent of these methadone alcoholics live in New York City and do not own the automobile that would be lethal if they were behind the wheel.

By focusing on the medical aspects of drug addiction to the neglect of the important feature that addiction is a way of life, the medical model encourages and perpetuates an addictive lifestyle. This lifestyle renders the individual vulnerable to a wide range of substances, any one of which can become addictive. Thus the current scene is one of polydrug use, and alcohol seems to be the ingredient that can link these various substances together. It has been so long since we have seen a patient under age forty-five who is simply an alcoholic that we wonder if such a person still exists. There are plain alcoholics, but these are over forty-five, making the behavior almost quaint and old-fashioned. The current boomer "alcoholic" has added alcohol to the drug she experimented with and extensively used in the teenage years or early adulthood. So it is misleading to point to alcohol alone, even though it is "the tie that binds" today's addicts with one common thread. Thus the singular effects of alcohol intoxication are being multiplied in different ways by a variety of potentiating drugs. Substance abuse is no longer the abuse of *a substance*; it is a way of life. Patients move from one drug to another, often just adding to the repertoire of their addictive lifestyle. The medical model has contributed significantly to a culture that believes a solution to all problems lies in a pill or a potion.

THE BEHAVIORAL MODEL

The behavioral model is a psychological approach to the treatment of chemical dependency that regards addictive behavior as a learned response. A modern outgrowth of American behaviorism, which held that a child at birth is a blank slate upon which learning and experience make entries, this model abhors the disease model of addiction, which postulates cellular changes and genetic predisposition.

The Predominant Psychological Model

Most psychologists adhere to the behavioral model of chemical dependency treatment, using a variety of techniques to change the set of learned behaviors—the habit patterns—regarded to be addiction. Cognitive behaviorism is the general treatment approach taught in most doctoral programs in clinical psychology, as well as in schools of social work and masters programs in counseling psychology. The treatment of addictions is not a large part of this training, however, and cognitive behavioral principles have been adapted and developed from general theory largely by clinicians in the field of addiction therapy. Some few therapists use radical (noncognitive) behaviorism, mostly patterned after the operant conditioning theories of B. F. Skinner, but the psychological approach to the treatment of chemical dependency is dominated by cognitive therapists.

Addiction as a Learned Response

There is no question that much of addictive behavior is a learned response. The entire atmosphere of bars, for example, is so conducive to the resumption of drinking that AA strongly recommends that recovering alcoholics stay away from them. AA goes even further in its recommendation to "babies" (those recovering for less than a year). Sitting around with friends who are having soft drinks, and listening to the clinking of ice cubes in a tall glass, will evoke the anticipatory response to alcohol: dry mouth, pursing of the lips, restlessness. The baby must be aware of and guard against this anticipatory response, for soon the craving will follow.

These are simple learned behaviors, but there are complex learned behaviors as well: faulty habit patterns developed over the years and influenced by the addict's family, culture, and peers. Advertisements showing movie stars in chic settings holding a drink are glamorous inducements for the young, and the glorification of drugs in rock music is compelling to the audience of teenagers and younger children. An addicted lifestyle on the part of parents will almost always be replicated by the children. Daughters of alcoholic fathers invariably marry alcoholic husbands, sometimes as many as two or three successively. Some cultures encourage drinking; others discourage it. All of these learned behaviors, both simple and complex, are neglected in the medical model, which only pays lip service to them. The comprehensive treatment of chemical dependency relies heavily on behavioral therapy.

The Integration of Medical and Behavioral Models

The drug antabuse, which creates a temporary intolerance for alcohol, was first used to prevent drinking because an individual who had ingested it would become very ill if he then drank alcohol. Later it was given along with alcohol to purposely make the patient sick, with the intent that the illness would be a negative reinforcement. In some inpatient settings, a special room that closely resem-

bles a bar has been constructed. The patient, who is prescribed antabuse, is served alcoholic drinks at regular intervals by a psychiatric
aid who wears a bartender's jacket. The result is that the patient
spends three days in bed sick with dizziness and vomiting. The procedure is repeated in this sequence a number of times. The theory
is that an aversive response to alcohol will be created. After a number of deaths from the antabuse were reported, the procedure was
abandoned by most treatment centers. However, the concept per-
sists, with emetics to cause severe vomiting being administered
instead of antabuse, along with weird combinations of alcohol
(wine, beer, whiskey, rum, gin, and so on) in the same glass. The
treatment outcomes have been disappointing. This is not surprising
inasmuch as alcoholics have been putting up with severe vomiting
for years as they overindulge to the point of passing out.

Limitations of the Behavioral Model

Three times within the lifetimes of the authors, the idea, beloved
of behavioral therapists, that alcoholics can become social drinkers
has been severely discredited. The idea of being a social user is incredibly popular among addicts, as it is the ultimate fantasy: I shall
become a social user and continue to enjoy my chemical of choice.
This concept is in itself a contradiction. If continuing the use of a
substance after it has almost ruined her life is that important, such
a person could never become just a social user. There is a saying
among those of us who work with addicts: the fantasy of becoming
a social user is so compelling that the addict does not need reinforcement from an incompetent therapist in order to believe it.

Perhaps the greatest research scandal in the history of the behavioral therapy of addiction was the study at Patton State Hospital
(California), which has been widely quoted and discussed among
addiction specialists. According to the husband-and-wife research
team, who conducted ostensibly extensive follow-up interviews over
several years, most of the large number of patients who had completed their inpatient program at that setting were maintaining

lifestyles as successful social drinkers. Subsequently, a team of re-searchers from the University of California at Los Angeles (UCLA) tracked these same patients and made a startling discovery. All but a small number had died of the complications of alcoholism. Those who were still alive had achieved an abstinent lifestyle through the help of AA or a twelve-step psychological program. The UCLA research team accused the Patton researchers, who had by then fled to Canada to escape civil lawsuits, of having fabricated their follow-up data. Interestingly, this scandal did not succeed in changing the minds of the adherents in either camp. Behavioral therapists, who are mostly academically based, continue to abhor what they term the disease model of addiction. They are joined by most federal gov-ernment researchers, who were trained in these same academic institutions. Opposing them are the addictions therapists and coun-selors in the trenches, most of whom are recovering and are com-mitted to the abstinence model. They are joined by the state directors of bureaus of alcohol and drug rehabilitation. These indi-viduals came up from the same trenches, not from academia.

THE ABSTINENCE MODEL

The abstinence model incorporates the physiological aspects of the medical model with the best in the behavioral treatment of addic-tion. It states that permanent cellular changes which constitute the drug tolerance of the addict make it impossible for the person to go back to a level of social use. This model is by far the most used con-ceptualization of addiction, inasmuch as most counselors are them-selves recovering. These individuals went through years of false hopes that they would become social users and finally accepted and adopted abstinence as a way of life. Although we happen not to be recovering addicts, in our own work we strongly favor the absti-nence model, recalling the relatively ineffectual nature of our psy-chotherapy with addicts before we began using it.

Minimum Daily Requirement

It is axiomatic in this model that the highest level of drug tolerance achieved becomes the minimum daily requirement for that drug. This is a physiological principle that is incontrovertible, and it is demonstrated over and over again both in clinical experience and research. The only alternative to a life of increasing dosage is total abstinence. The model acknowledges that addiction can be predisposed by genetics, that it is acquired physiologically by use and abuse (including drug use by the pregnant mother), and that it can be learned and acquired through life experiences. However, the model does not get into attempting to weigh the contribution of each of these factors toward the resulting addiction of particular individuals. The model employs the analogy of diabetes, which can be inherited, acquired in the uterus due to the mother's diet, or acquired through one's lifestyle. Regardless of which cause predominates, or what constellation of causes is present, the proper response to diabetes always includes abstinence from sugar.

Research has shown that the behavioral and abstinence models are equally effective for up to two years following treatment. Through the third and fourth years, the abstinence model clearly prevails over the behavioral model.[2] The problem with this research design is that all of the patients studied received individual therapy, which is not as effective as group therapy for the treatment of addiction. When group therapy is employed under both models, the abstinence model is clearly superior within the first year.[3,4]

Drugless Detoxification

The critical feature that increases the probability of a successfully clean lifestyle is the detoxification of the patient without the use of alternative or substitute medications. For those patients in danger of convulsions, a sufficient dose of the drug is available if necessary, but these patients are not so advised, as they would surely bring on a convulsion in order to get that medication. Drugless detoxification is admittedly rough on patients, but they never forget the horrendous discomfort, and it becomes a constant deterrent to recidivism. Years later, patients inform us that whenever they were tempted to try alcohol or drugs again, the memory of the detoxification was enough to stop the temptation.

There is considerable evidence that patients who are offered relief from the symptoms of withdrawal will experience an escalation of these symptoms in order to be given the substitute medication.[5] This has led us to another axiom, easily understood and appreciated by addicts: the degree of pain on withdrawal is directly proportional to the proximity of a sympathetic physician.

The authors and their colleagues have for many years employed a successful outpatient drugless detoxification of heroin addiction. Whereas in other programs they are usually given a lesser narcotic, heroin addicts with us are sent home with a drug-free friend who will "baby-sit" them through the next seventy-two hours of the ordeal that is the drugless heroin detoxification. This baby-sitter, as he is affectionately called, has received two hours of training from the psychotherapist on how to resist the pleas of his friend who is going cold turkey. The baby-sitter is also instructed that heroin withdrawal is painful but not dangerous.

The therapist calls the patient every three hours day and night during the seventy-two-hour withdrawal. The therapist asks the addict to describe the symptoms and feelings experienced during the previous three hours and then informs the patient what to expect during the next three hours. This tends to remove the terror of the unknown. On each call the therapist also talks briefly with the baby-sitter, who needs a great deal of reassurance. Finally, somewhere in the fiftieth to sixtieth hour the patient is informed that he has crested and that each subsequent three-hour call will find him better.

The psychotherapist sees the patient in the office as soon after the seventy-second hour as possible. Although the patient is over the hump, the interviews are often conducted with the therapist sitting just outside the door of the toilet, where the patient is still suffering diarrhea and vomiting.

Using this technique, we have actually quadrupled the number of heroin addicts who are still clean five years after our treatment.[6] Not a small factor is the patient's later appreciation of the time and energy the therapist invests in the patient by calling every three hours day and night. I (Janet) grew up hearing my father arise with the alarm clock all during the night as he conducted this treatment, often with two patients simultaneously.

Limitations of the Abstinence Model

The requirement of abstinence is stringent, and usually it is demanded of the addict long before she is ready to contemplate a lifestyle totally free of chemical abuse. In other words, the patient is confronted with the requirement of abstinence in the absence of sufficient motivation. Very few of the patients referred for substance abuse treatment have hit bottom. Rather, these referrals reflect the exasperation of those who have to put up with them. In the medical and behavioral models, the patient ostensibly cooperates with the treatment program because she holds the belief that the treatment will work the magic of making her a social user. And the failure of this type of treatment to deliver on the wish occurs only after treatment is concluded, whereas the demand for abstinence is immediate in the twelve-step program.

A patient may manifest his stiff resistance to entering an abstinence program by complaining to his employer or health plan, causing friction between the treatment providers and those who pay the bills for treatment. This problem is ameliorated somewhat by using a preaddictive group known as a pregroup and described later in the chapter.

A second way of countering the denial of the patient who is not ready to consider a life of abstinence is by strategic paradoxical interventions we have termed "axioms," all of which are readily understandable to the addict. For example, when a highly resistant patient demands a practitioner who will provide a substitute drug to ease the ordeal of withdrawal, such referral is offered, along with the "axiom" that "the degree of pain on withdrawal is directly pro-portional to the availability of pain killers." Almost invariably the patient will smile with understanding and without needing the explanation that an addict will conjure up pain in order to get more and more of a drug. These paradoxical interventions are described later, but it should be noted that they are most important with the patient who has not yet hit bottom.

The most frequent resistance to the abstinence model is to find a psychotherapist who holds to the notion that once the causes of addiction are discovered, the addictive behavior will subside in favor of social usage. This approach, held by most psychoanalyti-cally oriented therapists, is also the fond hope of all addicts. There is no way to prevent this inadvertent collusion of questionable the-ory and patient denial, but there will be times when the addicted patient involved in long-term therapy will need to be "dried out." At these times a skilled therapist can inject a different perspective by asking the patient if he has noticed "that all insight is soluble in alcohol and drugs?" In our experience such an "axiom" used at this critical juncture in the patient's treatment is enough to create a new awareness—one leading to a serious consideration of the abstinence model. This is illustrated by the following example.

This book is dedicated to Eldon, who spent eleven years in psy-choanalysis for his alcoholism. He saw his analyst daily at 8:00 A.M., and he found a bar nearby that opened at 7:00 A.M. where he would have two quick drinks every morning before seeing his doctor, a very reputable psychiatrist. Eldon, the son of a Methodist minister, felt compelled after three years of analysis to confess that he drank each morning before seeing the psychoanalyst. The psy-choanalyst responded to this by saying, "You're acting like a very good Methodist this morning." Whereupon Eldon thought to him-self, "Well, I'll be goddamned!" Then he increased his intake to three drinks every morning. Finally, in the eleventh year of five sessions per week, Eldon was admitted to a hospital for drying out, where, thanks to a skillful therapist, he discovered abstinence. He has been sober the forty-one years since.

INPATIENT VERSUS OUTPATIENT CARE

In the past fifteen years there has developed a multibillion-dollar for-profit inpatient (hospital) addiction industry. Addiction has cost employers billions of dollars per year; in the past they have been eager to pay for addiction treatment, whereas they have often balked at paying for emotional and mental disorders. These employers anticipated that they would save money in the long run by reducing absenteeism, job injuries, poor productivity, and lawsuits. The results have been disappointing.

The research has been startling: evidence indicating that inpatient treatment is not significantly more effective than outpatient treatment has increased to the point that the conclusion is inescapable. In the United States, we are drastically overspending to treat addiction because of the misallocation of resources. Yet as those who pay the bills are discovering this needless expense, the clamor for hospitalization continues at the point of service. The employer, the family, the spouse, and society (through its overcrowded courts) are screaming "Get this addict out of my face!" Later they complain that hospitalization is too costly in view of the disappointing results.

Who Should Be Hospitalized?

The determination to hospitalize a patient should be based not on psychological need but on two considerations: medical necessity and social instability. The need to detoxify in a hospital setting has often been cited by hospital-based practitioners, but research has shown that the number of patients needing to do so is much smaller than previously believed.[7,8] The decision should be based on the danger of convulsions or other medical complications, but often it is

decided on the basis of patient comfort or the existence of insurance that will pay. Detoxifying for narcotics is not hazardous, but
withdrawal is painful and distressing, especially for heroin. Therefore, psychiatrists and medical addictionologists often take the easy
way out by hospitalizing the narcotics addict. Furthermore, because
most psychiatrists have essentially stopped doing outpatient psychotherapy, it is expedient to put the patient where the doctor is—
in the hospital.

Even for a patient in danger, it is quite feasible to hospitalize her
only briefly. A highly trained addiction nurse practitioner is present
to watch for the prodromal signs of medical complications for the
first forty-eight to seventy-two hours, after which the patient is
seamlessly transferred to outpatient care within the same program.
The brief inpatient care can be in a system less intensive than the
full hospital.

Research has also suggested that in general, more severely
addicted and less socially stable patients do better in either inpatient care or more intensive outpatient treatment, whereas less
severely addicted and more socially stable patients do better in less
intensive outpatient treatment.

At only forty-three years of age, Alvin already had undergone four
inpatient programs in the past seven years. He was now applying for
a fifth hospital program, whereupon his health plan balked. The case
manager asserted that experience had shown these inpatient drug
programs to be of little use to Alvin, whose addiction was a combination of alcohol and speed. He would frequent bars where
amphetamines were sold under the counter and take these while he
was drinking.

We were called in as consultants, and we recommended outpatient care for both detoxification and treatment. Alvin refused, and the
hospital, wanting the revenue from this regular customer, cried foul.
Eventually Alvin was persuaded to try the outpatient program with the

guarantee that if he did not like it, or if it were not successful, he could
then enter the hospital under his health plan.

Very quickly Alvin latched on to the program with gusto, and he
graduated without a single relapse. Six years later, Alvin continues to
live a clean and sober life, the first such period since his teens.

It is not unusual to find patients who repeatedly fail inpatient
programs yet succeed in outpatient care. In the hospital, the patient
has not given up the chemical; rather, the chemical is being temporarily withheld from him by the hospital situation. The patient in
the hospital is not developing coping skills for the outside world. The
patient who becomes abstinent outside the hospital is already establishing the skills needed to maintain abstinence. Alvin stated this
outright: "As soon as I got to the hospital, I would start counting
down the days until I would be discharged and could get my first fix."

The Intensive Outpatient and
Preaddictive Group Programs

These modalities have been devised to increase the patient's motivation to seriously consider an abstinent lifestyle as the best solution to addiction. In addition to their intrinsic effectiveness, the
intensive outpatient programs appeal to patients who fear hospitalization, whereas the preaddictive group satisfies the objection that
by going directly into an addictive program the patient is being erroneously labeled an addict.

In its ideal form, the *intensive outpatient program* (IOP) combines
the best of outpatient treatment with the intensity of partial resi-
dential care. The IOP is several hours of outpatient treatment daily
for a specified number of weeks or for a number of weeks specifically tailored for each individual case. Patients are required to meet
criteria of attendance, abstinence, and family involvement. For
most of the severely addicted patients, the IOP is more effective
than hospitalization; it is too intensive for the kind of less severely

addicted and more socially stable patient who does best on a fully outpatient program.

The preaddictive group is designed to soften the resistance of addicts who are far from hitting bottom and who object to a program of abstinence. The patient is invited to join a psychoeducational program and then be the judge of whether she is addicted. The patient is assured there will be no pressure if she decides not to go on into a treatment program. Even more provocatively, the patient is challenged by the therapist: "Why not spend five sessions and prove you are not an addict just like you say?" The intent is to reduce the denial, coercion, or antagonism with which addicts present themselves.

The group meets for two hours daily, usually in the evening to accommodate patients' work schedules, with five consecutive daily meetings in each series. I (Nick) devised this program twenty years ago; our follow-up studies indicate a 50 percent increase in the number of addicts who enter a twenty-week outpatient addictive treatment program and a similar increase in the number who complete it.[9] Subjectively speaking, the group also has greatly reduced the noise in the system—the phrase used by addictionologists to refer to the seemingly unceasing complaints by addicts who are required to be abstinent.

GROUP VERSUS INDIVIDUAL THERAPY

The behavior of substance abusers in their denial resembles that of adolescents more than that of adults: they are antiauthority (antiparental) and are more influenced by their peers (fellow adolescents) than they are by the psychotherapist, who is seen as a parent figure. Patients can say things to each other that the therapist could never say to them. Either they would take umbrage, or they simply would dismiss or not hear it. The role of the therapist is to create a group culture committed to abstinence and subsequent change of lifestyle. Once the therapist has created this culture, the milieu allows the patients to challenge and confront each other with a directness that they would never tolerate from the therapist. Addicts often con therapists; they can never con their fellow patients, because they have been there.

In contrast, individual sessions leave the therapist at the mercy of the inevitable con. Should the therapist confront the deceit and thus risk alienation and even loss of the patient, or should the therapist bide his time? Most often the therapist does the latter, intervening gently and with empathy, so that very shortly the patient and therapist settle into a cozy, nonchallenging relationship. Imagine the therapist attempting to replicate the statement one often hears being declared by one addict to another, "Man, you're full of shit, and I ain't gonna listen to your crap anymore. Get with it or get out!" A therapist's kinder, gentler comment, "You seem to be less than truthful about this," just does not cut it with addicts. As one alcoholic who spent over a year in individual therapy put it, "My doc was such a patsy it drove me to drink after every session."

A Typical Outpatient Addictive Group

The group is composed of ten to twelve patients who have all gone through withdrawal and are abstinent. The patients are addicts of various substances. We seek this variety to help emphasize the nature of addiction: it is not what you ingest, shoot, or inhale that defines you as an addict; it is your lifestyle.

The group meets once a week for two hours, usually in the evening because it is mandatory that the patient return to work as soon as possible. All group members start on the same first session, and once the group begins, no one else is allowed to join.

The program spans twenty weeks, and during that time the patient has recourse to five individual sessions, but only in response to need. This approach allows for individual attention in a severe crisis but also does not detract from the patient's commitment to the group process. Attendance and abstinence are both required. If an individual is physically ill when the group is to meet, he must call in advance of the meeting. On the following week when the individual returns, the group votes on whether it is an excused absence. If deemed not to be, the absence counts as a fall. Each patient is allowed three falls. On the fourth fall, the patient has failed the program and is excluded. This patient may try again, but must wait until the group of which he was once a part has graduated before joining a newly formed group.

Each patient is allowed three falls, which may be either relapses into substance abuse or unexcused absences. The first order of business at each meeting is for the therapist to go around the room, looking each patient in the eye, and asking, "Are you clean?" If the patient says no, the group spends a few minutes to determine what happened, and then the patient forfeits the remainder of the session and must leave. Pleas of "I really need help tonight" are brushed aside with the admonition, "You get help by adhering to abstinence. Tonight any help will merely dissolve in your relapse." Occasionally someone will lie, but remarkably the group sees through the deceit immediately. A relapse counts as one of the three falls. Lying about it results in two falls, one for the relapse and one for the attempt to hide it. Fellow patients become keenly alert to what is known as "wet behavior." Once an addict has relapsed, certain behaviors and verbalizations naturally and consistently follow and are unmistakable to the group.

During the first session, the therapist tells the group that the ideal group size is eight patients but that ten have been accepted because two will flunk out. If twelve have been accepted, then the expectation is proffered that four will fail. This is a challenge that no addict can resist: to show the therapist and the rest of the group that it will not be she who flunks.

As previously noted, for less severely addicted patients with good social contacts, this type of group yields superior outcomes compared to those of the more intensive groups. The IOP is much more intensive and meets daily for two to three hours for one to four weeks. It is often desirable to refer patients who have succeeded in the IOP to the less intensive type of outpatient group.

Prerequisites for Group

As previously mentioned, *the completion of withdrawal* is mandatory. These patients have accepted the challenge and have been clean and sober from two, four, or more weeks. Most have been detoxified on an outpatient basis, with a knowledgeable physician doing the titration (if needed). A few will have been hospitalized for their withdrawal. It is preferable that the psychotherapist who worked with them through the discomfort of withdrawal will be the person seeing them in the twenty-week group program. Significant bonding occurs between patient and therapist during the withdrawal; they have a relationship that fosters the emerging recovery process.

There are occasions when the patient does not remain abstinent during the withdrawal period. Rather than being admitted to the group program, they must go back to square one and repeat the withdrawal in individual sessions with the psychotherapist. The patient who is medically withdrawn with substitute drugs must be free of those prescribed substitutes for at least two weeks before entering the group program. In other words, patients are going into a program of abstinence and must commit to it in advance through their behavior. If while working in individual sessions with the psychotherapist the patient fails three times to achieve even the temporary abstinence of two weeks, the patient is advised to come back when she is more serious. Patients are allowed the same number of relapses during withdrawal as they are once they are in the program. The patients who do not use up these allowances during withdrawal and the subsequent program are the ones most likely to recover.

Participation of the codependent (enabler) is mandatory for most addicts and desirable for all. This will be discussed fully in Chapter Eight.

Addiction Treatment and Managed Care

At the present time, the reimbursement mechanisms for the treatment of substance abuse are not in the best shape. Managed care companies, under pressure to reduce costs and weary of outcomes statistics that do not show robust results, have essentially restricted reimbursement to two levels of care, namely, detoxification and intensive outpatient care, the latter encompassing four hours a day for three days a week. This has resulted in a lot of patients falling through the cracks, but the managed care companies respond that this is no worse than the inefficient laissez-faire condition that existed before.

Along with the federal government, there are a number of provider organizations that are addressing the problem. Among these is the American Society of Addiction Medicine (ASAM), which is formulating a national strategy that will include standards and guidelines. Not the least of the major problems is what to do with the plethora of practitioners and providers, many of whom are less than competent.

As we enter the new millennium, the status of the field of substance abuse treatment is disappointing. The nation is spending less money on substance abuse treatment now than it did a decade ago. The managed care industry, which covers the behavioral health care for 75 percent of insured Americans, has not integrated chemical dependency services in its otherwise expanded continuum of care. And employers, who have been paying the increasing costs of care that has yielded worse-than-predicted results, have become less than enthusiastic advocates of treatment.[10] This somewhat bleak picture is complicated by the glut of providers, many with questionable competencies, as well as a plethora of treatment approaches whose efficacy has not been verified by outcomes research. The one bright spot is the emergence of outcomes research in response to the demand for evidence-based treatment. In the future those who pay the bills—employers, government, and the taxpayers—will be more savvy about what they are buying.

Notes

1. Cummings, N. A. (1991). Inpatient versus outpatient treatment of substance abuse: Recent developments in the controversy. *Contemporary Family Therapy, 13*(5), 507–520.

2. Quimette, P. C., Finney, J. W., & Moos, R. H. (1997). Twelve-step and cognitive-behavioral treatment for substance abuse: A comparison of treatment effectiveness. *Journal of Counseling and Clinical Psychology, 65,* 230–240.

3. Quimette, Finney, & Moos, *Journal of Counseling and Clinical Psychology.*

4. Center for Substance Abuse Treatment (1997). *Recovery from substance abuse and addiction: Real people tell their stories.* Rockville, MD: Substance Abuse and Mental Health Services Administration.

5. Center for Substance Abuse Treatment, *Recovery from substance abuse and addiction.*

6. Cummings, N. A. (1979). Turning bread into stones: Our modern anti-miracle. *American Psychologist, 34*(12), 1119–1129.

7. Saxe, L., Dougherty, D., Esty, K., & Fine, M. (1983). *The effectiveness and costs of alcoholism treatment* (Health Technology Case Study 22). Washington, DC: Office of Technology Assessment.

8. Saxe, L., & Goodman, L. (1988). *The effectiveness of outpatient versus inpatient treatment: Updating the OTA Report* (Health Technology Case Study 22 Update). Washington, DC: Office of Technology Assessment.

9. Cummings, N. A. (1979). Turning bread into stones: Our modern anti-miracle. *American Psychologist, 34*(12), 1119–1129.

10. Ross, E. C. (1997). Plans present mixed bag of results for providers, subscribers. *Tallahassee Democrat* (December 7), pp. F1, F4.

5

Diagnostic and Treatment Considerations

The treatment of substance abuse presents variations on problems unlike those you encounter in the treatment of neuroses and psychoses. Whereas most patients who come to us are prepared to accept some level of personal responsibility, the substance abuser's total denial blinds him to the cause and effect sequence of his own behavior. Consider, for example, the fact that all chemically dependent patients who come to us are in some kind of severe trouble and want our help to extricate themselves. How do you balance the patient's plea for you to intercede on his behalf with his need and right to confidentiality? On the one hand, disclosure of the patient's diagnosis can result in her losing her driver's license, life insurance, or job. On the other hand, failure to disclose may be in conflict with the patient's best interest when she needs the information and evaluation for her own defense. What are your responsibilities when the patient is ordered by the court to undergo treatment, and the judge expects to receive a "report card"? Should the report be honest, or should it be slanted in favor of the patient? Where is the balance between professional honesty and loyalty to the patient? What are the rights of a spouse who has put off a decision to divorce, awaiting the success of treatment? What is your responsibility toward children who have been frequently abused by a patient who is consistently drunk? Is there an obligation to disclose the truth when the patient might well go to jail for vehicular manslaughter? Does the family of those killed have a right to know the true cause of their loved one's untimely death?

QUESTIONNAIRES AND DIAGNOSTIC SCALES

Substance abusers are seldom, if ever, fully honest about their addictive behavior. Yet in subtle ways they reveal the truth as if a part of them is unconsciously seeking help. The practitioner must be alert to these disguised revelations, as they are easily missed.

Beware the Casual Aside

The practitioner who treats chemical dependency must be prepared to put many usual therapeutic considerations aside in favor of unbiased truth and fact. Ultimately what best serves society will prove best for the addict, whose own treatment will be served by the recognition of personal responsibility.

When a physician or psychotherapist asks a patient how much she drinks, the only question that remains is whether to multiply the patient's answer by two, four, or more likely ten. In denial, the patient will minimize the amount; what is fascinating is that at some time during the physician visit or the psychotherapy session, the patient will throw out a matter-of-fact statement that both hides and discloses the facts. For example, a frequent aside will be, "By the way, doctor, sometimes I have a shot of whisky just before I go to bed to help me sleep." The physician's, and often the psychologist's, response is, "That's fine. One shot of whisky occasionally at bedtime never hurt anyone. Besides, it's better than a sleeping pill." If the truth were known, this patient is "sucking on a lemon," the common alcoholic practice of going to bed with a bottle. Why would the patient bother even to mention the "one shot"? Because the patient has been worried and seeks reassurance. By throwing out this aside and receiving the answer, the patient can now go home and say, "I told the doctor, and he doesn't think I drink too much."

So when you hear such seemingly matter-of-fact statements, realize that they are of paramount significance. You need to follow through, asking the patient to tell how much he is actually drinking. The person who truly only occasionally has a shot of whisky before retiring would have no reason even to mention it.

"By the way, Doc, I sometimes have a glass of wine with dinner" has the same implications. The patient is seeking reassurance in the face of a growing fear that two or three bottles of wine a night may be too much. The psychotherapist's response provides that reassurance: "That's fine. A glass of wine at dinner never hurt anyone, and it helps relax you."

Another example of a heads-up sign is "I smoke a little grass once in a while," because this means several joints a day. In the same context are asides like these: "Once in a great while I have one drink too many" (probably several times a week); or "I like a couple of beers during the weekend" (most likely a full case or several six-packs); or "I've tried coke a couple of times just to see what it's like" (a regular cocaine user). The denial compels the patient to toss these bits at the physician or psychotherapist, and the comments will always seem so matter-of-fact that the practitioner will pay little attention to their meaning.

Read the Patient's Answers

It is interesting that on a written questionnaire or scale presented *within the health system*, the patient will candidly answer questions regarding drug behavior. In our own multiphasic health screening we include such questions as "Most days I have none, one, two or three, more than five drinks in one day [indicate number]." Another important question is "I use the following recreational drugs," and the choices after each are *never, rarely, occasionally, frequently,* or *regularly*. We have seen many patients who answer truthfully on the intake questionnaire and then contradict their written statements with a lie in the face-to-face interview. The same disclosure in the service of denial seems to be operating. The patient can say that the doctor knows the truth and is not concerned. And amazingly this is most often the case. Physicians and psychotherapists seldom pay much attention to the chemical dependency information on the very questionnaire they demand be completed by the patient. Yet they will take into account important disease or emotional factors revealed in the questionnaire. It is as if everyone wants to avoid opening a Pandora's box.

Such questionnaires, though largely ignored, still are very common and reside as part of the patient's permanent medical record. This is because alcohol and drug information is now within the province of the primary care physician (PCP). Thus it is subject to subpoena under many circumstances that would be excluded if the information were part of a separate psychological record. Be careful what you ask, as well as where you ask it; and if you ask, use the answer therapeutically, not just as filler in a chart.

A Word of Caution

Unfortunate scenarios abound. In a case in which we served as expert witnesses, a patient sued his employer for wrongful firing. Because the patient brought the suit, his privilege was relinquished, and the employer's lawyer subpoenaed everything in sight, hoping to find something useful. He did: three years earlier, in the patient's health questionnaire, the patient had acknowledged heavy drinking. The physician never followed up, and alcohol was never discussed. Now alcoholism was being used as the employer's justification in a wrongful firing suit. Ironically, the patient had sought help from AA on his own and had been dry for over two years. But AA sponsors are not recognized by the court as expert witnesses who can attest to abstinence, and the physician who had initially missed the entire matter could not comment one way or another. We were asked by the court to ascertain the abstinence. Eventually the patient prevailed, but only after the expenditure of much time and money. The health system, and especially the PCP, were embarrassed having to reveal in court that vital information had been ignored and appropriate treatment considerations had been overlooked.

ON BEHALF OF YOUR PATIENT

It is improbable that treatment for substance abuse can progress without directly addressing the trouble that brings the patient in. It is always the consequences, not the substance abuse itself, that bring the patient in. In the patient's mind, the purpose of the first session is to enlist the therapist as an advocate or intercessor in these terrible things that are happening. The psychotherapist, rather than regarding the patient's difficulties as real motivation for therapy, should seize on them as leverage to further therapy. The patient's denial and the resistance accompanying that denial are so overwhelming that you need to take advantage of the threat of incarceration, divorce, unemployment, loss of freedom, or any other misfortune in the patient's life as a legitimate motivation to get the patient on the road to abstinence. If it can be on the magnitude of a catapult rather than a measly cattle prod, all the better. This is not cynicism but reality. No addict comes into treatment for treatment's sake. There are many facets to this truism, and the following sections are intended to guide you through the labyrinth of denial you will face in the first session; the patient *and* the referring entity can readily lead you astray.

Victimization

All addicts are vociferous as to their plight as victims, and they do not require a well-meaning, compassionately misguided therapist to remind them of it. Even the slightest empathy is interpreted as agreement on the therapist's part with the belief that the world is unreasonable. Victimology, so popular in contemporary psychology, can be an extremely destructive force in the treatment of the addict. Tough love may be harder on the therapist than on the patient. We make ourselves feel good by being compassionate when we are really being called on to treat, not sympathize. Just as a patient undergoing surgery needs a surgeon who is not squeamish at the sight of blood, a psychotherapy patient has a right to a therapist who is not afraid of drawing psychic blood when psychological incisiveness is called for.

Whatever your thoughts are philosophically about victimization, you have a right to them. But for the well-being of your patient, you will need to put philosophy aside when treatment, not tea and sympathy, is needed.

Willie is a gifted and skilled addiction counselor who is one of the three recovering addicts to whom this book is dedicated. His story of how he cleaned up and returned to school after prison may be helpful.

Willie is an African American in his mid-forties who twenty-one years ago was a heavy-duty drug user headed for destruction. He grew up in the inner city and began at an early age to use any drug available. By his late teens he was a heroin-cocaine-alcohol speedballer. He was not interested in school, and dropped out at an early age. But Willie was remarkably intelligent. Unfortunately, he used his intelligence to con those who were determined to help him. He was in psychotherapy twice, once as a late teen, and later after his first prison term for assault and possession. Likable as he was, he seemed to have social agencies fighting over him to help him. He used them, but one must also point out that they were ripe to be suckered.

His first stint of psychotherapy was before his first prison term, through the juvenile justice system. Willie so conned his counselors that he essentially used them as his alibi whenever he was in trouble. However, after many arrests as a juvenile for possession with intent to sell, he was arrested for assault as an adult, and his friends at "juvie" were unable to save him from a prison sentence. He was a model prisoner and was released early on probation, providing he remained in psychotherapy.

There were two social agencies vying to get him as a patient, and Willie chose the easiest target, looking to repeat his favored status in the juvenile system. He agreed to go into outpatient psychotherapy, but he just went through the motions of being in treatment for almost three years.

His psychologist, a warm, understanding, and compassionately maternal white woman, immediately sided with him because of his victimization as an inner-city youth. She reinforced his belief that he had a right to be addicted; she could appreciate the reasons for his assaulting behavior; and she frequently apologized for his centuries of oppression and slavery. Whereas he was doing nothing in therapy, and freely admitted to his psychologist that he was using and dealing heroin and cocaine, she sent totally false, glowing reports to the court. She covered for him on more than one occasion and lied about his attendance record. (He was attending one scheduled session out of four or five.)

Eventually the entire collusion fell apart. Willie was arrested again and served the remainder of his probation of two years in prison. There he met a prison counselor, also African American and a former heroin addict, with whom he started treatment. In the first session Willie began the litany that worked so well in conning his two previous therapists. He intimated that as a brother the new counselor would understand if Willie arranged to have some dope smuggled into the prison and would look the other way on a number of other matters. His counselor stopped him in mid-sentence and said loudly and firmly, "Don't fuck with me, man, or I'll kick your lying ass right out of my office. The only difference we're talking about is that this place is full of stupid white junkies and stupid black junkies. You're just as fucking stupid as they are, so the con stops here." This was a new idea to Willie, who took an immediate liking to this man, continued counseling, and developed a drug-free outlook on life. When he left prison, he enrolled in the community college and finished a two-year

degree that he had begun earning in prison. He looks back on his
first years of therapy as useless at best, destructive at worst.

Admittedly, it would be misunderstood if a white therapist did
what Willie's African American counselor did. However, it is important to be thoroughly honest in confronting the patient's dishonesty. Willie deserved a lot more professionalism than he got from
his first two well-meaning but incompetent psychologists.

We take a nonjudgmental but very tough approach to the patient's difficulties. The patient brought all this upon herself, and if
she wants any reconsideration, it will have to be earned and deserved. Restitution and honesty are requirements; contrived contrition is useless. When the patient goes on the con (as is frequent),
the therapist laughs and expostulates, "Hey, that's a pretty good one,
but are you dishonest enough to pull it off?" or "Oh, come on. That's
a moth-eaten one and will never fly. Try again. You can do better
than that." One patient declared he had just discovered why he was
addicted and violent. He had read in the morning newspaper that
the FDA removed PhisoHex from the market because it had potent
side effects. "My mother used to rub PhisoHex on my skin as a child.
That probably resulted in my becoming an addict." His lawyer
thought this to be important and was going to mention it in defense
arguments. The therapist volubly congratulated the patient on an
originally contrived excuse. "I thought I'd heard them all in the past
forty years. You're marvelously creative." He then handed the patient
a Master Con Artist certificate. The patient later recalled this as the
turning point in his successful treatment and subsequent recovery.

We have compiled a list of potential problems with which we
can help our deserving patients, but we do so only with their acceptance of self-responsibility as well as the honest therapist-patient
partnership that must accompany that responsibility. When there
is insincerity, we remind the patient that she is talking to the psy-

chologist, not an overworked judge presiding over a crowded court calendar and looking for any excuse to get rid of the case. "The fifteen tons of phony contrition you throw at the judge won't cut it here. We look only at results." Soon our patients forsake victimology and espouse the mantra: results breed results.

Treatment as a Condition of Probation or Parole

Our jails are overcrowded, so courts are looking for ways to place first offenders and nonviolent criminals on probation. One way of appeasing society is to remand the offender to court-ordered psychotherapy. Judges can say they addressed the problem, prosecutors can say they got justice, the prison overcrowding is a bit less than it would be otherwise, and defense lawyers can say to their clients, "See, I got you off without jail time." Everyone is happy, including psychotherapists, who have few enough paying clientele in this era of managed care and so particularly appreciate a well-paying referral. The only problem with this approach is that it seldom works the way it is supposed to. Most cases go the way of Willie's first two therapies—nowhere. But court-ordered therapy need not go that way. A competent psychotherapist who is in charge makes all the difference.

Patients likely to be remanded to court-ordered psychotherapy are drunk drivers, men who batter their wives while drunk, and people who have committed a host of other offenses associated with inebriation. The courts are always looking for psychotherapists willing to work with the court on such cases, but very often it is the patient's lawyer who is shopping around. If you are a highly respected practitioner, and the case can benefit from a prestigious advocate, the lawyer may well seek you out. Or if the lawyer is looking for free therapy for the client, the lawyer may contact the health plan of which you are a staff member. You may be told you have to take the case because it is court ordered. This is not so. The courts can order the patient to seek therapy, but they cannot order you to see the patient. If you are an independent practitioner or a staff member of a private health plan, you are not obligated in any way to accept the referral. If the health plan you work for has a benefit package that includes court-ordered treatment, that would constitute an exception. Otherwise, the choice is yours, not that of the court. You may wish to see the patient, and most health plans want their addict members to receive treatment. But before the first session it is imperative to establish that you—not the court, the prosecutor, the defense attorney, or the patient—are in charge of the treatment. This must be accepted by all concerned, including the patient, who must wave rights of confidentiality.

Enlightened judges, tired of psychotherapists who mollycoddle their patients without any demonstrable results, are delighted to be working with a sincere, competent, no-nonsense professional. If you perform sound, competent therapy with your addict patient, with demonstrable outcomes, you will have to prepare to be deluged by the desperate court.

There are a number of working rules you must establish before the first interview with your patient:

- You are the psychotherapist, and you alone determine the treatment. The therapist provides the court with his therapy plan; once the court accepts it, the lawyers and the judge stay out of the picture from then on.

- The patient agrees to the therapy plan, which delineates a treatment program in which attendance, abstinence, and other features, as well as cooperation, are mandatory. If the patient exceeds the limits of these requirements (number of absences, relapses, and so on), then the patient fails the program. This is tantamount to failing conditions of probation.

- Once you become the patient's psychotherapist, that relationship continues until you release the patient.

The patient is not permitted to shop around seeking a less stringent treatment regimen.

- The patient agrees, in writing, that the psychotherapist will render a candid professional report monthly to the court. If the patient fails the program, or if the patient resumes addictive behavior, the therapist will inform the court immediately. Vis-à-vis the court, the patient waves the privilege of confidentiality. The patient is aware that the psychotherapist will report all matters as they are, not as the patient may like them to be.

- Reports to the court will assess the patient's progress but will not convey psychological matters that are not pertinent to the bottom-line assessment.

- The court (including prosecutor and defense lawyer) does not have access to the psychotherapist's notes, other than the periodic summary reports rendered.

- Special court orders, such as restraining orders, are part of the therapy requirements. Violation of any of the court's mandates results in an immediate report from the psychotherapist.

- The court agrees that if the patient fails the program as defined by the psychotherapist, the probation will be revoked.

- Participation in an appropriate twelve-step program is mandatory, and the psychotherapist and the patient's AA (NA, CA) sponsor are encouraged to communicate with each other.

- The conclusion of therapy may or may not, at the election of therapist and patient, coincide with the end of probation.

Once these ground rules are established, real psychotherapy can take place. Note that the therapist has taken advantage of all possible leverage to motivate the patient. Over thirty years of experience have taught us an important lesson: once the patient is in recovery, there is only gratitude, never resentment that the therapist went to such measures for the sake of the recovery. It is more likely to be the defense attorney who will try to interfere. Once patients are on the road to recovery, however, we have found that they muzzle their own lawyers.

Surprisingly, we have found that these considerations do not create a negative, legalistic atmosphere, especially if the patient is in a group program with others who are not court ordered. Rather, they cut through the patient's resistance and prevent the bureaucracy from taking its usual expedient course; either of these problems can wreak havoc on the treatment enterprise.

As we mentioned earlier, our outpatient programs are once a week for twenty sessions, after the initial withdrawal. Because the addict's body will not be producing its own endorphins and enkephalins in sufficient quantities until sometime between six months and a year after withdrawal, there is high probability of relapse. It is important that the patient continue in treatment after the three-month program and for the length of the probation. We also recommend a follow-up group program, and, as stated previously, participation in a twelve-step program (AA, NA, CA, or whichever program is appropriate) is mandatory. Offenders on probation frequently become very religious, even to the point of being "born again." Most, however, will object to religious influences and use this as an excuse to dodge the requirement of participation in a twelve-step program because of their strong "higher power" orientation. You should be suspicious of this objection as reflecting resistance to giving up chemicals for life, an objective of the twelve-step philosophy. Our successful patients, many of whom are avowed atheists, constantly remind us that AA is spiritual, not dogmatically religious, and that the objection is masking resistance to recovery.

Suspension of Driving Privileges

Frequently the courts will suspend a person's driver's license and make psychotherapy the avenue through which driving privileges may be restored. All the foregoing considerations apply here as well, but you should be aware that the court will require a letter recommending that the patient is now fit to drive. The court—not to mention you—will be disconcerted if a couple of weeks after your writing such a letter the former patient is arrested for DUI. Before you certify the patient as eligible to drive, it is imperative that you are reasonably certain of your assessment because the patient is actively engaged in a twelve-step program and is being seen at least once a month in follow-up therapy.

Reports to the Court, Appropriate and Inappropriate

Psychotherapists need to be frequently reminded that the court is not interested in the psychological details of a patient, such as his sex life, early weaning, toilet training, fantasies, and other issues. For some reason, psychotherapists feel compelled both to guard these details and to clutter up reports with them. The last thing a busy court wants is psychobabble. Complex reporting forms have come into existence because the courts have found therapists reluctant to state succinctly what the courts need. A report can be amazingly succinct as long as everything the court needs is there. If you include the necessary information in the report, it can be wonderfully brief, both for your sake and that of the overworked judge. The following are examples of appropriate and inappropriate periodic (usually monthly) reports.

Appropriate. The patient has attended every session and has experienced no relapses in the first month of the program. Adding the abstinence during the withdrawal period, the patient has now been clean and sober for seven weeks. His eager participation in the program also reflects his progress. His prognosis for changing to a clean and sober lifestyle is very good.

Inappropriate. The patient is doing well in psychotherapy. He has gained understanding into the oral deprivation imposed on him by a cold mother, and he no longer is obsessed with women with large breasts. As he gains insight into his oral addiction, he is expected to continue progressing.

Appropriate. The patient has had three relapses in the first month of the program, indicating that he has been clean and sober only one week out of the four. One more relapse and he will have failed the program. The court is alerted to the poor prognosis in this case so that it can, if one more relapse occurs, be prepared to follow through.

Inappropriate. The patient is having a difficult time in therapy, but this would not be the right time to remove him from the program. He has suffered a number of severe rejections in his life, beginning with a mother who put him up for adoption, and another rejection here would be unfortunate. I am continuing him in treatment in spite of four relapses in just one month.

Appropriate. The patient has come one hour late the last three group sessions and refuses to participate. Her attitude is belligerent and defiant. She has been warned that the three tardy sessions count as three absences. She declared that it's none of anyone's business if she drinks and that she wouldn't tell us, anyway. She is daring to be thrown out of the program and threatens to take me to court if she is. Prognosis: poor.

Inappropriate. This patient has never been allowed to be assertive. She knows only two modes: defiance or capitulation. Therefore, I have excused her being one hour late for each session, since her defiance is healthier than capitulation. She is reluctant to discuss her life situation, so I have asked her to write down and bring in her dreams. She will do well when she overcomes her fear of the group.

Employment Probation

Most employers are reluctant to fire an employee outright, occasionally because the employee is very valuable and should be salvaged if possible, but more often because a nonvaluable employee poses a threat of litigation. Companies have been sued because one of its executives accused an employee of being an alcoholic, and the courts have ruled in favor of the obviously intoxicated employee because the boss was not qualified to make a medical diagnosis. No wonder employers, faced with addictive behavior on the part of a worker, turn to the psychotherapist for help.

If there is an addict on the job, the employer generally has only two alternatives: firing the employee for cause other than addictive behavior (for example, absenteeism, hitting someone on the job, poor performance) or having the diagnosis established by an expert. If the employee refuses to see a doctor, the employer can, with difficulty, force compliance. Once the diagnosis is made, however, treatment can be made a part of job probation in most settings.

The situation varies, but it can be said generally that the courts have bent over backward to protect the employee, and the labor unions have tried to go even further. This may be a good thing in most instances, but unfortunately it tends to protect an addict's addiction rather than promote the addict's recovery.

Raymond finally had to come in for treatment of his alcoholism after being drunk on the job for over two years, more or less. He worked for the Veteran's Administration, and a new medical director laid down a shape-up-or-ship-out policy. There were too many physicians in the VA hospital that could readily make the diagnosis, and Raymond knew it.

A senior administrator at age fifty-eight, Raymond was the person whose duty it was to report for physical examination and blood test anyone who came to work intoxicated. When he sobered up,

there was suddenly a new-found epidemic of addicts at this installa-
tion. Raymond had been too drunk himself to report anyone else.

In some job settings, especially in a number of metropolitan police forces, if a police officer declares an addiction problem, the
police department cannot fire the officer if he is willing to enter
treatment. One can always find a less than competent therapist who
will go along with the officer's ostensible sincerity, allowing addictive behavior until the therapy "takes hold." Addiction, and especially alcoholism, is far higher than average among law enforcement
personnel. The mere existence of drunk cops is not reassuring to the
citizenry.

We established an effective program for the many officers in a
large metropolitan police department who had declared their addiction. The term for a slight alcohol or drug intoxication in this police
department was "having a heat on," and we were startled by the
number of officers who never went on duty without such a heat on.
This was also a culture that compelled bar owners to serve any officers on duty a quick shot if they wanted it, which was obvious from
their presence there. Most bar owners poured officers' favorite shots
as soon as the officers were seen walking through the door. Thus
officers could maintain a heat on throughout the shift.

The police commission worked with us in developing a fair but
no-nonsense treatment program, and enthusiastically accepted a
simple modification of our ten criteria listed earlier. Soon we were
able to really make a difference. Now, in this same community no
bar owner would dare serve a free drink to an officer on duty. It
could result in the revocation of the liquor license.

When the Spouse Leaves the Addict

Frequently the wife, and less often the husband, will leave the spouse,
threatening never to return unless the addict cleans up. The cry
"My wife left me" is the most frequently given reason for a man pre-

senting for psychotherapy. The sad fact is that it may be the third, fourth, or fifth time the wife has left, for she had taken him back after each occasion with only a modicum of evidence that her husband had actually changed. This aspect of substance abuse treatment is very complicated, and a discussion is better postponed for the later chapter on codependency.

THE PROBLEM OF DUAL DIAGNOSIS

As was said earlier, there is no premorbid addictive personality. The ubiquitous lying, cheating, rationalizing, and conning are all part of the addiction and its denial. Therapists frequently and erroneously conclude that the patient must have revealed this constellation of dishonesty before she became addicted and that such behavior fostered the addition. This would certainly be true in the case of a sociopathic personality that existed prior to the addition, but the premorbid personality of most substance abusers varies, just as personalities vary in the general population. This premorbid personality will become manifest with abstinence and usually will complicate recovery. Therefore, it is important for the therapist to be aware that all addicts should bear a dual diagnosis, the first being that of addiction and the second the premorbid personality. Once abstinence is attained, if the premorbid personality is not effectively addressed in the subsequent therapy, the patient is likely to resume addictive behavior. Ideally the therapist will be able to establish the premorbid personality within the first interview, thus making possible the early formulation of the treatment plan. It would be well to consider here the various kinds of personalities that precede the addiction and their implications for treatment.

Phobic or anxious patients often resort to self-medication. The agoraphobic finds that a drink or a Xanax helps her get out of the house. Soon she needs two drinks. Many phobics have to be somewhat intoxicated to get on an airplane, so bars at airports open at six or seven in the morning to accommodate them. The self-medication of the panic-disordered, phobic, or anxious patient is a very common phenomenon. Although such self-medication helps in the beginning, eventually it becomes a complex problem. There is such reinforcement that the patient becomes addicted relatively quickly; drug tolerance exacerbates the addiction.

Most programs would treat the panic disorder first, expecting that the addiction would go away once the need for self-medication is removed. As we have discussed, this is grossly in error: through addiction, the person's body has now undergone cellular changes; these changes are independent of the psychological problem that initiated the self-medicating behavior. Furthermore, by this time the self-medication does not work, and the patient is literally a scared-to-death drunk. This patient has to be detoxified knowing that the withdrawal will see the resurgence of the phobic behavior, but there really is no viable alternative. Even though the chemical is no longer effective, the patient has now avoided consciousness through intoxication rather than more self-medication. You cannot do psychotherapy with a drunk or a stony. We have also seen the danger of patients continuing with heavy use of their addictive substance, unbeknownst to the doctor, on top of the panic medication being prescribed. This is very dangerous stuff. There is no substitute for taking the patient through the withdrawal and then addressing the original phobic problem. Even then the patient should continue in a substance abuse program to prevent the return to previous addictive behavior.

Depressive patients who become substance abusers through self-medication are probably as common as phobic patients. Depression presents a special problem, as the drugs used by most depressives are in themselves depressants, augmenting the depression and complicating it. For example, it is common for a depressed person who drinks to become a crying drunk. Sleeping pills are another frequent recourse for depressed persons, especially women. Over time the depression is increased, and coming off the self-medication reveals a profound depression that needs more and immediate self-medicating.

The worst danger, however, is suicide. Most depressives commit suicide when they are bombed. Inhibitions are lowered, thought processes are clouded, and suicide seems like a very good idea. It is doubly important to get self-medicating depressives off of their abused substance. Again, giving antidepressants when the addicted depressive continues the chemical dependency, usually unbeknownst to the prescribing physician, is very dangerous. There is simply no substitute for addressing the chemical dependency first, instituting watchfulness during the withdrawal to prevent suicide, and then addressing the depression once the patient is clean and in a substance abuse program to ensure continued sobriety.

The *latent schizophrenic* patient often becomes addicted to hallucinogens, or just alcohol, which may induce hallucinations in a person with the underlying thought disorder. In this way the patient can rationalize that he is not crazy, that it is just the drugs. The temporary relief from their own thought disorder in favor of a drug-induced confusion is very compelling to many latent schizophrenics. In past decades when only alcohol was available, these individuals became alcoholics with the special label of "schizaholic." Now they can become addicted to marijuana and LSD as well as to alcohol and a variety of other drugs. They are frequently found living on the street, where they are exploited by more sociopathic street people.

Patients with *borderline and narcissistic personality disorders*, because of their inability to delay gratification, readily resort to substance abuse merely for the euphoria. Again, as with other patients with dual diagnoses, the problem of substance abuse is primary.

Of all the chemically dependent patients, the borderlines are the most troublesome. They can disrupt the group process, causing more vulnerable patients to flee the program. Much of their disruptive behavior is an effort to take over by intimidating the other patients. So difficult are these patients that when numbers allow, we separate them into their own addictive programs, incorporating into these groups many of the features that work so well in borderline group protocols.

The *sociopath* who becomes addicted is more of a problem in the criminal justice system, although a very intelligent and cunning sociopath may occasionally turn up in your practice. A habitual felon is most often both an addict and a sociopath. The chemical often impedes his agility, and he is repeatedly arrested and returned to prison. With the new three-strikes laws, the revolving door has closed in a number of states. The sociopathic inmate, however, has solved his addiction problem, as drugs are very prevalent in our prisons today.

In conclusion, it must be reemphasized that whatever the dual diagnosis, the addiction is primary and must be addressed first. Our experience in teaching addictive counseling is that no matter how often this is repeated, the therapist is very likely to get caught up in addressing the pathology of the premorbid personality to the neglect of the chemical dependency. Balancing the primacy of the addiction with the importance of the patient's premorbid personality in the first session is a skill that evolves with experience.

6

Establishing the Therapeutic Alliance

As you may conclude from the preceding chapters, in the ideal first session you will have identified the substance abuse, assessed its severity, determined the mode of detoxification (withdrawal), and formulated the treatment plan. There remains the most difficult aspect of the first interview: motivating the patient toward abstinence.

The task is not one of merely motivating the patient to enter a program; that is easy. The patient is in so much trouble that she will be eager to enter a program. The resistance is to entering a program of abstinence. In over half a century of work with chemical dependency, we have not seen a single patient who is willing even to seriously contemplate a life of abstinence, no matter how far down the hill she has slid.

The addict comes to "treatment" to extricate himself from trouble and is willing to cut down and even forgo the chemical for a time. The therapist will sprinkle a few words of wisdom upon the patient, who then will continue with the dependency under control. In other words, the patient comes in prepared to wiggle sideways, not to go forward. Toward this need, he is eager to imbue the therapist with magical powers. He will lavish praise and appreciation on the therapist, who too often falls for the flattery. "You, erudite and omnipotent one, will make me a social user. Together we shall bring forth a miracle: I shall be the first addict to become a social user, and you will get the credit." No, it is never this crass or obvious, but the bull is ankle-deep nonetheless. The weary therapist, drained by so many needy patients who never express appreciation, frequently falls for it. Welcome to the world of denial—it is a two-way street.

HITTING BOTTOM

As mentioned elsewhere, the prevailing philosophy in AA is that denial will rule until the patient has hit bottom—that is, the patient has sunk so low that she cannot sink any lower and is ready to surrender.

Bottom Is Relative and Sometimes Nonexistent

The difficulty with this approach is that there are great individual differences in what constitutes "bottom," and some addicts do not have a bottom. They continue to slide into skid row where they spend their last days panhandling for booze, drugs, and food, in that order. No matter how low an addict has sunk, there is another addict that is lower. Thus the addict who has lost a job argues that he was able to get another one. When the time comes that no one will give her a job, the argument is that she is not like the addict who lives in the street. When that time comes, the argument is that this is temporary. When all semblance of hope for ascending from the street vanishes, the addict can still point to the unfortunate person who is about to die: the addict who has descended to drinking gasoline milk. Too far gone to sustain his habit by panhandling, this individual resorts to gasoline. But the human stomach cannot hold gasoline without regurgitating it, so the end-of-the-road addict panhandles enough to be able to buy a small carton of milk. After the gas stations are closed and the pump handles are locked, one can still lift the bottom of the hose enough to drain a small quantity of gasoline to add to the milk. The person becomes roaring drunk and is the only addict that has no one else farther down to point to as the real addict. This addict does not even care. The brain is so damaged by the gasoline that all semblance of ego is gone. The person dies within days or weeks of beginning this practice. Fortunately, most addicts bottom out at a higher place along the downhill slide.

Rhonda, a suburban homemaker in her late thirties, had established a lifestyle in which she would get her husband and two sons off to work and school, and then as she did housework she would drink wine. She would usually pass out sometime between eleven and noon.

A few years down the road, she added sleeping pills to the wine, and she began passing out by nine-thirty in the morning. When the children came home from school, they would awaken her. She would shower and dress in a hurry, then put something of a dinner together before her husband came home.

One day the nine-year-old, Teddy, stayed home because he felt ill. He spent the day in bed, as did Rhonda in her usual drunken and stoned fashion. That evening the husband commented that Teddy was really ill and should see a doctor. Rhonda intended to take the boy to the pediatrician the next morning, but she passed out by nine-thirty. This was repeated two more mornings. Finally, the father looked at his son and said, "Teddy is burning up with fever." He rushed the boy to the emergency room, which promptly admitted him to the hospital. But it was too late. Nine-year-old Teddy died late that night of virulent meningitis.

Teddy's death was enough to bring Rhonda to treatment, but her denial was only damaged, not destroyed. She insisted that if she just removed the sleeping pills, she could continue the wine. Even in the face of the grief over loss of her son, Rhonda's addiction would not give up.

With the firm requirement of abstinence added to her guilt over her son's death, Rhonda succeeded to recovery and continues there to this date. But she remains a startling reminder to us that even

behavior that results in the death of a young son may not constitute
- bottom.

Recently we evaluated a drunk driver who on a city boulevard with a
forty-five-miles-an-hour speed limit plowed into the back of another
car at a speed of over one hundred. He killed the young mother of
three in the car he hit and demolished both cars, but he escaped with
superficial bruises.

Eleven years earlier while driving drunk, he demolished his own
car and killed his two preschool daughters who were traveling with
him. Since that time he had been arrested several times and charged
with DUIs, and he had had three twenty-eight-day substance abuse
hospitalizations.

In our evaluation, we pointed out that an alcoholic who did not
hit bottom when he killed his own little daughters will not bottom out
having now killed a young stranger. Another hospitalization would be
an affront to the people he killed and to those he would probably kill
in the future if he were allowed to continue driving.

We Can't Wait for Bottom

Most of our patients come to us in far less trouble than the addicts
in these two examples, so it can be said that they have not hit bottom. Should we, like AA, just say we'll be able to do something the
day the addict hits bottom? What of the families, employers, spouses,
police, and courts that are clamoring for our help? Either we should
devise ways to increase motivation for abstinence or else admit to
society that there is little we can do.

The therapeutic alliance with substance abusers is essentially to
get the patient to accept the imperative of abstinence and to commit to treatment that works toward the goal of recovery. Your responsibility to steer the patient in that direction begins in the first session
and continues in every session thereafter. Note that we are striving
for a commitment to the goal of abstinence, as we cannot at this

juncture demand "surrender." Surrender is an important concept in twelve-step programs and refers to the patient's acknowledging, "I cannot do it by myself; I surrender to a higher power." A form of "therapeutic surrender" occurs near the end of a successful treatment. The patient's depression lifts, and she develops a new, positive outlook on life. The patients who through their sobriety had become holier than thou about substance use now acknowledge that nonaddicts have a right to indulge, that it is only they who cannot, and they no longer resent those who can be social users. A remarkable change in attitude and optimism mysteriously pervades. We ask the patient, "When exactly was it that you accepted the fact you can never again drink [shoot, snort, smoke]?" The patient is at first startled, then recalls the exact moment the "surrender" to recovery occurred, after which a cloud of resentment and pessimism lifted.

MOTIVATING THE PATIENT FOR ABSTINENCE

Successfully motivating the patient in the first session rests on two important therapeutic principles of addiction: (1) the addicted patient is not really here to change, and (2) the secret to reaching the patient is through the obstinacy that is part and parcel of the addict's denial. If you cannot apply the first principle to the addicted patient sitting across from you, excuse yourself, leave the room, and repeat out loud ten times, "Addiction is denial." Come back into the office, and if as you look at this seemingly sincere, eager, likable, and appreciative addict who is smiling with anticipation, you still do not see the importance of this principle, leave the room again. This time repeat out loud one hundred times, "Addiction is denial." If this does not do it for you, terminate the interview and invite the patient out for a drink. If you can't lick 'em, you may as well join 'em.

Presuming you understand and accept that addiction is denial, let us move on to the second principle—the addict's obstinacy. In talking about obstinacy it is not our intention to be pejorative; the very nature of denial requires the addict to be oppositional. One manifestation of this is the way addicts are constantly rehearsing in their minds what they will say to the spouse, the employer, the police officer, or the doctor. As therapists, we fall into the general "doctor" category, so let us look at how the patient deflects the impact of what a physician might say. Told that the liver function test is very high and that if the patient continues to drink, cirrhosis is the probable outcome, the patient asks, "But I don't have cirrhosis yet, do I, Doctor?" (Translation: all I have to do is cut down a bit for a while until my liver recovers.) This is an excellent example of why scare tactics do not work with addicts. They have anticipated the doctor and have rehearsed an answer to whatever she might say.

Addicts are prepared for whatever you might say. What they are *not* prepared to hear is you talking as they would. When you confront them with their own words, addicts without realizing it begin to talk the way you would. You are thus engaging in a form of psychojudo, using patients' own opposing momentum to further the therapy by outmaneuvering the denial. You can never successfully confront denial head-on; the patient will simply tune you out. For example, the physician who insists that cirrhosis of the liver is imminent will not be heard; neither will the therapist be heard who insists to the patient that he has already progressed to serious addiction. Therefore, we employ a paradoxical strategy. We and our colleagues have found during the past thirty years that this strategy, skillfully employed, results in four out of five patients committing to a program based on abstinence.

The Challenge

At the moment the patient says "I want to quit," she actually believes this is true. The old adage that the best salesperson is the one who believes in the product is applicable. When the addict looks a therapist in the eye and says pleadingly, "Doctor, I've got to quit, and I want to quit," there is no greater sincerity in the world. This is why the psychotherapist, alert to discern a lie from the truth, erroneously accepts the statement at face value and proceeds accordingly. The difficulty arises within the next few minutes; once the addict sees some success in convincing the psychotherapist of sincere intent, denial takes over. The psychotherapist is quick to reassure the pleading patient that all will be well because the patient really wants to get well, and this reassurance results in the patient's concluding that all is well *now*. The addict is back to business as usual.

A preferable alternative is to challenge the patient's sincerity. How you will do this depends on your personality, but in any case you must do it firmly, resolutely, and consistently.

> PATIENT: For the sake of my family and my own health, I am finally ready to quit.
> THERAPIST: Your family still loves you, and your health is OK. Why are you in such a hurry to quit something that is so pleasurable?
> PATIENT: You don't understand: I've got to quit.
> THERAPIST: You're right. I don't understand why you've got to quit.

The nature of the denial will result in an increasing defensiveness in the face of the therapist's taking the role of the patient. A defensive anger is so much a characteristic of addicts that AA has made giving it up central to recovery.

At this point in the interaction, the anger escalates.

> PATIENT: You're wrong, Doctor. I really must quit.
> THERAPIST: But do you want to?
> PATIENT: What kind of a doctor are you? Can't you see I really want to? Can't you see you're wrong?
> THERAPIST: I've been treating addicts for a long time, and I average one mistake a decade. I've already made my one mistake for this decade.

PATIENT: What must I do to convince you I'm serious about quitting?

THERAPIST: Well, I'm not convinced. But there is one way that would change my mind. If you were to go clean for [period to be determined] I would really have to eat crow.

The amount of time given the patient depends on the longest the patient has been able to abstain in the past two years. For the heroin mainliner, we never demand more than seventy-two hours. For most alcoholics it is one week to ten days.

Properly presented, addicts cannot resist the challenge to embarrass the doubting psychotherapist. The response is a hostile, "I'll be back clean, and I'll show you!" The patient is told to call when the time agreed-on has elapsed and that an appointment will be given for that day.

This strategy is so different from the standard therapeutic approach that therapists learning of it for the first time are usually startled. They are skeptical that it can succeed, and express fear that the strategy can backfire, perhaps doing harm to the patient or more likely driving the patient away. It is understandable that most psychotherapists would question their own ability to pull off the paradox. Some object to the seemingly manipulative aspect of it. Having taught hundreds of therapists to successfully employ this strategy with American Biodyne (MedCo/Merck, then Merit, and now Magellan Behavioral Care), we understand all of these concerns. However, we have seen that most (but not all) therapists can acquire this skill if they take the time to do so.

Of importance in learning the strategy is not to proceed until the psychotherapist has practiced the dialogue through all of its possible permutations. We recommend that two psychotherapists who are comfortable with each other extensively role-play the presentation of the challenge, alternating with each other the therapist and patient roles. This role-play should be continued for weeks, or until each has experienced every conceivable patient response to the therapist's strategy and has developed a level of comfort that the possibilities are finite.

A psychotherapist should never attempt the challenge in a half-hearted or overly skeptical manner with a patient. The therapist must come across as firm and determined. Most failures are attributable to the therapist's lack of conviction that she can pull off the strategy. A second most frequent cause of failure is the therapist's prematurely ending the paradox. It is important that the patient leave the first session convinced that she must embarrass a pompous therapist by proving him wrong.

We have found that once therapists have experienced success, their skill and confidence increase rapidly thereafter. They experience the additional reward of having become far more effective in motivating a patient to abstinence than they were previously.

In our years of teaching this strategy we have found that the fear of untoward results is unfounded. The denial of the addict is so pervasive that she merely shuts out the unskilled challenge, just as she would other approaches presented without competence. The psychotherapist is dismissed, and if the addict is disposed toward finding the kind of therapist who will serve his denial, he will do so. We recall a social worker who was an otherwise skilled therapist but who could never master this strategy. She was attempting it on a patient who abruptly ended the session, muttering as she walked out, "You remind me of my Jewish mother." The patient demanded and received a transfer to another therapist who successfully presented the challenge in spite of the patient's having just experienced a bungled strategy. The patient became abstinent in defiance of the new therapist who doubted she could do so, and she successfully completed the twenty-week program.

Invariably the patient will call a few hours or a day before the time is up, and you must tell him to call back when the time is fulfilled. The patient will be furious and will call you unreasonable. Our response in these situations is something along the following lines: "I'm not surprised that you're mad because you can't con me.

I told you that you can't go clean for that time. You have come within a few hours of making it, but you can't hold on. By conning me into giving you an appointment early you can then get bombed and thumb your nose at me. It's like the guy who puts off for hours going to the toilet, but finally when he decides to go, he can't make the last few feet without wetting his pants. You're wetting your pants right now!" All patients are angry, and a few hang up. But all of them call back when the time is actually up.

When the now-clean patient is once again in your office, allow yourself to be unmercifully berated. A good response is, "I really underestimated you. I deserve anything you can throw at me. How did you do it?" The patient describes the technique employed, everything from cold showers and long walks to constantly clenched fists. But eventually the patient will become her breezy self, bragging that it was not as tough as you thought it would be. Denial is settling in again, and it is time to up the challenge.

THERAPIST: OK. You win this round. But I've seen a lot of addicts like you who by hook or by crook could get through a small period without their stuff. I bet you can't go the long haul. I bet you'd be too chicken to even think of committing to a twenty-week program of abstinence.

This challenge ups the ante. After a bit of arguing back and forth, in which your stance continues to be one of extreme skepticism, the patient will usually commit to twenty weeks of abstinence, if only to show you that he is not addicted. Do not worry about the patient's nefarious intent; you now have the addict for twenty weeks of a firm, continuously challenging, and successful program based on abstinence. The longer the patient is abstinent, the greater the inroad of therapy. It will be up to you to continue to outmaneuver the patient's denial throughout the twenty weeks.

In our program, we expect to successfully graduate into recovery about 60 percent of those who begin—a very high figure, indeed. This rate of success is dependent on the successful first session. If in the first session you are conned by the patient's facile denial, all is lost from then on. The abysmal record of recovery after one or two years resulting from most programs can be traced to an inappropriate beginning in which denial was a two-way street between patient and therapist.

A Variation of the Challenge

It is sometimes possible to elicit a long-lost wish from the patient and then reignite it in the service of motivating her. You need to inquire, "Is there something you used to think about and wish for a lot, but it somehow got forgotten and neglected?" This wish can be almost anything, such as the ambition to obtain a college degree or to return to the pursuit of a career that was long ago abandoned, or the desire to be reunited with one's children. There are patients who will immediately resonate to this question and go into an elaborate description of that lost wish of long ago.

At this point you can give an example of a former patient who had just such a longing and who by cleaning up his life, was able to fulfill the desire. It is important that the person in the example possess the same general demographic characteristics as the patient so that identification can take place. It is even better if you can provide two such success stories. Then, just as the patient begins to show excitement at the prospect, you become discouraging, focusing on the patient's degree of addiction and her lack of desire to give up the chemical dependency. As in the previously described challenge, the patient is forced to take your role, insisting it is possible and desirable to try. After which you can go into the standard challenge, "Well, I'm not convinced. But there is a way that would prove me wrong."

No, You're Not an Addict

Our patients come in to convince us they are not addicted. Be prepared to agree with your patient, but do it in a strategic way. First, you must establish the necessary rapport and communication that is the basis of any therapeutic alliance. You accomplish this by listening, understanding, and being nonjudgmental. Patients do not plunge into their denial immediately. Rather, they want to be good patients and will give you the straight facts at the outset, even though later they begin to retract and color them. You have plenty of time at the beginning of the session to establish good contact.

Once the patient resorts to the denial, you then begin the paradoxical strategy. The following are some scenarios.

PATIENT: My doctor says my liver is in bad shape. I've got to quit drinking.

THERAPIST: Why would you want to do that? Drinking is too pleasurable to give up. Why not just cut down for a while and give your liver a chance to recover?

PATIENT: My liver is too far gone for that. I would be risking cirrhosis. I've really got to quit.

PATIENT: My wife is threatening to leave me. I've got to get off the dope.

THERAPIST: How many times has she threatened to leave? She always comes back to you when you've laid off for a while. This is no different.

PATIENT: No, I really think she means it this time. She says I neglect her and I'm out of it with the kids.

THERAPIST: Don't give up so easily. Let's spend a little time figuring out how you might con her again. Just think of what you're saying, that you'll give up dope forever. No way!

PATIENT: No, no. I don't think it would work. I think it's time to shape up.

PATIENT: My boss has suspended me from work for two weeks. He won't take me back until I get into a program, and I really need the job. My credit cards are beyond their limit.

THERAPIST: Why did he suspend you?

PATIENT: Some friends and I every once in a while do coke and booze on weekends. I'm too wigged-out to go to work on Monday. He is really furious. I guess I've missed a lot of Mondays.

THERAPIST: How many times has he forgiven you? How can we convince him to overlook it again?

PATIENT: No, he won't without a letter saying I'm in a program.

THERAPIST: I don't write letters like that. My program is cold turkey, and you're not ready for the heavy, heavies. But I can send you to a guy that will write anything you want.

PATIENT: You mean, try to con the boss?

THERAPIST: Something like that. I don't do it, but there are guys in town . . .

PATIENT: No way, there would be hell to pay when he finds out I'm still snorting powder. Can you help me get off it?

THERAPIST: Let's not rush into this. Let's talk some more.

In the preceding example, the therapist is continuing the paradox because to do otherwise obliterates any inroads. When the paradox begins to work well, therapists too often prematurely abandon it. The strategy of going even beyond the necessary point is sound psychojudo.

PATIENT: This is my third DUI. My car is impounded. If I don't get into a program, I might not get to keep my car or my driver's license.

THERAPIST: I'd recommend a good lawyer, like the ones who advertise on TV that they specialize in DUIs.

PATIENT: I did that the first two times. He got me into a program each time. The court won't accept that program again. They say it didn't help.

THERAPIST: You need a better lawyer, a real shyster this time. Do you know any?

PATIENT: Yes, I talked to one. He's really expensive, and he wants the money up front.

THERAPIST: Shysters are like that. Why don't you go with it, anyway? It's easier than going cold turkey.

PATIENT: That's what I need, cold turkey.

THERAPIST: That's drastic, man. Besides, it's uncomfortable as hell. Are you ready for that? Let's talk a little more about the shyster.

In the preceding example, the therapist is not only continuing the paradox but beginning to challenge the patient, suggesting he can't tolerate the discomfort of withdrawal. An astute therapist will tailor the levels of paradoxical intention to fit the individual case. Again, this skill can be developed in role-playing in which every possible denial is confronted over weeks of practice.

In the next example, the patient had begun to experience blackouts and was appropriately told by his doctor that this is a form of brain damage caused by heavy drinking.

PATIENT: The doctor says it can get worse. The last time I blacked out for two days. I got home in a cab and had no idea where I parked the car. I went from bar to bar, looking in each parking lot, before I found my car.

THERAPIST: How much did you drink? Maybe we can figure out how to stop just short of the blackout.

PATIENT: No. I'm told that with time it takes less and less alcohol to bring about bigger and bigger blackouts. Besides, after two drinks I lose count.

THERAPIST: Oh, come on now. That's alcoholic talk. You're not an alcoholic.

PATIENT: I'm afraid that's what I am. I've been pretending too long that I'm not.

THERAPIST: Did your doctor put all those notions in your head?

PATIENT: Well, he started me to thinking. But I've also been reading a book and talking to a friend who belongs to AA.

THERAPIST: Well, if you are an alcoholic, you've got to go sober for life. Are you ready for that?

PATIENT: If I'm an alcoholic, I have no choice.

THERAPIST: There's a good way to find out. If you can stay off booze for a month, you can reassess the whole thing and decide if you want to live without drinking. If you can't stay off for even just a month, as concerned as you are about brain damage, you're an alcoholic for sure.

In the next example, the therapist is subtly placing the patient in a double bind along with the paradoxical intention.

PATIENT: Yes, I know dope has gotten me in some bad situations. But I'm not a junkie because I can quit any time.
THERAPIST: That would prove it, all right. But I don't think you can quit for even a week.

The patient described in this example of a double bind–paradox combination decided to show the psychotherapist. She returned in one week and took a great deal of time lording her success over the therapist. The therapist ate sufficient crow, but then opined that he had seen this happen before.

> THERAPIST: Most junkies can do this for one week. Now that you've rubbed my nose in it, you can hardly wait to get out of here and score.
> PATIENT: So you don't think I can do it for another week?
> THERAPIST: No, I frankly don't. You can almost feel the junk as we talk.

The therapist continued this paradox for three successive weeks; in the fourth week the patient saw through the strategy. Characteristically, she was not angry but grateful. She told the therapist, "While you were doing your number, I was scared silly inside that I really could not go one week. Now I've been off four weeks, and I feel great. Where can we go from here?"

A variation of the foregoing example is the patient who first insists she can quit anytime, but then reverses herself when challenged. The first stance is, "I'm not really addicted." The reverse stance is, "I'm addicted and not responsible." Psychojudo is again indicated.

> THERAPIST: *(Sighing)* Yes, I agree you're hopelessly addicted. I would agree it would be an exercise in futility to even try to go clean.
> PATIENT: I'm not that far gone.
> THERAPIST: Well, I see a lot of patients, and you're pretty far gone.
> PATIENT: I think you're a smartass.
> THERAPIST: Then prove me wrong, or you are the smartass.

With an addict it is not only permissible but helpful to use the patient's own words and rationalizations. You can be as outrageous as your patient, and the two of you will establish a bond because of it. This young woman had for a time lived on the street and had a tough exterior masking her scared interior, and the tactic worked very well. One would never use this language with a perfectionistic suburban housewife who is desperately hiding her addiction to downers.

MOBILIZING RAGE TO SUPPORT HEALTH

Rage is the most galvanizing emotion in the human repertoire. Although love may be the greater emotion in the long run, rage is immediate and directed. All addicts have trouble with hostility. A great many are mild, lovable people when sober, and hostile, mean people when drunk or stoned. In several of the foregoing examples, the therapist skillfully mobilized the patient's rage against the therapist, but in the direction of a healthy outcome. The mobilization of rage in the interest of health enables you to cut through a wall of denial that otherwise would be impenetrable. Let us consider some examples.

Glenda's Grandmother

Glenda's indolent lifestyle on the West Coast was made possible by a regular monthly check from her wealthy grandmother in New Jersey. Twenty-year-old Glenda was ostensibly attending nursing school, but instead she pretended to paint while she was heavily into drugs. Her grandmother had grown suspicious; checking with the nursing school, she learned that Glenda had not attended classes beyond the first week almost two years ago. The grandmother was furious, as she had received regular letters from Glenda describing her nursing classes and indicating how well she was doing. She consulted a psychologist in New Jersey, who referred her to us. After we spoke with the grandmother on the telephone, she agreed to making the monthly checks contingent upon Glenda's entering therapy.

The patient breezed into the first session as one who is used to getting her own way. She was confident that she could talk her way out of anything, and immediately initiated an ingratiating manner designed to draw the psychologist into a plot to appease her grandmother. The psychotherapist sidestepped this thrust and sought to learn as much as he could about Glenda. Hers was the tale of a sordid lifestyle made possible by too much money in the hands of parents who lacked stability. Her mother had been married and divorced seven times. Glenda's father had died of a combination of cocaine and alcohol when Glenda was eleven. The patient was deposited in a series of expensive boarding schools from New England to Switzerland, and managed to get thrown out of several of them. Three years ago, her mother was killed in a head-on collision while driving at ninety miles an hour. Her blood alcohol level was .21 according to the autopsy. The grandmother, long ago having realized the self-destructiveness of Glenda's mother, had arranged to take charge of the family fortune. Glenda inherited nothing until her grandmother died, so Glenda was completely dependent on the very generous checks, which were to keep her more than comfortable while she was attending nursing school.

Succinctly, Glenda was a spoiled brat. But at twenty she was also a lonely, frightened, abandoned little girl who had not one clue as to how she might conduct an adult life. It was with this person that the psychotherapist connected. The patient latched onto the therapist in her needy, frightened fashion, but it was evident in her cynical smugness that she thought she had conned the therapist and was about to manipulate him. So she was stunned when she was told the psychologist would not see her because she had no intention of giving up drugs and entering school.

"You have to see me. If you don't, Grandmother will be furious." The psychologist replied, "I am a psychologist, not a baby-sitter hired by your grandmother." There followed a series of rationalizations in which Glenda escalated her volubility, all of which were deflected by the psychologist. Little by little, the patient began to talk as if she were the therapist, culminating with her sobbing, "I don't want to die like my drug-ridden father and drunken mother."

By the end of the first session, Glenda agreed to enter treatment subject to a series of conditions as part of the therapeutic contract. Her $6,500 monthly allowance was cut to $2,500, and she would have to pay for her therapy sessions out of that. She would refrain from all mind-altering substances. She would resume school at the beginning of the next semester, which was to be in three weeks, and she would succeed in school. Any violation of the therapeutic contract would result in the suspension of both her therapy and her allowance. If her grandmother did not agree to those conditions, the therapist would not see the patient.

An amazed grandmother eagerly agreed but was properly skeptical. The patient entered an incredibly turbulent treatment. She alternately soaked up like a sponge the parenting of which she had been deprived, and heaped on the therapist all the hostility intended for her parents who had betrayed her. She was seen for more than two years, illustrating that our goal is not always a twenty-week program but an effective and efficient therapy that is appropriate to the case.

Desmond's Deceitful Dodge

This forty-three-year-old married man was an anomaly in this day and age, in that he looked like an old-fashioned aging matinee idol. Graying at the temples, pencil mustache meticulously tailored, and pinstriped suit pressed to perfection, Desmond was a secret alcoholic. Certainly his wife, Melinda, knew it well, but she aided him in hiding this from the world. Melinda had money, and Desmond was a kept man. He made frequent pretenses of going into business, and several times his wife sustained heavy financial losses as she bankrolled his various doomed ventures. At heart Desmond was a playboy, and it was remarkable that his wife continuously forgave his infidelities. Finally she reached her limit and was about to throw him out of the house. Desmond cleverly convinced her that he wanted to get over his attachment to the other woman in favor of saving his marriage. He convinced her that therapy takes time, and pleaded with her to be fair and patient as he struggled with the neurosis he was suddenly more than willing to declare. The wife fell for it, and why not? He had been conning her for over fifteen years. She required only one concession: that Desmond go into therapy with me (Nick), who had helped her father through a very painful, suicidal depression years earlier.

Desmond came to the office oozing charm and casting flatteries with every sentence. It was an honor to see a psychologist who not only had seen his father-in-law but also had been president of the American Psychological Association. I waited for Desmond's rehearsed speech to end, and then asked what I might do for him. Desmond described his extramarital affair, admitted he needed the kind of torrid sex he got from Lorna but that he loved Melinda and wanted to save his marriage without hurting his mistress. He added, "I know it takes therapy a long time to sort things out, but both Melinda and Lorna have promised to be patient even if it takes two or three years."

I exploded with delight, calling the patient a genius for having conceived of a plan that allowed him to keep the home-and-hearth and the chickie at the same time, perhaps indefinitely. There was only one hitch; as a therapist, I was committed to treating needy people, not playing games. Desmond was stunned: Did this therapist really think he was playing games? Not only did I believe the patient was playing games, but I marveled at the ingenuity of the plan. "You don't need me. I'm sure you can continue to con these women without my help."

Desmond grew angry. He lost his usual suave demeanor and yelled, "I have never been so insulted in my life." He continued to berate the therapist for the next several minutes. I had by this time picked up the telltale signs of advanced alcoholism and replied, "Nothing like the way you insult yourself when you're being a common drunk and your wife has to bail you out. You've been hiding behind booze and skirts all your adult life." The secret that Desmond thought was well hidden was out. For about five minutes he railed in a rage, then settled down, asking, "I really do need therapy, don't I?"

I agreed that Desmond very much needed therapy but doubted that he was ready. Why not stick to the tried-and-true con game with women? I made a big point of complimenting the patient on how slick he was (along the lines of "You almost even had me fooled"), and recommended he simply polish up the behavior that was just temporarily derailed. Desmond became insistent that he should be in treatment, and grew increasingly angry that I was so skeptical of his intentions. He readily agreed to several conditions: no alcohol or any substitutes for two weeks, during which time he would get a job. He would also have to choose between Melinda and Lorna. The choice was his, but he had to choose. This time he would need to be employed, not start a business on Melinda's money. He was to call in two weeks verifying he had done both of these things so as to earn the second appointment. He gave his permission for the therapist to talk with Melinda, who agreed to the treatment plan. Desmond was cut off from access to her money; he would have to get a job.

It took Desmond almost two months to qualify for his second appointment. Yes, he did see Lorna a couple of times. No, he didn't have a job yet. Yes, he did have a drink, but it was only one drink. Finally Desmond swallowed his pride and took a menial job, admitting that he was not eligible for anything better. He was maintaining sobriety, and he had broken with Lorna. He entered the addiction program and maintained the conditions of work, fidelity, and sobriety throughout. To my delight, he shaved off his mustache, stopped getting facials and manicures, and started looking like a real person instead of an aging matinee idol.

LEVERAGING THE BLACKOUT

It is important to ask in the first session whether the patient has experienced blackouts. If you do not ask, the patient will never think of telling you, because his denial has already relegated the blackouts to the realm of insignificance. In fact, blackouts are extremely important because they are an early sign of alcoholic brain damage.

A blackout can occur for one or several hours at a time, and in later stages it can encompass a day or more. During the blackout the patient walks and talks normally, and most observers would not guess the patient is intoxicated. When the patient comes out of this state, usually the next morning, she remembers nothing about the time period involved. The persons she was with will retell things the patient said or did, none of which the patient will recall. When the first blackout occurs and the patient is later told of events that were blacked out, she tends to accuse the friends of making it all up. But as this occurs again and again, the patient becomes painfully aware that these are blackouts.

There is an old saying among alcoholics that "the more you drink the more you can." This has to do with tolerance, of course, but in time this saying reverses itself. After blackouts have set in, it takes less and less alcohol to produce longer and longer blackouts. Alcoholics who are potentiating the alcohol with other drugs will begin experiencing this state earlier than they would have otherwise.

It is horrifying to the patient to be told the blackout is early alcoholic brain damage. You can use this knowledge to increase the patient's motivation, but not directly. As soon as the patient begins getting over the realization that the brain has been damaged, denial kicks in to minimize the importance of the damage.

It is at this point, still in the first session, that you can begin a paradoxical strategy. Impress upon the patient that the brain damage is irreversible and progressive, and at the same time grossly minimize the importance of the central nervous system involvement for him. Yes, you know of persons who got so bad that only one drink would black them out for hours or a day, but there are great individual differences, and your patient might be one of the lucky ones who is only slightly affected. A case example is useful here.

Our favorite case illustration is Carl, who at the age of only forty-one had been experiencing blackouts for several years. They grew in magnitude, and decreasing initial amounts of alcohol resulted in blackouts of frightening lengths. Carl, like all patients in a blackout, would not be aware of the condition and continue to drink to the level to which over the years he had become accustomed. As a result, the blackouts grew to encompass days at a time.

On the particular occasion that brought Carl to his first appointment, he had blacked out for eleven days. His drinking bout began in Sacramento, California, after work on a Friday evening, and he came to in a hotel room in Kansas City, Missouri. He remembered nothing of how he got there. His car was missing, and he could not recall what he had done with it.

It was only after Carl retraced his journey through his credit card charges that he learned of his itinerary. When the bars closed at 2:00 A.M. in California, he drove to Reno, where the bars are open all night. His car got stuck in the snow on Donner Summit, and he was given a ride into Reno by a passerby in a four-wheel-drive vehicle. After two days in Reno, Carl rented a car and drove to Salt Lake City, stopping along the way to buy drinks. In this fashion he eventually got to Kansas City. He recalled nothing of renting a car, so he did not even look for it in the hotel parking lot. No one along the way realized Carl was intoxicated.

After telling this story to a patient, we like to stress this is an extreme case. Although it could happen to any alcoholic, we say, "There is no reason to believe you will be the next one. Of course, the scary thing is that once those brain cells have died, they're gone for good. But, as we've decided here, that will never happen to you. After all, only a little over half of alcoholics ever have blackouts, so you have a one in two chance of beating it."

As expected in this strategy, the patient takes the therapist's role and protests that he does not want to take that chance. One in two odds are not very good. Besides, he needs all his brain cells for the tough job at work. From here, it is relatively simple for the therapist, by doubting the patient's sincerity, to lead him through the challenge.

THE SQUISHY THERAPIST

In an effort to be compassionate, empathic, and understanding, most psychotherapists are easy targets for the skillful addict in denial. The addict has nothing but contempt for those she can con, and the list includes spouse, family, employer, friends, police, and psychotherapist. Addicts are especially contemptuous of well-meaning psychotherapists they call "squishy"; they figure that therapists should know better because they are supposed to be experts in human behavior. Furthermore, a part of them is unconsciously hoping for help and sees the therapist's incompetence as betrayal. This contempt then justifies whatever deceit and manipulation they heap on the hapless therapist.

In contrast, addicts have tremendous respect for the therapist who can outmaneuver their con. It is as if deep inside, buried below the layers of denial, there is a frightened person who longs for someone strong enough to save her from destruction. During the hangover and the other regular forms of depression that consistently beset the addict, she gets a clear picture of where she is heading, with its clear and inevitable ending. Quickly, then, the addict must obliterate the frightening image with a drink, a snort, a pill, a pop, or whatever her fix might be. But even the denial cannot hide the image, and as the addiction progresses and the images during the sober periods become more stark, the addict must be stoned more and more, until she is stoned all the time. Even then she longs for someone strong enough to tell it to her straight.

The working through all of this is a remarkably choreographed ballet that we call "the games." Addicts love the games, especially if they can be outmaneuvered while playing them. Let us now turn to these games.

7

Further Interviewing Strategies
The Games

There are a number of behaviors stemming from the addict's denial that are so consistent and enduring that we call them "the games." Eric Berne was the first to describe games in his book *Games People Play*.[1] The term was further popularized by Chuck Detrich, the founder of Synanon, a heroin recovery community in Sausalito, California, during the late 1960s and early 1970s. At Synanon the term "games" was directly related to the concept of addiction. The suddenly mushrooming American drug culture flourished in San Francisco and New York before it swept the rest of the nation. The Haight-Ashbury district of San Francisco was glamorized, but we became concerned as we saw the first ravages of drugs experienced by young people who had come for the Flower Power. I (Nick) was practicing in San Francisco at the time and knew firsthand the pioneering efforts of such programs as Synanon House and Delancy Street. I was also a member for twelve years of the San Francisco City and County Mental Health Advisory Board and was instrumental in obtaining government funding for the newly established free clinics.

The games described here are our applications of the concept to addiction and did not have names until it became apparent to us that it would be helpful if we gave them names that would be readily understandable and easily identifiable for addicts. Labeling the games made a shorthand available for use during the group process;

one addict could say to the other, for example, "You're playing the blame game." Everyone in the room would immediately be able to see what the patient had been doing and getting away with (until caught at it).

THE GAMES

The games, eleven in all, appear in the first session and persist throughout the treatment program. Not all will come up in one interview, but all will have made their appearance time after time over the course of several interviews. Some patients favor some games over others, and they put them through remarkably inventive permutations. Because addicts will proffer a never-ending supply of variations, you must be forever alert. In the group process, we are fortunate in having addicts who spot these creative inventions in their fellow substance abusers. The games are nothing more than derivatives of denial. Stated another way, they are among the vehicles through which denial operates. Let us look at each of them, and also think back to many of the previous case examples that reflected game playing.

The Woe-Is-Me Game

This game is a form of self-pity that the patient's denial has ingeniously adapted in the service of the addiction. It says, "I wouldn't have a chemical dependency problem if my life were not so turbulent." In effect, this rationalization turns the facts upside down: it is not the substance abuse that is causing all the troubles; rather, the addict claims that if it were not for so many problems there would be no need to drink (shoot, snort, smoke, inhale).

This game is ubiquitous, as every addict will use it in some variation over and over. The addict believes it to be true and succeeds in convincing a surprising number of nonaddicts to pity the unfortunate individual who has been driven to addiction by life's circumstances.

The manner in which patients use this game ranks high in the annals of unconscious cleverness. Because of the turbulent life, the addict ostensibly needs a different kind of treatment than that offered. Essentially the patient is saying, "If I could straighten out my life, the chemical dependency would go away. I do not need an addiction program; I need a therapist who will help me cope with life's problems."

The woe-is-me game is used as an excuse to resume alcohol and drug activity after a brief period of sobriety. A cross word from a boss, a depressing headline in the newspaper, a busy friend's impatience, a nagging spouse—all are seized upon as reasons to resume chemical indulgence. In fact, addicts frequently precipitate crises in order to justify going on a binge, and a common ploy is to incite a previously nagging spouse who has curtailed that behavior through counseling to begin nagging again.

In contrast to the victim game (described next), the woe-is-me game refers more to a blindsiding, a sudden event that justifies the momentary intoxication, although these events come so rapidly that they add up to a life of alleged turbulence. The possible permutations are infinite; a few examples will convey the flavor of the suddenness:

I missed the last train to the suburbs.

My father didn't even bother to come to my law school graduation.

I just found out my wife slept with my best friend.

The boss said the report on which I worked so hard has to be done over again.

On the way to work I got a lousy speeding ticket.

The bank bounced my rent check.

My car needs a new transmission.

At church there were two other women with my same dress. I was mortified.

Some damn pickpocket got my wallet.

Sam got the promotion instead of me.

My husband was rude to my mother.

My son's teacher says John is getting into fights at school.

I've got to get my mother into a rest home.

My wife thinks our teenage daughter is sexually active.

The landlord raised our rent again.

I was hurrying so much I ripped a hole in my best suit.

Every one of these events is reason for the addict to say, "Woe is me, I need a drink." Yet all of these are frequent events in most people's lives, and they do not make addicts out of nonaddicts. It is appropriate for you to exclaim with a sympathetic smile, "Woe is me; you poor guy [gal]. How could you possibly get through this without booze [dope]?" When challenged, the addict will readily relinquish her latest excuse, but this does not mean that she will not bring up many more similar trite excuses. Woe-is-me is a way of life.

The transitory nature of woe-is-me is illustrated by a five-minute segment in the first interview with Rob, a forty-three-year-old actuary with a large insurance company. Note how the patient, discerning that the therapist is not altogether impressed by his plight, jumps from one woe-is-me to another with ease, finally abandoning the entire line of rationalizations in order to deny alcoholism.

ROB: Some days my boss is so impossible that I have to have a drink right after work and before I start for home.

THERAPIST: How could you stand such a boss otherwise?

ROB: Well, if he isn't a bastard all day long my nagging wife starts in on me the moment I come through the front door. The only thing that will drown her out is a drink.

THERAPIST: What a terrible life. A bastard for a boss at work and a nag for a wife at home. It's enough to drive you to drink.

ROB: Well, I can somehow put up with both of them, but have you tried the commute across the Golden Gate Bridge lately? That really drives me to drink. Sometimes I have to stop halfway to Mill Valley for a couple of drinks. No wonder I got a DUI last week.

THERAPIST: There is nothing like a DUI to drive a man to drink. With all this you must be well on your way to alcoholism right now.

ROB: Well, actually, no. I'm pretty tough after all. I can take it.

We have seen very similar strings of woe-is-me preferred by food-aholics as to why they overeat.

The Victim Game

In the victim game, the addict sees the cause of his addiction as stemming from a more permanent or pervasive source than the sudden annoyances that beset everyone. These victim games require a more supportive response from you in the first session, even though in later sessions you can be more candid. In an addiction group, however, the response is likely to be brutally frank. Consider the following actual interchange; the therapist's response is from the first session, and the group's response came up once the program was under way.

PATIENT: My husband hasn't loved me in years. Liquor and pills are my only solace.
THERAPIST: Do you really think this is a solution? That this will stop your loneliness?

GROUP: No husband in his right mind could love a pill-popping drunk.

The group collectively has the wisdom and the peer authority to nail the patient's victim game for what it is. In this instance, the patient had begun her addictive behavior first, which contributed to her husband's subsequent and growing alienation from her.

In a recent interchange, a man attributed his chemical dependency to his Jewish parents having sent him through Catholic schools from grades one thorough twelve. He complained that he was subjected to twelve years of anti-Semitic torment, which warped his personality for life.

PATIENT: I fixed everybody by becoming a Jewish drunk.
THERAPIST: How does that hurt your tormentors more than it hurts you?
GROUP: Have you tried becoming an Albanian?

In the first session, you have an obligation to point out the futility of such a response, but gently, whereas the peers can confront the utter absurdity of the excuse. More believable scenarios involve growing up in the inner city, being shunted as a child from one foster home to another, chronic childhood illness or a physical or mental disability, an inherited obesity (foodaholic) and other such serious inequities. Your approach in the first session is to sympathetically reject these more serious events as causative. It is important to remind yourself that 90 percent of persons growing up in these circumstances do not become addicts, and there is a significant percentage of those growing up with privilege that do become chemically dependent. Be empathic and bide your time. In the group will be addicts who have been through it and will confront the victim games as they come up. The compassionate therapist must keep the faith.

No matter how much credence the patient's story has, it is being put out there to trap you, to con you into relieving the patient from taking charge of his life now. This is particularly heady bait, for psychology has gone overboard on promoting victimization. As we have mentioned elsewhere, you must separate the philosophical concept of victimization from your beliefs and actions as a clinician. Failing to do so will likely hurt the patient clinically, especially in addiction treatment, where a positive psychology (optimism, personal responsibility, coping skills, forgiveness, and so on) is more relevant. This does not mean that poverty, abuse, abandonment, social injustice, and other such factors are not contributory to addiction. To avoid misunderstanding, we fall back again on the condition of diabetes. Knowing that the failure to produce insulin on the part of the islets of Langerhans in the pancreas is the cause of the condition, we don't help the patient if we say, "You poor diabetic; no wonder you cannot stay off sugar." Such sympathy is not productive while the patient is suffering from conditions ranging from retinopathy to heart disease, all complicated by the failure to stay on the medical regimen.

The Rescue Game

The addict spends a great deal of time rescuing friends, coworkers, family, and everyone else who may want help. The more unworthy the prospective recipient, the greater the likelihood the addict will expend energy to rescue that person. If someone in the office needs a few dollars before payday, the addict will volunteer a loan, especially if the person already owes money and has no intention to repay. Addicts receive telephone calls at all hours from friends and acquaintances who want to tell them their troubles. No matter how undeserving the individual, the addict listens for hours at a time and attempts to rescue the caller. Why does the addict expend so much time and effort in rescuing the unworthy? It is an investment.

In the magical world of addiction, someone is keeping score. Our rescuer behaves as if there were a depository of owed rescues, and when she herself requires rescuing, no matter how much she has screwed up, someone will ride to the rescue. These patients believe that when they get bombed, someone will see them home; that

when they are fired, someone will intercede; that when they are arrested, the courts will forgive; and so forth. The message is, "I have
earned the right to be rescued."

The rescue is performed in such a way that it perpetuates the
addictive behavior of the person rescued. It softens the blow, holds
the hand, and excuses the misfortune. The addict's compulsion to
rescue every addict in the world also perpetuates his own addictive
behavior: in addition to earning and guaranteeing his own rescue,
the addict shifts the question of who is the real addict from the rescuer to the rescued.

The addict will present you with this rescuing behavior in the
first session, establishing her credentials as a good person and de-
flecting the question of Who is the addict? You need to see this as
another diagnostic sign. The following question is appropriate:
"Have you noticed that after you have rescued everyone else, when
you need rescuing you may as well be standing alone in the middle
of the desert? No one comes." Invariably the patient agrees, as this
imagined abandonment has been experienced many times. On the
second or third rescue game story from the same patient, the therapist can lament that the scorecard in heaven must have broken
down, for surely the patient has earned the right to be rescued herself the next three times she is in trouble because of her substance
abuse.

In her first session, Ellen, a woman in her late thirties, made a point
of telling the psychotherapist that a number of her women friends
carried her phone number, which they would give the bartender if
they had too much to drink. Ellen would drop everything in favor of
going to the bar, driving the woman home, and tucking her into bed.
She had done this frequently for the same women. Recently when
she was drunk in a bar, she called several of these friends, but no one
was able to come after her. Consequently, she tried to drive herself

home, had a serious auto accident, and was charged with felony drunk driving.

Ellen told the therapist that he was obligated to be as helpful to her as she had been toward her friends, and was incensed when the therapist advised her he could not rescue her with the court. She was playing the rescue game; in her mind it was time to collect.

AA takes this destructive rescue game and turns it into something constructive. The recovering addict maintains sobriety by initiating and sponsoring others through the twelve steps. The goal of an effective program is to transform addictive games into constructive games, but the addict cannot go from destructive games directly to constructive games. It takes a lot of working through in the program to make the transition.

The Blame Game

The blame game differs from the victim game in that the player purports to hold someone else directly responsible for an unfortunate event that has happened. If the boss fired me, it is not because of my drinking on the job but because he was prey to false gossip by coworkers who want my job. If my spouse leaves me, it is because of an extramarital lover, not because my addictive behavior has ruined our marriage. If my grown children want nothing to do with me, it is because they are ungrateful, not because I am drunk whenever they visit. If my diagnostic workup shows chronic pancreatitis, it is because of poor medical care, not my chemical dependency. If I keep gaining weight it is because my physician has not given me the appropriate diet for my physiology.

The addict needs the blame game to account for the continuous series of bad things that happen. Each successive event requires a new cast of characters to be blamed. In the first session, the patient will inform you of the entity that is actually responsible for the present plight, exonerating herself and avoiding the addict label.

A gay man who had just learned he was HIV-positive blamed infected men who engaged in sex without informing their partners. As the interview progressed, it became apparent that this man, who was responsible about protected sex when sober, was irresponsible when drunk and inhaling poppers (amyl nitrate). He preferred to blame the gay community rather than look at his own addictive behavior. The patient was an alcoholic who did not behave in his own best interest when drunk. He was well aware from past experience that when drunk during a sexual encounter, he would throw caution to the wind, risking infection. The therapist seriously inquired, "Is it true HIV seeks out men who are drunk during sex?" The patient was quiet for several minutes and then tried to blame his partners who were infected. The therapist interjected: "Now, I understand. Alcohol and condoms don't mix," upon which the patient admitted he had been foolishly irresponsible.

The blame game can be startlingly unreasonable. A man complained in the first session that his wife was unfairly leaving him. He had driven her to the hospital, as she had gone into early labor. On the way he plowed into another car, provoking a miscarriage. She blamed him for the loss of the baby. Had he been drinking? Yes. But his wife knew he would enjoy a six-pack of beer every night before going to bed. She should never have chosen that moment to go into labor! She should have done so when he had drunk only one or two bottles, or she should have waited until the next morning. The therapist responded with a straight face, "Don't you think you should blame that damn impatient baby instead of your wife?" The patient lapsed into quiet assent.

The Feeling Game

The addict is adroit at playing the feeling game, so the unwary therapist may be fooled into accepting counterfeit feelings as genuine understanding and contrition. The addict's friends have been fooled for years. It is a common experience to be shocked upon learning that a friend and neighbor who has always been highly admired for sincerity, concern, and honesty turned out to be an addict who has been neglecting and abusing his family for years. The skeptical therapist can say to the patient, "Things just don't seem to add up the way you say." Then watch the patient switch from feelings of concern to those of annoyance, irritability, and even outright hostility.

Tears of remorse are common, and at the moment she is expressing them the patient experiences them as genuine. However, they quickly disappear as the patient plunges into defending her behavior. It escapes the patient, who is busy conning the therapist, that innocent contrition is a contradiction, perhaps even an oxymoron.

We were impressed in one first session by the patient's telling us that the night before, he had been overcome with tears while watching an old rerun of a *Lassie* episode on TV. Timmy and Lassie were separated, and the pathos of the situation touched him deeply. He almost cried in the session as he told how the episode had tugged at his heart. We might have remained impressed with his tenderness had it not unfolded that this man was neglectful of his children and abusive toward his wife. And to top it all off, he was cruel to the family dog.

Chronic inebriation breeds irritability and short temper, not warmth and kindness. Be wary of the patient whom you suspect of substance abuse, who presents as just too wonderful. It is our addicted patients, far more than our depressives, who use up our Kleenex. With our *Lassie* devotee we were able to say, once the entire picture was presented, "You must have been very drunk to have shed more tears for Lassie than for your family. I wonder what your wife and children would tell us about that." This evoked admission of heavy drinking, accompanied by verbal self-flagellation, which enabled us to set the stage for the paradoxical strategy.

The Lassie case demonstrates that part of the feeling game is to feel counterfeit emotions while avoiding genuine ones. Addicts cannot handle real feelings. In fact, one of the first complaints you will hear from a patient who is newly clean and sober or the foodaholic who is losing weight is that he is overwhelmed by his feelings. It becomes readily apparent that these feelings are those that nonaddicts regularly experience in their daily lives and that should be no big deal were it not for the fact that the addict has long ago forgotten how to respond to genuine feelings. Looked at another way, the feeling game is also the nonfeeling game.

The Insight Game

Addicts enjoy playing the insight game, which they can do with impunity while continuing their addictive behavior. Therapists who believe that insight leads to changes in behavior will be sorely disappointed, for substance abusers offer insight in lieu of change. To the extent they can enthrall the psychotherapist with classic psychodynamics, substance abusers will heap insight upon insight, meanwhile avoiding the confrontation of their addictive behavior. Even among therapists who do not regard insight as paramount in treatment, the quality and ingenuity of addicts' insight can be seductive. Consider the following samples we have culled from actual cases.

This is our favorite: Tom, a suave fifty-one-year-old married lawyer, told us, "My mother was cold and harsh, and weaned me at an incredibly early age. My grandmother would hide me in the closet where my mother could not see that my grandmother had given me a bottle. I just realized that the bar represents the cozy closet where I can get away from my harsh mother, who is now represented by my cold wife, and enjoy the bottle grandmother has given me.

Alice, a forty-two-year-old suburban housewife and mother of three: "My mother and father would have awful fights after I went to bed. He would frequently hit her, and I would be very scared. I learned to stuff cotton in my ears and pull blankets over me so I couldn't hear, and I was able to sleep through the fights. Today sleeping pills are like pulling a fuzzy blanket over my head and shutting out all the awful things going on in my life."

Frances, a twenty-four-year-old single heroin addict: "My mother was a lush, and my life with her was hell. She would often have to go to a hospital to dry out, and I would go to live with my father, who was captain of a freighter. He arranged for me to sail with him. These were the happiest times of my life. I would lie on the deck and let the roll of the ship tranquilize me. That's how heroin makes me feel, tranquil and safe with Daddy. Without heroin I'm still afraid Mother will get me."

Patrick, a forty-eight-year-old perpetual bachelor: "My grandfather would take me to the pub with him to show off my singing voice. It was a happy time for me, as all the patrons in the pub adopted me. I spent all my time with these adults and missed growing up and playing with kids my own age. I guess this left me socially retarded. Even now I am the happiest interacting with people in a bar. The trouble is, you just can't sit in a bar without drinking. It's not that I'm an alcoholic; I just don't know how to socialize unless I'm in a bar."

The implication on the part of the patient is that if she were to get over the psychological problem, the chemical dependency would disappear. Psychologically, however, even if these were true causes, the behavior now has functional autonomy.

Sylvia was a twenty-two-year-old foodaholic who weighed over three hundred pounds. She described her mother as being totally unable to express affection toward her. Whenever she wanted to do something for Sylvia she would give her gifts of candy and pastries. The patient explained her compulsive eating as an attempt to get from her now-absent mother the love she never got. The therapist asked, "Now that you know this, how will it help you stop overeating?" The patient responded, "Now that I know this, I can remind myself of it whenever I am tempted to scarf." Therapist: "How long have you known this?" Patient: "All my life." Therapist: "Obviously this isn't going to help you. What do you think you really ought to do to lose weight?"

In countering the insight game the psychotherapist only needs to point out the ineffectualness of the "insight." With pill popping Alice, she was asked whether, now that she has made the connection, resuming stuffing cotton in her ears would get her off the sleeping pills. She had to agree it was doubtful. Similarly, Tom was admonished to create a room in his house that would represent grandmother's cozy closet and to do his drinking there. He responded, "I guess it is a silly excuse, isn't it?" Patrick was asked if he could substitute membership in a church choir for singing in the Irish pub, while Frances was instructed to find a boyfriend who owned a boat. Such pointed suggestions and inquiries invariably bring a reluctant admission on the part of the patient that the insight is being used to perpetuate the addiction. During the first session, you must guide the patient through the concept that all insight is soluble in alcohol and drugs and that abstinence precedes understanding. Then, of course, the stage is set for the paradoxical strategy.

The Rubber Yardstick Game

The rubber yardstick, also called the rubber ruler, is the game by which the addict measures substance abuse. The beeraholic, the most common type of addict in the United States, assures the traffic cop that he only had two beers. Beer drinkers generally rationalize that because they are not drinking spirits (whisky, gin, vodka, and the like), they are drinking less. However, as discussed in Chapter Two, the amount of alcohol in a bottle of beer is equivalent to that in a martini. Thus, the person who drinks a six-pack of beer may as well have drunk five or six martinis. Wine drinkers similarly rationalize. But four ounces of wine is more than equivalent to a martini.

Our all-time favorite one-glass-of-wine story involves a couple in which the wife dragged the husband in kicking and screaming. He was employed in construction, which involved beginning work very early in the morning. He was home early each afternoon in time to take care of their nine-year-old daughter when she came home from school. The wife's complaint was that when Gina came home, her father was passed out drunk. He countered that he was merely asleep, insisting, "How can I be drunk on one glass of wine?"

He told the therapist that he grew up in an Italian family and that all Italians drink wine, throwing out a cultural trap that the therapist ignored. When he was a child, his parents gave him one small glass of wine with dinner each night. He grew up with the dictum that just one glass of wine can never hurt anyone, not even a child.

The problem was that the size of the glass grew steadily through the years from a regular wineglass, to a goblet, and now to a plastic sixty-four-ounce Big Gulp soft-drink container he had saved from the convenience store. Each afternoon, on returning from work, he would fill the Big Gulp glass from a gallon jug of inexpensive Italian red wine.

His "one glass" was two liters, a little less than two regular bottles of wine. The rubber yardstick even works with the metric system.

If it were not so dangerous, we would be amused with the individual who claims to have only one drink at home before driving to join friends. The one drink is served in a ten-ounce tumbler. Alcoholics in a bar joke about the amount of gin that is displaced by the olive in a martini, and accordingly they ask the bartender to omit the olive. The real reason they do this is that at the end of the evening, they do not want to see seven toothpicks in the ashtray, as they want to believe they had only three martinis.

These substance abusers are playing the rubber yardstick game, and the variations on the game are infinite. The rubber yardstick will always reveal itself in one way or another during the first session, and you must challenge this form of denial by pointing out the actual count in each case.

The rubber yardstick must be challenged directly and straightforwardly. For example, the therapist can say, "In forty years of practice I have never had a wife drag her husband in here because he was drinking one glass of wine a day. How big was your glass—a tumbler or a bucket?" Or "It is impossible to get a DUI with a .15 blood alcohol level with only two beers. How much did you really drink before driving?" For the foodaholic, it is appropriate to state, "No one gains weight on the salad with lemon (instead of dressing) you have for lunch and dinner. Compulsive eaters never count what they eat while standing up or what they eat between meals. How much do you eat a day when you actually count what you're not counting now?" With still other patients it is appropriate to ask, "You have one drink every evening after you get home. Do we multiply that by two, four, or ten?" When so confronted, the addict almost always renders an honest report, only to forget the actual amount by later repeating the rubber yardstick. At such a time the therapist needs to confront the rubber yardstick by reminding the patient of the honest measure she had reported previously and holding her to it. Therapists who do not as a matter of course confront the rubber yardstick in their patients will be surprised how honest addicts can be (at least temporarily) when so confronted.

The rubber yardstick can be compressed as in the foregoing examples, or it can be stretched. An addict will often convince herself that the period of sobriety has been six weeks, when actually it has been only ten days. This is an unconscious ploy commonly used in the first session. By telling the therapist that she has been clean for over one-and-a-half months, the addict implies that there is no real chemical dependency. You must probe and ascertain the actual amount of time. It is not unusual for an addict to come in with a belief that she has been clean for two months, when actually it has been two weeks. Although the two weeks might seem that long to the addict, the most likely reason for the "mistake" is that an employer or a spouse has said, "Don't come back until you can get a letter from a psychologist that says you've been clean for ninety days." The stretched rubber yardstick gives the patient a seeming head start.

Some of the most obvious uses of the rubber yardstick are by compulsive eaters. The foodaholic will say that the giant-size bag of potato chips that he just demolished was only a quarter full, when it was actually seven-eighths full. A box of chocolates eaten at one sitting is remembered as a one-pound rather than a two-pound box. Other forms of the rubber yardstick among compulsive eaters involve not counting anything that is eaten while standing up, and refusing to own a full-length mirror in which the person's girth is painfully apparent.

Alcoholics have a need to limit their drinks if they are at a party given by the boss or at any other event in which they have to make a good impression. They use the rubber yardstick to avoid relying on memory, which would recall only two drinks regardless of the number; a common practice is to tally the drinks with a pen on the shirt cuff. Once he has tallied the second drink, the alcoholic from then on inspects his cuff and reassures himself that he is on the second drink. He enters no other tallies, and the rubber yardstick ends up replicating with the shirt cuff what the alcoholic would have done relying simply on memory. What he attempted to prevent occurs; he gets drunk and embarrasses himself.

A frequently overlooked manifestation of the rubber yardstick game involves the patient who is purposely seeing multiple physicians and obtaining prescriptions from each for the drug to which she is addicted. The person may be seeing five and as many as ten doctors, but on inquiry will recall only two and at most three. There is serious danger involved if the drug of abuse is a benzodiazepine, especially if it is Xanax. The titration from benzodiazepines is protracted. For Xanax it can be as much as six months, or even one year in some extreme cases. During that time, anyone who has been taking large quantities of Xanax is in danger of severe seizures. This danger is not usually present with patients suffering from phobic and panic disorders who are prescribed and taking a therapeutic dose. It applies to the abuse of any of the benzodiazepines, and the danger is compounded if the physician doing the titration is unaware of the extent of the addiction. If during the first session you hear any mention of Xanax, the most abused of the benzodiazepines, be skillful in cutting through the rubber yardstick.

The Vending Machine Game

The vending machine is a familiar sight in modern society. It gives us coffee, soft drinks, sandwiches, donuts, candy, and even money through a vending machine called the ATM. In this game, the substance abuser conceptualizes life as one big vending machine: you put in your money, and you get your commodity. The rescue game described earlier combines well with the vending machine game, for the coins put into this vending machine are quantities of "goodness." Thus the addict will say, "I've been clean for two months [that is, I put the coins into the vending machine], so why hasn't my wife come back to me?" Or, "I haven't missed a day of work in a month, so why hasn't the boss given me the raise I asked for?" It does not occur to the addict that this wife and this boss have been burned so badly in the past by the patient that it will take much more than one little "payment" to overcome the skepticism.

In the first session, it is appropriate to point out to the patient that the complaint you are hearing resembles a type of game called the vending machine. Ask this same patient, "If you were in your spouse's [boss's] shoes, how long would it take before you could trust again under the circumstances?"

The vending machine can viciously be turned on to the psycho-therapist, as the next case shows.

Terrence was actually clean for over three months when we first saw him. He had been charged with DUI, and he could not understand why the psychotherapist, in the middle of the first interview, would not agree to write what we call the my-patient-is-a-good-kid letter to the judge. Terrence was demanding that we certify him as not being an alcoholic, something he had "earned" with the last twelve weeks of sobriety.

· We explained that a person often is scared into temporary sobri-ety and that we were not convinced he was not an alcoholic, espe-cially because he was playing the vending machine game with such vehemence. He was furious, and next we heard from his very nasty defense lawyer, who hounded and threatened us for days. The lawyer tried to have the psychologist removed; the court, which knew us and was well acquainted with the tactics of DUI lawyers, refused.

Realizing that he was stuck with us, Terrence settled down, and he asked for treatment. He was accepted as a patient; along with the attendance, abstinence, and other usual requirements, the thera-peutic contract included the agreement that the lawyer would never again meddle in his client's treatment.

The File Card Game

This game is among the most difficult to detect, yet failure to do so will result in a relapse or other severe setback to treatment. It is named after the old-fashioned practice of entering into a calendar or file a reminder of anniversary, birthdays, or other important dates and events that require response. The file card game is a mnemonic device, but the addict sets it up and uses it unconsciously. Simply stated, the patient decides that if a certain thing happens, he has the right to resume substance abuse. Once he has determined what this crucial thing is, the patient develops amnesia with regard to this decision. Then, at some time in the future when this event occurs, the addict automatically resumes wet behavior without having gone through any conscious decision at that moment to do so. This is not an easy sequence for the psychotherapist to grasp, and examples are important.

Having just been fired after eight months of abstinence, David came to the first session hurt and bewildered. He was a forty-six-year-old research biologist who had been put on a six-month probation following a history of missing work as a result of binges with coke and alcohol. He had fulfilled the six-month probationary period with two months to spare, and he could not understand why the boss was so swift in firing him for one relapse in eight months when previously his behavior involved absences at least once a week.

During that first interview a file card came to light. Several times during the previous eight months the boss had asked David to work weekends. On the last occasion, less than two months ago, the boss promised the patient that he would not ask this favor again for a long time. The patient recalled during our session that at that moment he vowed, "If this happens again before two months, I have the right to go on a toot." So when David received the new request to work on the weekend, he plunged into substance abuse automatically and without having given it any conscious thought. The file card had become due. Instead of working, he spent the weekend stoned, leaving an angry boss in the lurch. The file card not only caused a relapse but also cost David his job. When this sequence was detected by the therapist he explained his use of the file card and asked if this were characteristic of him. Suddenly and to his own surprise, the patient became aware of another file card. "When I made this appointment, I said to myself that if you sided with my boss I would go on a binge and blame you. Then I forgot about it until now."

The file card can also pop up during treatment. It is swift, sudden, and baffling, and you need to look for it and learn to recognize it. Be particularly wary if a patient has gone through a recent experience that should have aroused anger or anxiety but instead appears to have promoted indifference. The feelings may have been bound in a new file card, and the absence of feelings is a heads-up for you.

During treatment a patient's mother suffered a severe stroke on top of a chronic severe heart condition. The patient attended to the medical and other arrangements, visited his mother in the hospital daily after work, and was remarkably placid in the face of his mother's impending death. The psychotherapist, baffled by the lack of anxiety and concern, probed and was able to help the patient restore a file card to consciousness. The patient had determined, "When my mother dies, even my psychotherapist cannot deny me a drink." With the removal of the file card, the patient's anxiety over his mother's condition increased markedly. The patient was now experiencing the appropriate emotions; in addition, he had prevented his own relapse.

All addicts at one time or another use the file card game, but for some substance abusers it seems to be a favorite form of denial. Such patients are likely to manifest the file card on the first session, and it is important to identify it immediately. Earline was a single twenty-five year-old alcoholic and barbiturate user who had several experiences of being date-raped while intoxicated. She had brought suit simultaneously against three different men whom she was accusing of having taken sexual liberties while she was drunk and stoned. Because of the frequency of the offense, one of the defense lawyers petitioned the court and obtained an order to have Earline examined psychologically. She was given an appointment with Janet for two weeks hence, for which she showed up mildly intoxicated. She apologized, stating that if she had known Dr. Cummings was a woman she would not have come in stoned. I (Janet) was alerted to something important and probed intensively. The following sequence emerged: When referred by her attorney, he did not know Dr. Cummings' gender. She thought to herself, "If it is a man I will show up stoned, he will take advantage of me, and this will serve the judge right for ordering a psych examination." She called the office, and Nick responded with his usual, "Hello, this is Dr. Cummings." The patient hung up, forgot the entire incident and its implications, and on the morning of her appointment she began to drink and pop pills. The therapist, having identified the file card, confronted the patient with it and wondered how often the patient played the game. To Earline's own surprise, she was able to recount several instances, accompanied with the amazement that she could plan to do something and then put it out of her mind so the event took place (in the patient's own words) "like it was automatic."

The Musical Chairs Game

Many of our patients will try to beat the consequences of their substance abuse by switching among comparable drugs (those in the same class). The original addictive substance has begun producing side effects, or it has come to the attention of the boss, the courts, the athletic commission, or whomever. By invoking the same high from another drug, the addict seeks to continue the addiction.

Reggie, a man in his early thirties, was a heavy drinker who was offered his dream job: that of being personal driver to the CEO of a large company. He was given the offer because he grew up in England and could resurrect his accent at will. He also looked like the proverbial British gentleman. The CEO was a bit of a snob, and he wanted to impress his fellow CEOs that he had an English driver. Reggie knew he would not have this job long if he continued to drink, so he switched to Xanax during working days and drank only on weekends and his days off.

For almost two years this worked very well. However, as addiction is always a progressive condition (because of drug tolerance), he began to drink more and more on his days off, which resulted in his needing increasing doses of Xanax during working hours. Eventually this practice caught up with him; he had two traffic mishaps, both minor fender-benders, but sufficient to alert the CEO. The boss gave him warning, which increased Reggie's stress level, leading him to try to solve the problem by mixing small quantities of alcohol with comparably small quantities of Xanax. His thinking was that one would leverage the high of the other but that neither would be enough to be detected. This tactic did not work, and he smashed the CEO's Mercedes Benz 600. His blood test score was marginal and Reggie came to therapy to save his chauffeur's license, even though his job was long gone.

Addicts often come to the first session already having played musical chairs, and the therapist must look for its manifestation. Patients will not talk about the switch unless the therapist asks. Quite common is the alcoholic who comes to the first interview free of alcohol for several weeks and suggests that since he has not missed drinking, he must not be an alcoholic. Unless the therapist asks what the patient is taking, he will not volunteer that he is overusing Valium,

Xanax, or some similar drug or drugs, prescribed by more than one physician, all of whom are unaware the patient is seeing several doctors. It is necessary to confront the patient with his musical chairs game and insist that abstinence means refraining from all substitutes.

A surprisingly common substitute is coffee, which is not usually the subject of our interventions. In these cases the patient is attempting to achieve a high with as many as thirty or more cups of coffee a day. These patients are easily identified because they are tremulous, on edge, jangled, and squirming in their chair. It is important to immediately restrict the coffee because caffeine is an upper whereas alcohol is a downer. The upper in a patient who craves downers will cause the craving to escalate dramatically, so this patient is very close to relapse.

The most common forms of musical chairs are the substitution of compulsive eating, drinking large amounts of sugary sodas, and compulsive gambling. The first two will joke that they gained ten or fifteen pounds since they quit drinking. The gambling musical chair will come up as an aside: "Since I quit drinking I have so much time I have to find things to do." This is a heads-up for the therapist. Ask how the time is filled, and you will find that the alcoholic is now a compulsive gambler. Often missed on the first interview with a formerly obese patient who is now skinny are the musical chairs of bulimia (both vomiting and laxatives types), anorexia, and excessive exercise. She has not gone from obesity to emaciation as a normal sequence.

Patients who play musical chairs will not present the pattern; you will have to probe. Reggie presented only the use of Xanax, minimizing its extent and claiming he was taking it in accordance with the doctor's prescription. The question soon arose as to which of three physicians. Reggie admitted to abusing Xanax, but he did not confess to the drinking until the very last minute of the first session. He had tried to pretend that the drinking was an isolated event on the day of the car crash.

There are patients who play the equivalent of musical chairs by becoming what we call a cafeteria addict. This individual ingests whatever is put before her, thus always remaining high on something but denying addiction because she does not crave one specific drug. Cafeteria addicts are hard to detoxify because no one, including the addict, knows what chemical has been abused over the past several days or even the past several hours.

The Special Person Game

Down deep inside themselves, all addicts believe that they are special persons and that some day this fact will manifest itself to the world. Although the phenomenon is found in the general population, in the addict it takes a peculiarly specific and concrete form. They do not talk about this spontaneously, as it may be somewhat delicate or embarrassing, but they will discuss it if you ask in the right manner. The therapist can ask quite directly, "How are you special and different from everyone else and when and how will this eventually be proven?" Inwardly, they are proud of this special person. The destructiveness of this game stems from the fact that it perpetuates the addictive lifestyle: as long as the substance abuser believes that any day now the special person will make her appearance, it is not important to change the addictive behavior.

The special person is never vague but is highly differentiated in the addict's fantasy. Most male adolescent addicts have a persistent but unstructured fantasy that they will someday be a very remarkable adult, accomplishing great things, and this will come about because an older man will appear who will appreciate and care for them—in short, that this older man will save them from self-destruction and reveal their special person. A great deal of this fantasy results from the lack of fathering in these adolescents' earlier childhood, and the deep hope that a loving and caring father will appear not only is persistent but also renders these boys (especially those who are runaways) vulnerable to male predators.

The special person has sometimes been fostered in childhood by a doting parent figure, or the absence of such so that the patient has to create a loving figure. The special person is always inside the addict, although the vehicle for its revelation may come from outside. One patient, Roland, had a very specific special person. He was either the son of the president of the Chase Manhattan Bank or of the U.S. ambassador to the United Nations. Roland had been born out of wedlock, and his mother refused to tell him who the father was. In his mind, she was protecting a very important national figure. He spent countless hours indulging this fantasy, but it never occurred to him that the U.S. ambassador to the United Nations at the time he was conceived was not a man at all, but Shirley Temple Black.

He fantasized that one day his father, just learning that he was dying, would appear to claim and proclaim his son. Roland would be elevated to his rightful place in the world. Why, then, should he worry about his marginal life now, and especially why should he be concerned with his chemical dependency?

The fantasy was persistent, and when the therapist told him about Ambassador Black, Roland simply narrowed the focus of his expectation to the president of the Chase Manhattan Bank. The group required Roland to confront his mother in an effort to ascertain his father's identity, and it pointed out to him that he had a wet attitude toward learning the truth. Finally, Roland talked with his mother, who convinced him that his father was in fact an unemployed musician who was passing through town and with whom she had had a one-night stand. With his special person gone, Roland settled into serious treatment.

A very common version of the special person game is, "I shall be the first addict to become a social user." Until this myth is exploded, life change is not possible. This is the most frequent manifestation of the special person on the first interview, and it is important that the therapist identify it as an addict's game.

One patient, Marcus, became very argumentative when this special person was revealed in the first session. Marcus was a prominent research physiologist who could run circles around the psychotherapist on matters of cellular biology. He set out to prove that it was physiologically possible to be a social user, and rather than get into a futile duel with this man, the psychotherapist challenged him to remain abstinent until he proved the premise with an addict other than himself. Marcus accepted the challenge and remained clean week after week; he completed the program, during which time he gave up his fantasy.

Another prominent scientist mentioned during one group session that he had obtained temporary possession of a NASA moon rock. The psychotherapist, always alert for the bizarre hope among addicts, asked what he intended to do with it. He confessed sheepishly that he had hoped to discover the cure for cancer with it. Questioned now about his special person, he confessed that in his childhood his mother often told him the following story.

When she was pregnant with him she went out on the back porch one dusk. Just as a shooting star crossed the sky, she felt him kick for the first time. She said to herself, "This is going to be a very special child. He will grow up to do something wonderful, like discover the cure for cancer."

The therapist merely asked, "Really, Charlie, don't you think it's time to accept the truth? You are a brilliant scientist and a recovering addict, not a special person." Initially angry at the thought that he would never alone discover the cure for cancer, Charlie settled down in the intervening week and declared at the next session, "I may never discover the cure for cancer, but I don't have to die a junkie either."

The earlier the special person is detected and eradicated, the faster the therapy will progress. The goal is for all patients to lose the special person before the conclusion of the program. The prognosis for those who do not elicit their special person is poor, whereas it is excellent for those who discover it in the first session.

ADDICTION IS PERFECTIONISM

In spite of failures, blunders, and troubles, addicts are perfectionists. It is easy to lose sight of this fact when the person sitting across from you is a disheveled drunk, an emaciated speed freak, or a spider-tracked hophead. Although perfectionism is found in a number of different kinds of patients seen in psychotherapy, the perfectionism in the addict is, indeed, a game because it is a form of denial in which the perfect self-image is maintained in spite of behavior and a lifestyle that are totally contrary. The skid row drunk may be passed out in the gutter, but in his denial he is perfect and sooner or later the world will agree with him. It is nurtured by a steady stream of denial that may seem superficial to the casual observer but is integral to being a perfectionist. For example, addiction is denied by thinking of oneself as perfect, but "just down on my luck." To the very end the addict preserves a facade, denying the addiction. Words like *alcoholic, amphetamine user,* or *heroin addict* help him maintain that denial. It is difficult to ignore first-order words such as *drunk, speed freak,* and *hophead.*

Consider even the patient who is suffering from Korsakoff's Syndrome, a type of permanent brain damage resulting from years of alcohol abuse. This person cannot remember very much, but to the end she maintains a pretense. She will confabulate rather than admit memory loss. An interviewer might feign, "Remember me? Last night we attended a black tie dinner at the Waldorf Astoria." The patient will confabulate, "Oh, yes. That was a very fine event." As outrageous as this question about the black tie dinner and its confabulation are, ask the patient, "Remember all the times we got drunk together and ended up in the drunk tank?" The patient will vehemently deny this, as the ego defends itself to the very end.

This perfectionism has contributed to a life of deceit, coverup, and pretense. It has involved family and friends unless these finally bail out. When the perfectionism manifests itself, no matter how slightly, you must address it, starting with the first session and continuing throughout. You must do so because the perfectionism will set the patient up for failure: "If I can't be the best, I'll be the worst." Thus when the patient suffers a small relapse, he will say, "I blew it with one drink, so I may as well drink the whole bottle." To the perfectionist, there are no degrees of relapse.

Confronting Perfectionism

One of the ways of addressing perfectionism during the first interview is to use first-order words. Doing so is difficult for therapists brought up with the fear of hurting people's feelings. Yet in working with addicts it is imperative to cut through the denial. You should begin this process gently and progress in accordance with the feel you are getting. Consider the following dialogue:

PATIENT: My wife is worried that I drink too much.

THERAPIST: Why does she think you might be an alcoholic?

PATIENT: No, not an alcoholic; that I might be a problem drinker.

THERAPIST: An alcoholic is someone who consistently drinks so much that it worries those around him. How does that differ from a problem drinker who is someone who consistently drinks so much that it worries people around him?

PATIENT: Well, she worries that I'm an alcoholic. The problem drinker stuff is my words, not hers.

THERAPIST: How often do you drink too much?

PATIENT: Several times a week, I'm afraid.

THERAPIST: So you are drunk almost every day or night?

PATIENT: Not drunk, just had too much to drink.

THERAPIST: Does your wife say you're drunk?

PATIENT: Yes.

THERAPIST: So your wife is afraid you've become a drunk?

PATIENT: When you put it that way, it sounds horrible. But yes, that's what is worrying her.

THERAPIST: Congratulations. You've just taken the first step toward cutting through the bull. Now we can start. Tell me, with no bull, what's going on?

Until the addiction progresses to the point that she cannot work, the addict is very conscientious about her job. She is perfectionistic on the job while being drunk every night at home. She dresses better than her fellow workers, works longer hours, cuts her lunch hour short, and seems like an ideal employee. Addicts are such perfectionists that they often make good employees in spite of their chemical dependency. We have talked with cynical employers who have kept an employee despite knowing that her absenteeism is the result of alcoholism. As one supervisor put it, "I don't expect her to come to work on Mondays, because she is nursing a terrible hangover from the weekend binge. And I know she will miss work on Fridays because, not being able to hold off until the weekend, she begins to drink Thursday nights. But on Tuesdays, Wednesdays, and Thursdays I'll get two weeks' worth of work in three days."

Preventing the Unraveling of Treatment

The main reason to confront and ameliorate the perfectionism is because it will interfere with treatment. Too often we have seen a relapse result in the addict's dropping out of the program: "If I can't go through it perfectly (that is, without a single relapse), I won't go through it at all." Frequently a foodaholic who gains one pound will go off her regimen and gain ten pounds by the following session. To the addicted perfectionist there is no degree of difference between one pound and ten. It is all too common for patients to argue with us that our program should not allow three relapses before the patient is excluded on the fourth one. Or patients become holier than thou, a recognizable characteristic of what might be termed *reformed* addicts as opposed to *recovering* addicts. The former resent anyone who can have what they cannot, and their holier-than-thou attitude will lead them right back to addiction. They are now perfect (abstinent) and will have nothing to do with persons who are not perfect, as manifested in their having even one drink. The latter have accepted a life of abstinence as a personal matter and do not resent nonaddicts. We strongly address the holier-than-thou attitude and any perfectionism as enemies to recovery.

In this chapter, we have demonstrated how critical it is to get addicts out of their usual ways of maneuvering conversations. Our suggestions for handling these gambits must begin during the first session. Waiting never works.

Even though successful recovery depends on the addict giving up the games and accepting responsibility, it helps if the primary enablers learn about their contribution to the games addicts play. Disarming the enablers in the addict's life isn't easy. We turn now to strategies for involving enablers in the treatment of the addict.

Note

1. Berne, E. (1964). *Games people play: The psychology of human relationships*. New York: Ballantine Books.

8

The First Interview with the Enabler

It is easy to become frustrated with the people in an addict's life who seem to unravel any progress the addict makes in therapy. Addiction is a family problem that affects all the members and also extends to people involved with the addict at work and through friendship. Enablers, or codependents, are the people or entities that are dependent, for one reason or another, on the addict's continuing substance abuse behavior; because of their dependence, enablers strive unconsciously or unwittingly to perpetuate that behavior. Co-dependents complain when the addiction gets out of control, but once it is back within the desired limits, they behave as if to encourage the substance abuse. Every substance abuser needs an enabler who makes the addictive process possible. This is why it is difficult, if not impossible, to treat an addict without involving the codependent.

When approaching members of the addict's support network, it is important to keep in mind Al-Anon's three C's: you didn't *cause* it, you can't *control* it, and you can't *cure* it. Although it is important to make clear that enablers never cause addiction and that they should not be held responsible for curing it, they can certainly learn to become part of the solution instead of part of the problem by learning to take responsibility for their own happiness and well-being. Along these lines, codependents also have much to learn about the ways they contribute to maintaining the very problems that so frustrate them.

Before discussing the methods of involving the enabler(s) in the first session, it is important to look at the variations on the codependency theme.

WHO ARE THE ENABLERS?

The enabler can be the addict's spouse or lover, a family member or the entire family, a friend, or even an employer. Not surprisingly, the courts or some other government agency, such as the welfare and rehabilitation department, and even psychotherapists can be enablers.

The Spouse as Enabler

The most common type of codependent is the addict's spouse. To a much lesser extent, the enabler can be a lover or close friend, but these are more tenuous relationships that lack the gusto and commitment that a married codependent can provide. (A frequent exception is found in some lesbian relationships, in which the tenacity of codependency can rival that found in the most committed marriage.)

Most enabling spouses are women, but this does not mean that male codependents do not abound. It seems that in our society women get more praise and support from friends and families for hanging in with a drunk or addicted husband than the other way around. One will often hear such comments as, "Mary is a saint for putting up with that awful man, just for the sake of the children," whereas the opposite is true for husbands: "Why is Bob so stupid, putting up with that bitch?"

A common codependency pattern for single women is what we term the der Stunken relationship. Der Stunken are men who "lie on the hip," doing dope all day while pretending to write poetry. The woman is working to support both and also does all the cooking and housework. This woman has very low self-esteem and was never appreciated by an irresponsible, drunken father whom she tried to save. In this relationship, der Stunken serves as a replicate of her father, and she is determined to succeed in saving him this time. Her low self-esteem has convinced her that this is the only kind of man she deserves (why should she be more fortunate than her mother?) and that without him her life would be sheer loneliness.

We do not regard this type of woman as a candidate for co-dependency treatment. She needs to extricate herself from this man and all subsequent der Stunken whom such unfortunate women find as replacements for the first one. She needs psychotherapy for herself, not for the sake of the addict she supports. Der Stunken quickly find other women with low self-esteem to care for them. In fact, our patient, once she successfully extricates herself from the relationship, is stunned by how many women are waiting to snatch him. We sadly point out that there are so many women with low self-esteem that there is a shortage of der Stunken.

The enabler spouse who requires a codependency program concurrent with the addiction program for her husband is exemplified by Merle in the following case.

Merle and Lon had been married for many years and had grown children. Lon was an alcoholic who periodically would be admitted to the hospital with severe alcohol-related medical problems. Following these episodes of hospitalization, Lon would become abstinent until Merle brought the sobriety to a halt. Lon would have found a way to eventually resume drinking without Merle's help, but his wife's behavior accelerated the process; she unconsciously did the scheduling. After Lon was sober a few weeks she could not stand it in spite of her declarations to the contrary. She would invite all of her female friends in for a margarita party, announcing to all as he served the drinks, "Lon is on the wagon and can't have any." It does not require rocket science to predict that before the day was over Lon would be very drunk on margaritas. Then Merle, now unconsciously rewarded, could resume her complaints far and wide about her alcoholic husband.

It is also not surprising that their younger daughter, Pamela, became the one to smuggle alcohol into the home where Merle had ineffectively banned it. This constellation is classic, and Lon will never achieve an abstinent lifestyle unless both Merle and Pamela become part of Lon's treatment program by joining a codependency group.

The enabling by Merle and to a lesser extent by Pamela has many variations.

Some enabling behaviors seem so obvious that they escape awareness only because they fulfill the psychological needs of both the addict and his codependent. Ken and Lucille were a financially struggling, middle-aged couple as a result of Ken's alcoholism and consequent poor job record. This all changed when Lucille became co-owner with her brother of a liquor store in a part of the city where business was brisk. Periodically Ken would be hospitalized for drying out, after which characteristically he remained sober for two or three weeks. During these periods of sobriety Lucille would insist Ken help out in the liquor store. Of course it was not long before Ken was sneaking bottles of whisky out the back door and would be drunk again.

No one but an enabler would consider urging an addict to work in a liquor store, serve as bartender, help out in a pharmacy, or other such job where the temptation would be overwhelming. However, it must be emphasized that the codependent does not cause the addict's substance abuse; the addict would abuse chemicals without the enabler. The term codependency means just that: two people have found each other and stay together because the substance abuse of one serves the psychological needs of both. Does the enabler's behavior help the addict rationalize his substance abuse? Yes.

Does the enabler cause the addiction? Resoundingly, no! Is it possible for an addict who has cleaned up to remain so while involved with her enabler? Probably not. But such a temporarily clean addict may stay with the codependent as an excuse to eventually resume the abuse of chemicals. In our treatment of the addict we stress that it is his responsibility to divest himself of the enabler if her codependency treatment has not curtailed the enabling behavior, just as with the codependent we constantly seek out what is psychologically in it for her.

It is not uncommon for two substance abusers to marry each other so that both continue in the dual roles of addict and enabler. The most frequent dyad is the alcoholic male and the compulsive, overeating female. They not only enable each other's indulgences, but there is an unspoken understanding that, since they are both vulnerable, "I can't call you fat and you can't call me a drunk." Men who cannot have a close interpersonal relationship with a woman will seek out an addict and enable her, while a sexually unresponsive woman can use the excuse, "How can I get turned on by a sloppy drunk?" The psychological reasons are many, but each person in treatment must accept personal responsibility for his or her own behavior.

Codependent husbands are equally blind to their own enabling behavior.

Derrick was a pharmacist who initially helped his wife along the road to Xanax addiction by supplying her with extra medication above her prescription when she asked for it. Alarmed that she was ingesting dangerous amounts of the drug, Derrick stopped being her supplier and properly insisted that she go to an outside pharmacist to fill her prescription. This is something he would ethically have done in the first place were he not his wife's enabler. However, once her addiction was discovered and her addictionologist physician had her in the slow, often dangerous titration that Xanax withdrawal requires, her husband manifested a new type of enabling. Several times he came home with a bag full of Xanax samples, complaining that he had noticed them after he had closed and secured the pharmaceutical part of the drugstore. He could not leave them exposed overnight there, but apparently it was all right to expose them to his Xanax-addicted wife, who snatched and hid most of the sample packages. This woman's treatment for addiction was complicated as long as Derrick chose unconsciously to enable it. Ultimately she had to realize that she was responsible for her recovery, not Derrick. After several more relapses in the face of Derrick's persistent enabling, she left him and subsequently entered successful recovery.

Medical education and knowledge do not prevent someone from being an enabler to a spouse. We have treated scores of physician's wives whose husbands were perpetuating their addiction, in contrast to the way these doctors vigilantly monitored their patients' chemical dependencies. These physicians can manifest vigilance with their patients and not with their wives, or, more commonly, they are blind to all addicts. Often the latter results from having to deny that a parent was addicted while the physician was still a child.

One prominent vascular surgeon, who stored large quantities of medications in his home, was oblivious to how many downers his wife was swallowing. She began mixing these with alcohol, with severe results. Several times he carried her into his own hospital while she was in a coma, never realizing she had been doing copious amounts of alcohol and downers. He found himself too busy to attend a co-dependency program once she showed interest in getting treatment for herself. It was not until she informed him that she was divorcing him that he came to grips with her addiction. When an enabler is uncooperative, often the only viable alternative for the substance abuser is to leave the spouse.

The Family as Enabler

Those of us working with substance abusers are well aware of the family systems that enable several family members each to have different kinds of addictive problems, spanning several chemicals, while functioning as each other's enabler. A frequent constellation is an alcoholic man married to a foodaholic or Xanax-addicted wife, whose children are potheads and doing very poorly in school. There is an unspoken rule that no one point the finger of addiction at anyone, thus avoiding having the finger pointed at himself or herself. The system gets out of kilter when one family member's addiction swings out of control and the other family members have to cry foul.

Bob was a sixth grader whose dealing drugs on the school grounds came to the attention of his teachers. When the parents ignored three requests for a parent-teacher conference, the school notified the police. Their investigation confirmed that Bob was dealing marijuana and amphetamines, and he had built up a considerable clientele in the school. The parents had flagrantly been looking the other way while their addicted son was supporting his own habit by dealing. Once summoned by the police, however, they disavowed Bob as a rebellious and possibly incorrigible son.

During the evaluation by juvenile authorities, the family history came to light. Bob's father was an alcoholic and a periodic cocaine user, and his mother was a benzodiazepine addict who spent most of her time placing two-dollar bets at the track or with her bookie. She was a small-time compulsive gambler in addition to being a pill addict, and she was seldom, if ever, there for Bob. Thus, while serving as each other's enabler by looking the other way, they were also addicts themselves.

> The evaluation revealed that the father had twice been admitted to inpatient detoxification programs, and the mother had numerous entries in her medical charts indicating physicians' suspicions that she might be misusing prescription medications. The fact was that the mother was seeing three different physicians, all of whom were prescribing without knowledge of the existence of the other two. Whenever one physician cut back on her dosage, she added another physician.
>
> The only solution for this family was for each member to go into his or her own *separate* addiction program; family therapy was a consideration only after all were clean. The rationale for this will be discussed later in the chapter.

We have seen many tight-knit family enabling systems fall apart for reasons similar to those described in the foregoing case. In one, the fourteen-year-old daughter almost died of an overdose; in another, the father went to prison. For many, the system suffered collapse because the main breadwinner lost her job. In one, the family enabling system experienced disarray when a child was born with severe fetal alcohol syndrome (FAS). But probably the most frequent form that the enabling of child or adolescent substance abuse takes is that of parents being unable to confront and thereby prevent addictive behavior in their offspring. Some parents have not resolved their own adolescent rebellion or their own dabbling in illegal substance use. Others have abdicated the parental role through timidity or overpermissiveness, wanting to be pals with their kids. And over and over again we have seen the destructiveness of the following capitulation: since you are going to do drugs anyway, we want you to do them in front of us. Other family enabling systems disintegrate because someone, usually the substance abuser, oversteps the unspoken limits of what is to be tolerated. This is illustrated in the following case in which the family enabling had been stable for years, only to fall apart suddenly.

The family of a middle-aged alcoholic were his staunch enablers. He was a prominent businessman, but he was essentially incompetent because of his drinking. He was "successful" in the eyes of the community because the family fortune had been built in this business generations before he took it over. The business ran itself, which allowed him plenty of time to be known all over town as a well-dressed, affable partygoer. His wit and well-bred manners made him a welcome and even sought-after guest at all snooty events.

His beautiful wife had been recruited as a keeper of the family secret, and she, in turn, had trained the children to be enablers. The whole system came apart at the seams when the wife, tiring of being just something on display, filed for divorce. The straw that broke the camel's back was that the family mythology called on her not only to continue to cover her husband's alcoholism but also to stand by him during his latest scandal involving still another infidelity. The upheaval mobilized the enabling family, which, failing to change the mother's mind, now pressured their prominent town drunk to go into treatment. The family members were shocked when told they all would have to enter a codependent program if the patient's treatment were to be meaningful.

The Employer as Enabler

The employer can exhibit enabling behavior for a number of reasons: (1) the boss may be genuinely trying to salvage a valuable employee but going about it in such a way that the addictive behavior is enabled rather than reduced; (2) the employer may fear a wrongful-firing suit in this litigious era; (3) the employment policies may inadvertently promote or foster addictive behavior; or (4) the enabling may reflect the boss's own unresolved issues. The first three require extensive organizational and legal consultation, with subsequent revision of the company's human resources policies.

There may be times when we might be of help to the employer in modifying these policies, but it is the fourth cause that is the most frequent concern of the addiction therapist.

One of our major employer contracts provided for consultation to the executive suite. These kinds of contracts are not uncommon, as addictive problems in the highest echelon can adversely affect an entire organization. Management is interested in addressing these problems in the most effective yet discreet manner.

The CEO of this company requested these services for his vice presidents more often than most, but the surprising feature was that each referral involved an addictive problem. Every time, the CEO would refer the VP for what had been thought to be stress resulting from the demands of a recent promotion. And each time, the CEO was surprised to learn the case involved alcohol, cocaine, or both.

This CEO had an uncanny ability to hire and promote addicts. He argued that this was a fantastic coincidence but agreed to have us evaluate a man he was contemplating for promotion. The CEO was certain that this man had absolutely no chemical dependency. Yet, again to the CEO's surprise, the candidate was an alcoholic.

Dismayed and feeling chastened, the CEO agreed to treatment for himself, during which he learned that for years he had been hiding from himself and the world that his father had died of alcoholism when the CEO was sixteen years old. Once the boss had resolved this issue, we were never again called to evaluate a VP who turned out to be addicted.

In a much different case, a union local in the Midwest asked for our help with a family of three members: a father, mother, and grown son. The three of them had been hospitalized a number of times for alcoholism, and were now claiming for the third time a very liberal benefit. The contract called for a ninety-day hospitalization for those members for whom less protracted hospitalizations had not worked. For three years, the three family members alternated, with one being in the hospital at all times. As one completed the ninety-day stint, another succeeded, until all three had been hospitalized for ninety days each. Then the rotation would begin again the following year. It appeared as if this annual ritual would go on indefinitely.

We interviewed the three family members and ascertained that although they were alcoholics, there was no serious intent to receive treatment. Rather, they looked on the ninety days as an opportunity to catch up on the nutrition they had been neglecting, as well as to take a holiday. We advised the union that a modification of the benefit was called for, but because this benefit had been won after hard-fought negotiations, the union leadership was loathe to tamper with it. The union continued to be this family's enabler.

Examples of enabling by the employer are numerous and varied, and the inability to obtain company cooperation may render treatment improbable. Similarly, the courts are reluctant to send substance abusers to our overcrowded jails, and they thus remove the leverage the psychotherapist needs in order to do an effective job.

The Physician or Psychotherapist as Enabler

Here we are not looking at the addicted professional, known as the impaired physician or psychotherapist; that problem will be addressed in Chapter Nine. Here we are discussing the professional who, as a function of his or her own unresolved issues, inadvertently is enabling the patient's chemical dependency.

Len was a favorite primary care physician (PCP) and one of the most competent in a large group practice in a metropolitan community. He prided himself on being psychologically minded, and he frequently referred patients for psychotherapy. Every one of his female referrals was an alcoholic; in contrast, his male referrals varied.

Len had labeled all of his female referrals as suffering from "housewife's stress syndrome," and he had worked with each woman for a long time. He firmly believed that the PCP was the first line in the treatment of neurosis and that the behavioral care specialist should be called for only the most difficult cases.

Len was quick to prescribe tranquilizers or other medications, and was constantly surprised when these exacerbated the symptoms. Unbeknownst to Len, these women were now drinking on top of their medication, potentiating its effects. Finally, in exasperation Len would make the belated referral.

His lack of insight into his female referrals baffled him, and he sought a series of consultations. As a result he entered a codependency program, with dramatic results. He learned that his wife, daughter, and mother were all alcoholics and that he enabled all of them through his ministrations and medications while never even suspecting the real problem. His blind spot extended to his women patients.

An employee colleague had difficulty in assessing chemical dependency in his patients. He attributed the lack of substance abusers in his caseload to the luck of the draw, but his supervisor time and time again was able to point to patients he was seeing who were, indeed, chemically dependent. Once the addicted patients were pointed out to him, this employee was able to treat them fairly appropriately; his blindness involved the initial identification.

Eventually the reason for the employee's blind spot became apparent. At a clinic function that included the families of employees, his three teenage children manifested serious substance abuse. He had not wanted to see the problem in his own children, so he was blinded to the unmistakable signs in his patients. Both at home and in the office, this otherwise skillful psychotherapist had been an enabler.

Once the reason was exposed before the entire staff, he felt too humiliated to continue in his current job, and he moved on to other employment. We have no knowledge whether the issue was resolved, but for the sake of his three teenage children and his patients, we hope so.

INTERVIEWING THE ENABLER

Interviews with an enabling spouse, family member, or friend are much less complicated than those with the substance abuser. At this moment in time the codependent is clamoring for the addict to receive treatment and is eager to push, drag, or cajole the patient. In stressing the need for cooperation from the codependent, the therapist must initially accept at face value the enabler's expressed wish to be of help. By stating, "I know you want to help in your spouse's [father's, son's, friend's] recovery," the enabler will charge forward with very good intentions.

It can be said that motivating the enabler requires almost the opposite strategy than that required for motivating the addict. This is the time to enlist cooperation, and the enabler, who has hidden behind a facade of cooperation for years, will jump at the chance to cooperate. This is *not* the time to confront the codependent's enabling behavior. That will come in the codependency group program. Consider the following examples of appropriate and inappropriate responses to two enablers' statements:

ENABLER 1: Very often when he is about to start drinking again I start to warn him that I can see it coming. I threaten to leave him if he starts drinking again.

INAPPROPRIATE THERAPIST: Did it ever occur to you that this kind of nagging may be just the thing that sets him off? Why would you want to do that?

This therapist has already begun to confront the enabling behavior, which is a mistake at this point. Such confrontation usually has the effect of alerting the codependent of things to come, causing her to avoid joining the codependency program.

APPROPRIATE THERAPIST: I can understand how desperate you must feel at that moment when you see the drinking bout coming. You're groping for a way to keep him dry. I believe we can help you be able to help him.

This therapist does not challenge the enabling behavior, but rather allies with the healthy part of the codependent.

ENABLER 2: Just because he is on the wagon doesn't mean I shouldn't have my charity group in for cocktails, does it?

INAPPROPRIATE THERAPIST: By doing that you are tempting him to drink again. Did it ever occur to you that that's what you might be trying to accomplish?

Again, this therapist has begun treatment at the inopportune time. The task is to recruit the enabler, not chase her away by hanging her behavior out to dry.

APPROPRIATE THERAPIST: It is difficult to know what to do when you're married to an alcoholic. Our program can help answer so many of your questions, which will ultimately help you help him.

This therapist is engaging the enabler in such a way as to increase her motivation to participate in the program.

Guidelines for Working with Codependents

If you do not prematurely challenge the codependent's belief that he really wants the addict to quit, and if you always keep in mind the simple guidelines we will be describing in the next paragraphs, the enabler almost always enters the codependency program and completes it satisfactorily.

1. *The codependent must actively participate in the codependency program throughout the substance abuser's treatment.* Without the participation of the enabler, the addict has a greatly diminished chance for recovery. When an addict has entered therapy, the time is right for the enabler to participate, and it is relatively simple to enlist him. Remember, however, that the enabler is cooperative now because the codependency equilibrium has been upset or is out of control. Once the old status quo is restored, the cooperation will vanish, and the enabler will return to being just that, an enabler. So the codependent must become actively involved and vested in the codependency program before the old interpersonal conflicts seek restoration of the addict's behavior. In the absence of a firm investment in the codependency program, the enabler will drop out and begin to sabotage the addict's recovery. As long as the codependent is an active participant in the program, enabling behavior can be addressed in the group as it arises.

This was the situation with Flora, who initially dragged her husband into treatment against his will. To her surprise and delight, Frank took hold, completed his withdrawal, and entered a program of abstinence. Flora seemingly eagerly attended the first codependency group session, but then for one reason or another missed the next three. On one occasion the seven-year-old son was sick, and the following two weeks she was visiting her mother in a distant city.

By the time she returned, Frank had been clean and sober for a little over a month. Flora began her systematic nagging, which always sent him straight to the bottle. Before the next session, Frank was drunk. Flora attended the fifth codependency session; in her absence the group had gelled into a cohesive culture for abstinence. The group spent most of the session with Flora and was able to get her on board and to salvage Frank's treatment.

---

2. *Do not attempt to work with the addict and the enabler together in the same room.* We have seen disasters occur when the therapist is challenging the addict for sobriety. The enabler sees through the paradox and effectively sabotages it. The codependent will likely do anything from vehemently defending the addict to skillfully turning the addict against the therapist. A variation of the following is common: "Darling, this doctor is very good. He is tricking you right into sobriety before you even know it."

We have yet to see a successful challenge while the codependent is in the room. The codependent is good at enabling, having spent years rescuing the addict from the jaws of recovery. Having this happen in your office may be a wonder to behold, but it is not very rewarding at the end of it to be standing in shambles.

Seeing the addict and the codependent separately is imperative for successful treatment. We generally have the enabler see a colleague, preferably the one who will be conducting the codependency group.

3. *If the codependent is found to be addicted, do not enroll this person in the codependency program.* Rather, this spouse, family member, or close friend needs to be in an addiction program of her own. It is appropriate while interviewing such individuals to switch from encouraging participation in a codependency program to making a recovery challenge.

4. *Do not initiate marital counseling or family therapy immediately.* It is popular in many programs to do so, but we have found this approach to be counterproductive. Both the addiction and the codependency must be addressed first. The time to begin marital or family therapy is after the addict has completed the program and is committed to abstinence.

It is also understood that before other therapies are undertaken, the codependent has done as well as the addict in moving toward recovery. Otherwise, the codependent undertakes the job of enabling the addict to resume chemical dependency. Thus the marital or family therapy has failed, and the addictive behavior has returned with a vengeance. In such instances we have not only failed but also trained the cast of characters in how to resist and defeat treatment in the future. We refer to such persons as "trained seals," and the field of addictionology is cluttered with patients and enablers who have the skill to temporarily manipulate and ultimately defeat any program.

5. *If a patient has more than one enabler, it is best to separate them from each other as well as from the addict.* Two or three enablers from one drama constitute a subgroup within the codependency group, and together will cause all kinds of problems. They may not only prevent themselves from understanding their codependency but also inhibit the success of others.

6. *When the employer or an institution is the enabler, the problem is best handled by consultation or through a series of problem-solving meetings.* Occasionally an employer or bureaucrat will want to participate in a codependency program, but this is rare. On one surprising occasion, a domestic relations judge asked for and received participation in a codependency group. She claimed it helped her with her decisions from the bench.

THE CODEPENDENCY GROUP

These groups, composed of eight to twelve enablers, have two types of participants. The majority of the group are enablers whose addict has qualified for and entered a program of abstinence. The second type of participant is the codependent whose addict has not entered a program but who wants to know how the relationship contributes to the perpetuation of the addiction. The outcome for this latter group, once the codependent is no longer enabling, will be either that the addict does eventually enter treatment or that the former enabler, no longer needing to be codependent, leaves the relationship. Some codependents come into treatment without the addict, who steadfastly refuses to enter treatment. Just as in the addiction program the participants are highly encouraged and in very resistant cases demanded, the codependent is encouraged to attend Al-Anon meetings. We have found that the group culture in our program becomes one that leads almost all codependents to become active in Al-Anon. In such cases the codependent often has the implicit contract in meeting with the psychotherapist to get the addict into treatment rather than learn about her own behavior. There is a second type of enabler; she comes for the first interview with her addict, who did not accept the challenge, and she hopes that by participating herself, the addict will enter a program in the future. It is appropriate for the therapist on initial interview with such a codependent to refrain from challenging her wishes; first, get her in the program.

The group meets for three hours each week for a total of twenty weeks, a program that roughly coincides with the addicts' participation in their recovery program. As previously noted, the group leader is different from the one who is treating the addicts.

The first part of each meeting is psychoeducational, beginning first with aspects of codependency and concluding with alternative behaviors to that codependency. The majority of the meeting is given to group process, with considerable interaction among the participants. The emphasis is on understanding of one's behavior and how it contributes to addiction within the relationship. Of special importance is the codependent's increased understanding of the secondary gain to the codependent when the addiction is active. Relaxation techniques, guided imagery, and other forms of stress reduction are included, and biofeedback is available as an adjunct.

The success rate of these groups is quite high. It is not unusual for the codependent to successfully complete a program while the corresponding addict does not. In such cases, however, we have often seen recovery on a subsequent try, now enhanced—a true partner in recovery—rather than enabled by a codependent.

Certainly, the challenge of getting both the addict and the support network working together toward recovery is begun during the initial therapeutic contacts. Being able to confront not only the addict but also the primary enablers is a significant therapeutic skill that takes practice. We turn now to the primary obstacle to being able to actually do everything we have discussed so far: the therapist's countertransference.

9

Countertransference
Denial Is a Two-Way Street

There is no other health endeavor more subject to bias, both at the level of the individual therapist and at the societal level, than the treatment of chemical dependency. The therapists' individual beliefs and training determine the interventions she uses. But aside from those kinds of choices society, through its allocation of resources, reflects its attitudes toward the substance abuser.

Present-day societal attitudes toward chemical dependency run the gamut from being lenient to overly punitive. Mothers Against Drunk Driving (MADD) has complained in the media for years that even those repeatedly arrested for drunk driving are let off with light sentences and most often without having to do jail time, often resulting in the death or severe injury of innocent persons. But mandatory sentencing and the so-called three-strikes legislation have overcrowded our jails with drug addicts. Within the broad range of attitudes from lenient to punitive, other inconsistencies abound. As just one example, powder cocaine users are usually white-collar individuals and generally receive lighter sentences than crack cocaine users who are mostly from the inner city. Society is composed of the entire spectrum of moral, political, ethnic, cultural, and economic attitudes and cannot be expected to reflect the exquisite balance among personal responsibility, surrender, and recovery exemplified by AA (and NA, CA, OA). Nonetheless, biases found among some in authority, as well as many of our policymakers, indicate that society is a long way from achieving a cohesive and effective approach to the enormous chemical dependency problem in America.

Because the two of us have for so long been identified with the treatment of addiction, we are often drawn into discussions with people who reflect attitudes that are troublesome to those of us who are treatment oriented: Is the drunk worth saving? Wouldn't we be better off if junkies just overdosed? What about adding something carcinogenic to drugs, like they did when they sprayed herbicides on marijuana plants? Then, of course, we hear the opposite. Drugs should be decriminalized. All substance abuse is caused by victimization by a sick society. No one should be held responsible for acts committed while intoxicated.

As soldiers in the trenches, we have little time or stomach for these armchair debates. A number of years ago, however, when the U.S. Supreme Court was deliberating over whether addiction is a disease, I (Nick) made an exception. On my own and at my expense, I filed an amicus brief on behalf of all the patients who would die of the complications of addiction if the court declared addiction to be a disease.

Many found my action curious, inasmuch as I do believe addiction results in tissue changes that could be described as a syndrome. The reason is simple: I am a pragmatist who believes that we must use every possible weapon to counter the addict's denial. Excusing the behavior as a disease would result in depriving weary therapists of any leverage, for if addiction were a disease, the addict would bear no responsibility. As we have seen, it is trouble that brings the patient to treatment, not a desire to clean up. We therapists need every bit of help available to combat the wall of denial, which would only be strengthened if the court declared addiction to be a disease. In its wisdom, the Supreme Court rejected the premise.

BIAS IN THE TREATMENT ROOM

There are psychologists and counselors who still believe addiction is a character flaw that should be regarded as a moral weakness. This is an old-fashioned notion; it is politically incorrect. The opposite position holds that substance abusers are victims who are responding to victimization in the only way they know how. This is currently a very popular view; it is politically correct. For those of us who work successfully with chemical dependency, both positions are wrong.

The strength of character required of those who attain abstinence in the face of addiction is more than most human beings are called on to exhibit in their entire lifetimes. We are constantly in awe of recovering addicts' accomplishment, and fully empathize with how much strength they need to take things one day at a time. For this reason we find it insulting to regard such persons as hapless victims who have no alternative. They do have a choice. We know this because every day we help them make those choices.

Some therapists and many patients regard the need for surrender to a higher power a sign of weakness and deride the concept. In contrast, we admire recovering addicts' humility and their recognition that they cannot accomplish sobriety by themselves, and we respect their surrender to a higher power. In our estimation, that surrender takes the greatest strength of all. Recovering addicts are everywhere in our society, among its most successful members, yet not long ago they were headed for self-destruction. Of all of us, they are doing the most to lead others to sobriety.

We cannot help but be impressed by the energetic hands-on work being done by such institutions as AA and the Salvation Army, as well as that of the many competent, dedicated therapists. We are less than sanguine regarding the thousands of ineffective hours spent with substance abusers by ineffective or biased therapists. What our colleagues do in the treatment room is of great concern to us. We have seen over and over again that denial can be a two-way street, with the therapist almost as much in denial as the patient. It is to these countertransference issues that we now turn.

RELUCTANCE TO CONFRONT AND ACTIVELY ENGAGE THE ADDICTION

Most therapists want to like and be liked by their patients. They see the road to such a relationship through being kind, compassionate, understanding, and accepting. We would like to add *therapeutic*, for that is why we are here. If we have all the foregoing qualities yet are not therapeutic, we are merely paid friends. This point was poignantly made clear by a member of Congress, a recovering alcoholic who almost lost his career because of his drinking. One day when I (Nick) was working the halls of the House of Representatives on behalf of the APA, this member volunteered his admiration for the psychologist who had finally led him to sobriety:

I hated that little son of a bitch. I hated his bald head, his tweed suits, his half glasses, and his whole damn professorial look. I hated him because I felt inferior to the strength this man had in his short, little body. But I kept going to him because he was the only one with the guts to kick my ass. My two previous therapists treated me like a congressman, with deference. It was as if they feared me. Here I was a drunk, and they treated me with awe.

This new psychologist, when I launched into my bullshit denial, he would fix me with an icy stare. The first time, it was preceded by his hope that I was more truthful when I was on the floor of the House than I was being in his office. From then on, it was just the cold stare. That was the coldest look I have ever seen, and I would shiver all over. I knew that I might be fooling me, but I wasn't fooling him. I got to the point where I preferred the truth to that icy stare.

Then I got mad. I was self-destructing with booze and destroying everything around me. He knew it and was going to let me do it.
Here I was the congressman, and this little son of a bitch was going
to let me go down the tubes. Well, I'll show him who's boss. Then in
my anger I realized what the icy stare meant. He was not going to
clean me up; he couldn't. I had to do that myself. But first I had to
quit lying to myself. I am alive today and still in the Congress because
of the sheer guts of that brilliant little man.

Needless to say, this U.S. Representative has profound respect for
psychology, in contrast to most members of Congress, who see psychotherapists as naive dreamers. If there is a bit of ambivalence along
with the admiration in the congressman's tone, we are certain that
our psychologist colleague puts effectiveness ahead of being liked.

Psychotherapists are trained to be accepting and nonconfronta-
tional. To many colleagues, challenging or confronting a patient
means being judgmental, in spite of the fact that the challenges in
substance abuse treatment are strategically purposeful and effective.
Paradoxical intention is a strategy, not a judgment. But even when
a psychotherapist comes to grips with this idea and is determined
to become adept with the procedure, his inherent distaste leads him
to be easily sidetracked.

The tendency to get sidetracked is the most common failing
among psychotherapists who are attempting to overcome their reluctance to appropriately confront an addict. The following two
examples are from actual taped interviews by a therapist we were
supervising. Her interview with the first patient took place before
she had become comfortable with the technique, and she was readily sidetracked.

PATIENT: I guess I'm always tense, but I get really uptight when my
wife starts nagging me. When she is in one of her nagging moods,
she never stops.

THERAPIST: What brings about her nagging?

PATIENT: She gets it from her mother, who is the nag-in-chief. When her mother is visiting us, its nag, nag, nag all day long. When they get tired of nagging each other, they both turn on me. That's when I really get uptight.

THERAPIST: Have you discussed this behavior with your wife?

PATIENT: No, it wouldn't do any good. I just keep it to myself and get uptight.

THERAPIST: (Now totally distracted) Every marriage requires communication. If you do not talk with her about what is bothering you, how will she know?

In the interview with the second patient, conducted after she had gained more experience, she stuck to the problem of alcoholism.

PATIENT: My wife waits until I'm sober, and then she begins to nag me.

THERAPIST: What do you do that makes her want to nag you?

PATIENT: Nothing.

THERAPIST: Nothing?

PATIENT: Well, I'm not doing all the things I let go while I was drinking.

THERAPIST: So in your own way you are sitting back waiting for her to nag you.

PATIENT: Maybe, but her nagging is enough to drive me back to drink.

THERAPIST: Could it be that you are actually provoking her so you have an excuse to drink? You know, we can provoke people by doing nothing.

PATIENT: *(After a long pause)* I hate to think I get her to nagging just so I can have a drink. If I want a drink, why don't I just have a drink?

THERAPIST: Because you are pretending to her and to yourself that you really want to stop drinking, and that you probably could if only she didn't nag you.

PATIENT: That's pretty disgusting.

THERAPIST: Not any more than all of your other ploys we have discussed. As you said, any excuse to have a drink. Your gullible wife believes you when you con her that you'd be sober if she were not such a nag. Your grade is A for alcoholic on this one.

This therapist is a highly skilled social worker who specialized in marital therapy in a private practice that had, unfortunately, dwindled. She was comfortable in the communication theory of marital relationships, and in the first example she retreated into it with the first sidetrack the patient accorded her. By the time she had seen the second patient, she had seen a number of alcoholics and drug addicts and had not only learned to avoid the pitfalls but also was comfortable in outmaneuvering the patient's denial. Her response of giving the patient an "A grade" is one that addicts enjoy. It lets them know with good-natured humor that they not only were clever in their original ploy but also did well in seeing through it.

Good-natured humor is how addicts like to communicate. Such humor is in that brief zone after the second drink and before the third drink begins to produce irritability. The addict tries to bring that ten- to twenty-minute period back with more drinks, resulting eventually in stupor or ugly mood. Addicts are delighted when humor can be achieved naturally, without chemicals. They relate to and accept information dispensed in this manner. The tongue-in-cheek award certificates we present in the group program are appreciated in the same vein.

There are colleagues who regard any kind of tough love to be anathema. There are others who are willing to challenge the addict but are uncomfortable doing so; they consequently often do it in a clumsy fashion. Another social worker we worked with was quite controlling in her personal life. She was not a very well-liked figure in the center because of her constant meddling. For example, she would scour the psychology interns' appointment books to ascertain whether they were seeing enough patients, an activity that was totally outside her province or authority.

To compensate for this overcontrolling style, her usual approach with patients was to bend over backward to be overly accepting. This resulted in her challenge of a patient being done in a clumsy, half-hearted manner. When she tried to challenge her first patient, a thirty-something woman addicted to sleeping pills, the patient stood up and exclaimed, "You remind me of my Jewish mother," whereupon she stormed out of the office. She requested another therapist and was given one who completed the challenge with her in their first session. This patient was uncanny in her assessment of the first attempt to motivate her. Our colleague fortunately had an affable sense of humor. She laughed about it as she concluded, "She sure nailed me." Yet this social worker decided not to work with addicts in the future, probably a wise decision and one that benefited both her and her patients.

INABILITY TO SEE
THE ADDICTIVE PROBLEM

We never cease to be amazed at how many colleagues marry addicts or personality-disordered individuals whose acting out includes multiple addictions. Because they do not have insight into their spouse's behavior, these therapists are blind to manifestations of addiction in their patients. The blindness in their personal lives is replicated in the manner in which they fail to diagnose substance abuse in their patients. Some of them have a need for a spouse or lover they can alternately rescue and berate, leaving them with a kind of power over their partner. In the rescue phase, however, they are among the most enabling of codependents because they can misuse psychological knowledge. Also, colleagues in this role are highly resistive to either their spouses or themselves going into appropriate treatment as an addictive dyad.

One of the most aggressive, resistive addicts we have seen was a woman in her late twenties whose husband, Bill, was a master's-level counselor and the head of a treatment center in town. Pamela was a flagrant borderline personality disorder whose six-foot height, in itself, would have been intimidating to most therapists, even without a husband who not only justified her behavior but also threatened to sue any therapist who diagnosed her to be a substance abuser. Bill told Pamela and the world that she was suffering from bipolar disorder, a diagnosis so outrageously inaccurate that it would have been laughable were it not that every professional in the community ran for cover from this dynamic duo.

Bill demanded and received treatment from their health plan in accordance with his misdiagnosis. Treating Pamela with lithium was not only ludicrous therapeutically but sad in that it prevented her from getting the appropriate treatment. With this couple, denial was a two-way boulevard. The blind spot extended, of course, to all the addicted patients seen in the center of which Bill was the director.

We have had to let go of several very gifted therapists whose spouses were addicts of some sort or had personality disorders combined with substance abuse. No matter how much we tried, we could not help these therapists cut through their denial so long as they were married to their chemically dependent spouses. Two of these, in looking into their denial with patients, decided to enter into codependent programs in our own centers, where they achieved the understanding that led to their dissolving the marriages.

A divorced mother of a full-blown borderline teenager conducted agoraphobia groups for us. She was aware that any phobic who was addicted to alcohol or drugs must first go through a program of abstinence. However, she was never able to spot a chemical abuser, even . when he was glaringly obvious. She would put several in each group, destroying the impact of the phobia program.

We later learned that her husband and father had both been alcoholic, and her daughter was heavily into drugs. Needing to deny the substance abuse in her family resulted in her not seeing it in her patients. The only solution was to have other therapists screen the candidates for her agoraphobia groups.

It is not uncommon for psychotherapists to have had an addicted father or mother. In fact, their family background could well be one of the reasons they went into psychology, hoping to learn something about their parents and their own upbringing. Often such colleagues do very well as psychotherapists. Seldom, however, have we seen them do well with chemically dependent patients. There are exceptions, of course, but they seem to be just that.

PAST DRUG USE

The current generation of psychotherapists grew up in an era when experimentation with drugs during one's youth was very much in vogue. This should not prevent any of them from treating chemical dependency, unless, of course, they have not resolved their feelings about the matter. For most of these colleagues, drug use is something in the past. For others, it is either an ongoing problem of ambivalence, or a continuing problem of use. The kind of brutal honesty required in dealing with hard-core addictions precludes many of these otherwise fine colleagues from treating chemical dependency.

Is it possible to be a social drinker and still treat alcoholics and other addicts? Yes, because social use of alcohol is legal and a familiar behavior readily accorded therapists by their patients. The *illegal* use of drugs is another matter altogether. We acknowledge that there can be social (nonaddictive) use of illegal substances and that such use may be OK as part of one's personal lifestyle, but not while one is attempting to treat hard-core substance abusers. It must be kept in mind that many of our patients are felons, and most have been in trouble with the law. To them, survival is an all-or-nothing, do-or-die issue. For them there is no incremental use, as all use has become abuse. They are putting their lives in our hands, and brutal honesty is required, as these patients are uncanny in discerning the slightest deceit or compromise. They would not admire, respect, and follow a therapist who is breaking the law. As one patient candidly put it, "It's like being an armed robber and finding you're putting your trust in a petty thief." Another patient chimed in, "Yeah, its like being in therapy for heavy-duty nervousness and looking over at your therapist who bites his fingernails. No way, Jose!"

INABILITY TO LEAVE THE PARENTAL ROLE

Therapy, by its very nature, resembles the parent-child relationship. The patient comes to the therapist for help, defining from the onset who is the expert and who is the needy. Many psychotherapists do things to minimize this inherent hierarchy, especially in the newer "constructive" therapies, as they have come to be called. In the treatment of substance abuse, however, something different even from minimizing the parental role is required. The therapist literally, but temporarily, relinquishes the parental role and adopts the role of the child. Specifically, the psychotherapist must begin to talk like an obstinate, rebellious, or manipulative adolescent, which results in the patient's assumption of the traditional doctor's (parental) role. This switch is difficult and even impossible for many therapists to accomplish. The following examples illustrate the parental and the adolescent kinds of therapist response.

1. *The therapist has just looked at the patient's pictures of her children.*

PARENTAL ROLE: Those are beautiful children. I know you love them very much and want to win them back by going clean.

ADOLESCENT ROLE: Those look like great kids, all right. But your husband has probably turned them against you for all time. You'll never win them back. At least having a drink soothes the pain.

2. *The patient has just told how he lost a job with a top accounting firm for regularly drinking his lunch.*

PARENTAL ROLE: You are a good accountant and deserve a top job. Clean up, get another job, and show them you can perform your duties responsibly.

ADOLESCENT ROLE: Haven't you noticed that all accounting firms are stuffy? Who needs it? Screw them. Get a job with one of their competitors, and let them be sorry when you give away their secrets to the new firm.

3. *A heroin-addicted mother has lost custody of her ten-month-old child.*

PARENTAL ROLE: This is a terrible blow. Losing your baby is really hitting bottom. No smack [heroin] is worth losing your baby over. I have confidence that now you'll start on the road to recovery.

ADOLESCENT ROLE: Those damn bureaucratic social workers have no right to take your baby away. And that judge is in cahoots with them. To hell with all of them. Who needs a baby right now, anyway?

This adolescent behavior is so antithetical to what we have learned in training that it is very difficult to pull off. Comfort with the technique grows as you achieve more and more success with the paradox. The first sign that the novice therapist is on the right track is the rapidity with which the patient jumps into the therapist role.

OVERIDENTIFICATION
WITH THE PATIENT

The foregoing section described the therapist's briefly assuming the patient's denial as a therapeutic tool known as the challenge. The psychotherapist using the challenge is very much in charge of the treatment and in no way has really become an adolescent. In contrast, there are psychotherapists with their own unresolved parent-child issues. They go through life in a perpetual antiauthority stance and behave with their patients much like the parent who vicariously lives her own rebelliousness through encouraging her children to rebel. Such parents, and their counterparts among psychotherapists, are not helpful to the process of recovery. Again, denial is of such magnitude in chemical dependency that the patient does not need an incompetent therapist to augment it.

These antiauthority psychotherapists are not rare. When treating adolescents, they form a rapid alliance by siding with the teenager against the parents, the school, and the juvenile courts. They prefer to work with teenagers, and the cheap rapport they establish often fools other psychotherapists into thinking they have a special talent for bonding with teenagers. This kind of therapist eventually finds his way into the treatment of substance abuse because it is the presenting problem with so many teenagers. Eventually he branches out to include adult substance abusers, where he perpetuates the same kind of adolescent rebelliousness.

The message such therapists give is simple but absurd: "You can have your cake and eat it too." The theme of therapy becomes that of beating the system, and not getting caught is the measure of success. This is music to the ears of the chemically dependent patient, and the two, therapist and patient, appear for a time to be making great progress. The illusion soon vanishes, but not before the therapist has had to rescue the patient a number of times from the consequences of addictive behavior.

NARCISSISM

Perhaps the greatest source of countertransference is the therapist's inability to accept a "clean life" as the standard of success for treatment because this high standard is so difficult to achieve. Those who see abstinence as the gold standard have to be able to tolerate more failure than success, a fact that twelve-step programs recognized and accepted decades ago. A predominant lack of success is hurtful to most psychotherapists' narcissism and sense of omnipotence, and colleagues who need a steady stream of narcissistic supplies from compliant and grateful patients should not go into the treatment of chemical dependency.

An alternative, of course, is to redefine the criterion of success. This is exactly what one colleague did, and accordingly claimed a 95 percent success rate with his chemical dependency treatment program. His brochures stated that one year of controlled drinking was rated most satisfactory on his scale; six months was very satisfactory, and ninety days was just satisfactory. Furthermore, controlled drinking was defined as drinking that did not lead to job loss, marital separation, or DUI arrest. Because 95 percent of his patients achieved at least a satisfactory rating (ninety days or more), the therapist claimed this unprecedented level of successful treatment. We were amazed that the profession did not object to this gerrymandered brochure and concluded that countertransference issues are pervasive. Patients and the profession saw what they wanted to see.

Similar, but far less crass, standards for successful outcomes are employed both by many treatment centers and, more disturbing, by research projects. Level of improvement can be defined by the number of relapses in a month, number of binges of two days or more in a three-month period, and so forth. The ratings can be further defined in such ways that most research subjects will demonstrate improvement, even though such improvement falls far short of a standard based on abstinence.

SUBSTANCE ADDICTION

In the parlance of the health professions, the polite word for addicted is *impaired*. There is no doubt that there are psychotherapists who are themselves chemically dependent and thus less than fully effective in their work. Some even attempt to treat addicts, with predictable results. Most overly identify with the patient and thus are unable to proceed with the tough love that addicts need. A chemically dependent therapist, remembering his own discomfort when he was unable to get a fix, is putty in the hands of a strung-out addict. He is willing to give the addict the store. In contrast, some impaired psychotherapists are punitive and rejecting, as if to repudiate their own addiction.

It would seem obvious that an addicted psychotherapist is disqualified as a therapist for other substance abusers. Yet the field of chemical dependency has spawned a surprising subculture of addiction counselors who go on planned binges. They supposedly remain squeaky clean between these monthly binges. We first heard of this behavior when the director of one program confided that he saves five days a month to go on a chemical binge. His bag was alcohol plus cocaine, and he would drive to a distant city, rent a hotel room, and spend five days doing nothing but drinking and snorting. He would have just enough booze and coke for the prescribed period, and at the end of this he would sleep it off, shave several days of beard, otherwise clean up, and then drive home. He claimed "This really helps."

We thought this to be an isolated or rare instance, but then it came to our attention that one of our own clinical managers was disappearing for three days at a time while he abused the designer drug Ecstasy. Before we made this discovery, we had had to fire this man for unsatisfactory performance, undoubtedly resulting in part from his drug behavior. A short time later, the prevalence of this subculture made itself surprisingly apparent to us:

One Sunday morning, I (Nick) was called by a colleague, Cyril, who said he needed to go to the emergency room but needed a sympathetic colleague with staff privileges at that hospital to accompany him. I did not know this colleague well but had met him on a number of occasions. He was a well-known therapist in one of San Francisco's better rehabilitation programs.

I made a house call, and found this man, who was in his late thirties, in bad shape. He was tremulous, malnourished, and disheveled. I drove Cyril to the ER and remained with him for a time. Cyril had been on an alcohol and heroin binge, something he did monthly. This time the binge did not end on the fifth day as it was supposed to do. Rather, it continued, leaving Cyril in bad shape. He expressed gratitude for the help and said, "I've got to hang on to you."

It developed that he asked me to be his therapist. It seemed that Cyril was part of a group of addiction counselors who went on planned, "controlled" binges monthly. The therapist with whom he was paired, stated Cyril, "is not doing a very good job for me." Hence, he asked me to take that role.

Because I questioned the wisdom of this entire procedure, Cyril offered to hold a meeting of the colleagues involved to explore the usefulness of what seemed to me an oxymoron—controlled binges. I went to the meeting expecting to see half a dozen colleagues and was shocked to find twenty-three addiction therapists in attendance. They were determined to convince me that the presumably therapeutic use of the controlled binge has become a widespread and legitimate phenomenon.

Our informal follow-up of this group revealed a disaster for those engaging in the behavior. We cannot help but conclude that in the months this practice went on, and before these counselors one by one lost their jobs, their patients were shortchanged in the quality and veracity of their treatment.

The illusion for these colleagues is the same as that for health professionals of all specialties: I know too much to get addicted.

BIAS IN FAVOR OF THEORY OVER EXPERIENCE

Academically based clinicians are overwhelmingly behavioral or cognitive-behavioral in their approach to the treatment of addictions. They are insistent that chemical dependency is learned behavior that can be unlearned, and for years they have waged war against the disease model of addiction as if it were the Great Satan. We are troubled by well-trained researchers who underplay and even discount genetics and physiology. They are strongly determined to prove the validity of controlled drinking, a drive that seems fueled more by theoretical considerations than by concern for the patient.

Behavioral therapy has contributed enormously to our knowledge, and it does not need to validate controlled drinking in order to justify its preeminent role in psychotherapy. It is curious that so many therapists ignore so much biological evidence to demonstrate something that is irrelevant. Perhaps it is because so many prominent behavioral researchers have stuck their necks out in the past on the issue of controlled drinking that it has now become more of a religious tenet than an aspect of scientific theory. We use behavioral techniques extensively in our work with chemical dependency, but we do so in the service of achieving abstinence, not the elusive controlled drinking. Behavior modification is just as real within the context of certain biological conditions. For example, a child who is born deaf will learn to communicate differently than the hearing newborn. This in no way obviates the importance of learning theory.

Given the fact that controlled drinking is tenuous at best, we would be delighted to see all of this energy going toward the research elicitation of the effectiveness of behavioral treatment within the realities of the mounting genetic and physiological evidence. There are many conditions with a strong biological component for which behavioral therapy is nonetheless a necessary treatment.

TWELVE-STEP BIAS

As was previously noted, most substance abuse counselors who are themselves recovering look down on their colleagues who have never been addicted. They believe they know the process from the inside, having earned their stripes through addiction and subsequent recovery. They feel justified in proffering their recovery as a substitute for formal counselor training and credentials. We admire the dedication and effectiveness of these counselors, but object to an attitude that not only excludes qualified therapists but renders an overly zealous appraisal of the outcomes of twelve-step recovery programs. This zeal has produced more faith than research.

Bill Wilson was emphatic that a recovering addict must help others to sobriety without ever being compensated for it. It is this activity that strengthens the recovery process, for by helping others, the recovering addict is helping herself. Bill cautioned that if the day ever came when the recovery movement was paid for its services, the corruption of the twelve-step movement would begin like a rapidly spreading infection. If Bill were alive today, he would be shocked at the legion of paid counselors who are themselves recovering. He would point to those who believe in their own controlled binges as a manifestation of that corruption. He would be appalled at the number of recovering counselors who for the sake of a paycheck compromise the twelve-step movement by working in slipshod programs of dubious effectiveness. When we remind our recovering colleagues who look down on us of Bill's prophetic exhortations, they fall silent. We have never had to justify ourselves to our patients, who are well aware of our dedication and commitment to their recovery.

THE EXQUISITE COUNTERTRANSFERENCE

A discussion of countertransference would not be complete without addressing the countertransferences that might be inherent in the abstinence model. We have noted one above: the bias that only a therapist in recovery is suited to treat chemical dependency. This has manifested itself in the frequent disparagement to a patient of her nonaddicted, not-recovering therapist so as to undermine her confidence in the treatment. It is common for twelve-step therapists to refrain from referring to therapists who are not in recovery, often depriving the patient of an available, helpful resource. Other biases also exist, but in noting them we also insist that in spite of the countertransferences found in the twelve-step model, such programs are among the most effective. We have chosen a paradox and an oxymoron, *exquisite countertransference*, to indicate that a bias that only abstinence works is ultimately helpful to the patient. Often more revivalist than scientific, the twelve-step approach has been developed, applied, and championed by those who have hit bottom and have found the road back to sobriety. Their zeal often stems from the fact that they must help others achieve abstinence to maintain their own sobriety—a form of countertransference by virtue of is compelling nature.

The zeal to help others is a fire in the belly that results in a dedication seldom seen in the usual low-key, nine-to-five practice of psychotherapy. This dedication makes the therapist available at all hours of the day and night, often "baby sitting" the most disgusting aspects of inebriation and drug reaction. In its extreme it results in a therapist becoming what is known in AA as an "AA junkie," going overboard in rejecting any approach that does not fit his rigid reinterpretation of the twelve-step model and through this countertransference doing more harm than good.

In spite of these limitations, decades of experience has led us to conclude that for the overwhelming number of individuals benefiting from the abstinence movement, this exquisite countertransference is a positive force.

It is now time to see how all of the issues we have discussed are demonstrated in an actual first interview with a difficult patient manifesting severe polydrug use.

Appendix

A Structured First Session
Kevin's Cacophony

Kevin was a single man, twenty-eight years old, who arrived at my (Nick's) waiting room shortly after the noon hour and without an appointment. He was in a state of severe drug withdrawal, very disheveled; he demanded to be seen.

I had just begun my first appointment of a completely scheduled afternoon. The receptionist knew it was my practice to see such a needy patient as soon as I had finished with my scheduled patients, and she informed Kevin that he could be seen at five o'clock. However, aware of his extreme discomfort, she offered him the option of being seen immediately in the medical drop-in clinic. He abruptly refused, insisted that he see Dr. Cummings, and spent the afternoon in the waiting room exhibiting a variety of high-anxiety behaviors. He was either pacing or in yoga or meditation positions, desperately searching for tension relief. If he was not drinking at the water cooler, he was in the men's room with frequent urination. His perpetual sighing, grunting, and grimacing were considerably disruptive in a waiting room filled with the psychotherapy patients of a number of colleagues.

THE FIRST SESSION

Once in my office, Kevin dismissed the offer to sit down and talked as he continued to pace. Before I could say another word, Kevin rebuked me in advance.

KEVIN: Don't ask me how you can be of help. Man, can't you see I'm strung w-a-a-y out? I need some kind of fix. I'm hurting something real bad. That's what you can do for me. I don't want any of your fancy therapist talk.

THERAPIST: What are you on?

KEVIN: Everything. Everything and anything. It's gotten all mixed up, and nothing I take brings me down. I just keep getting more strung out. You know what I mean? I've gone to several doctors, and they've given me stuff, tranquilizers and things. They don't help. They tell me you're the man. That's why I came to see you.

This patient is what I have called a cafeteria addict, someone who engages in an extreme form of polydrug abuse, taking any chemical offered, staying constantly stoned, but bragging that he is not addicted to any particular substance.

THERAPIST: With all that, you may belong in detox.

KEVIN: Man, get off it. I've been in detox, and detox, and detox. I clean up and then get strung out all over again. I need a new menu, understand what I'm saying?

THERAPIST: Yes, but I don't do that. Once you've got the monkey, I've never seen the perfect high. Know what I mean?

KEVIN: (Half expecting my response) Yeah, yeah. What else is new?

THERAPIST: What are your main bags?

KEVIN: Booze. Smack [heroin]. Nose candy [cocaine], but I usually mainline it. And lots and lots of booze. And then when I'm with people, I take whatever they're taking, from quaaludes to LSD. It don't make much difference what it is. But it's getting harder and harder to party, 'cause I just get sick. It used to make me real mellow; not any more.

THERAPIST: How long since it made you real mellow?

With this last question I am trying to determine not only the severity of the abuse but also the chronicity. Detoxification with the cafeteria addict is quite problematic, to say nothing of the psychotherapy.

The patient did not immediately answer the question. He launched into his history in a manner that only a "trained patient" can do. Kevin obviously had been through this before, to no avail. It was almost cynical the way he told me who he was, as if to merely fulfill the perfunctory so that he could get his miracle prescription from "the man." Yet everything he said rang true. He had obviously tapped into my reputation in the drug culture of San Francisco, and on some suppressed inner level he was hoping for a different life.

Kevin was born in Indianapolis, an only child. While still in high school he began to drink heavily in the afternoons, often passing out at the dinner table with his face in his soup bowl. His parents would laugh, having no idea of their son's drinking. His mother would say, "Kevin, stop clowning." He voiced real contempt for his working-class parents, who he said were "out to lunch." He graduated from Purdue University as a teacher. On the third day of his first week of teaching, he panicked, went out to the beltway that surrounds Indianapolis, and without returning to his (parents') home, hitchhiked to San Francisco with just the clothes he was wearing and what he had in his pockets. He was introduced to drugs, and within a few weeks he was living a lifestyle in which he was never sober or free from chemicals. He also confided, as if to solidify his status as a severe case, that all through college he was very isolated. His social life consisted mainly of returning to his parents' house on weekends and going to skid row with a couple of bottles of cheap wine, where he could get himself and the alcoholics intoxicated and then perform fellatio on them.

KEVIN: I'm pretty bad, eh? Am I the worst case you've ever seen?

THERAPIST: Sorry, you're way in the back of the line for that title. In fact, you're still alert enough to dodge the question. When was the last time you could say you were mellow?

Here I have not only challenged the patient's evasion but also given him hope by slipping in sideways the fact that I have seen far, far worse.

KEVIN: (*Subdued and no longer arrogant and demanding, he finally sits down.*) About three years. (*Long pause*) You're not going to give me a paper fix [prescription], are you? Some guys I know that you treated warned me that you can be a real hard-ass.

THERAPIST: And you still wanted to see me? Why?

KEVIN: Maybe it's time I really cleaned up.

This comment represents another form of denial. Even if the desire to be drug free is real, it is on a very submerged level and not relevant here. The patient's immediate thought is that by being clean for just a little while, he will enjoy taking drugs but will not be addicted. His hope, of course, is that I will see him as sincere and deserving.

THERAPIST: So you can get back to the halcyon days when you could get mellow instead of more strung out?

KEVIN: Something like that.

THERAPIST: No way, Jose. I don't know how to do that for you. The only way I know to get mellow once you've got a "Jones" [addicted] is to go the natural way, to learn how to get a natural high by living without drugs. Otherwise, once a Jones, always a Jones. You're nowhere near ready to go clean.

KEVIN: I could, but why should I? *(He stands up again and begins pacing rapidly about the room.)* I'm not really as bad as I look. I put on a show because I know shrinks won't see you without an appointment unless you're real bad. I really put on a great show for you, didn't I?

The patient has switched forms of denial. He is no longer a hopeless addict who needs a miracle fix from "the man." He now needs no one at all. He is telling me to get lost. He is angry because he is not getting his way.

THERAPIST: Yes, Kevin. You put your face in the soup bowl. Do you expect me to believe you're just showing off? That way I'd be stupid like your parents, and you could have contempt for me, too. Get your face out of the soup, sit down, and level with me. This clinic has already closed, and I'm still here listening to your crap. If you can't level with me, I'm going home.

I now have a feel for this patient, and I know how far I can go in confronting him. With defiant addicts, you can be as bombastic as the patient, and the patient will secretly admire you for cutting through the verbiage and thus demonstrating that you are stronger than the patient's addiction. Note that all along with Kevin I have liberally used the language of the street. This informs him that this interview is for real and not a pushover with a well-meaning but naive do-gooder.

KEVIN: Fuck you! You can't do that. You're supposed to help me. You're no shrink; you're a son of a bitch.

He launches into a string of epithets, berating me and becoming more vituperative with each exclamation. Finally he runs out of bile, sputters to a stop somewhat like a car running out of gas, and falls limp into his chair. He is silent for ten minutes or more.

It would be a mistake to become so inundated by Kevin's cacophony that his very significant move toward compliance is overlooked: he sat down as instructed. This is only a partial compliance, for he fell silent and had not begun to level as he had been admonished to do. But with a defiant patient this partial compliance is an important signal that the therapist is connecting.

At this point the patient could go forward toward further compliance or rekindle his defiance. The interview had reached the critical stage, and I could not back down. Timing was of the essence, and Kevin, still silent, gave the opening as he began to stand up again. Before he could get more than halfway out of his chair, I made the defining move.

THERAPIST: Enough, Kevin. If you stand up you can just walk yourself out of my office. If you stay, you've got to stay in your seat and level with me. I've run out of down time. It's either up time or it's out with you.

Kevin slumped back into his chair. He glared at me for about a minute, then his countenance softened. He had made the decision to play it the way I wanted, at least for the time being. Note, however, that this is still a far cry from his actually getting into treatment. It is merely the other half of the first compliant step.

KEVIN: OK. You really are living up to your reputation as a nononsense psychologist. (He is smiling nervously, but his speech is more that of a college graduate. I follow suit and abandon the street talk.) I had two purposes in coming here. First, I was hoping you had the ultimate drug. The other . . . (long pause) is that I need to be recertified as emotionally unfit for work so I can continue to receive my welfare check.

THERAPIST: You said recertified. Are you already on welfare? Why don't you go back to the doctor who certified you originally?

KEVIN: He got busted for being a script doctor.

As mentioned elsewhere in this book, the term *script doctor* refers to a physician who writes prescriptions for addicts, either for money or because of a personal addiction that renders the physician overly identified with the patient's severe craving. Often it is both. Kevin explained that this physician had been signing his welfare certification annually; the physician's arrest put Kevin's eligibility for welfare seriously into question.

KEVIN: I was told I would have to get recertified by someone with an impeccable reputation with the welfare department. My social worker even said, "Someone like Dr. Nick Cummings." She mentioned a couple of other names, but I remembered yours because I had heard of you from several friends you treated.

THERAPIST: Are these friends now clean and sober?

KEVIN: Yes. (*Long pause*) Is it true you only work with addicts who want to clean up? Would you work with me?

THERAPIST: No, because you are not ready to go that route. You would be looking for a period free from drugs long enough so that you could recapture the original euphoria before drugs became a necessity just to get through each day.

KEVIN: I'm not saying you're right, but would that be so terrible?

THERAPIST: You're back on the con, Kevin. You've tried that route several times before. You know it can't work because once you resumed even a little drug behavior you were back to full speed within days.

I followed with a little more psychoeducational information here, but briefly and only enough to reinforce what Kevin knew experientially.

KEVIN: I know you're right. And I know it's time I cleaned up and turned my life around. In my more honest moments I say that to myself. Wouldn't it be great to get that monkey off my back? I'm really hurting right now. I don't want to just keep going through this over and over again.

THERAPIST: Oh, I'm not so sure. Alcohol and drugs really work for you, so don't get carried away. You probably deserve to take one more shot at being clean and sober for a couple of weeks so you can get back to being high without being strung out.

KEVIN: Yeah, but you won't help me do that.

THERAPIST: So what! There are plenty of other therapists in town. Ask your social worker for the other two names you've forgotten. Or better yet, ask your wigged-out friends who the doctor is who's carrying them.

Here I'm using a type of paradoxical intention in which the therapist repeats out loud what the patient is saying inwardly. This prompts the oppositional patient, of which an addict is a prime example, to inadvertently take the role of the psychotherapist.

KEVIN: But I'm getting sick of living that way. Some of my wigged-out friends look awful. They're not high anymore. They just need drugs so they can breathe.

THERAPIST: But you're smarter than they are. You're a college graduate. You'll figure out how to be the first addict to beat the inevitable slide to oblivion. Come on, Kevin. You've already got a plan.

KEVIN: Yeah, and it's a lousy plan. It's never worked before. Why should it work this time?

THERAPIST: Just fine-tune it. It's worth at least one more try. Come on, Kevin, you know you can make it work. Even the attempt is preferable to working with a hard-ass like me. You've already seen I have no mercy.

KEVIN: No, no. I want to work with you. I want to become clean and sober. I know it will take time. But I'm hurting pretty badly. Can I come back tomorrow?

THERAPIST: Absolutely not! You are nowhere near ready to give up your chemicals.

KEVIN: (*Obviously annoyed*) How can you be so sure?

THERAPIST: I've treated hundreds of addicts. I have a real feel for when a person is ready.

KEVIN: (*In a shrill voice, openly annoyed*) Are you never wrong?

THERAPIST: I make one mistake every ten years, and I've already made one for this decade.

KEVIN: (*Pleading in a shrill voice*) What do I have to do to convince you? What? What?

THERAPIST: (*After a couple of minutes of silent but obvious reflection*) Well, maybe there is a way, but I doubt it. Kevin, what is the longest time in the past six months that you've been able to go without any chemical of any kind: alcohol, drugs, illicit or prescription? I mean absolutely nothing.

KEVIN: About three days.

THERAPIST: Well, I'm still skeptical, mind you. But if you were to go seventy-two hours with nothing—squeaky clean—I think I would be convinced you mean it this time. But both of us know how unlikely you are to even attempt this.

I have ascertained the optimal length of the assignment: for Kevin to go seventy-two hours without chemicals is doable yet difficult enough to give him a sense of accomplishment. Kevin grabbed the offer after it was carefully explained that he would be eligible to call for an appointment only after the clean and sober seventy-two hours had transpired.

Having inaugurated a bonding through tough love, I now augmented it with a dose of well-deserved compassion.

THERAPIST: I know how much you are hurting, Kevin, and I admire your guts in undertaking this task of proving I'm wrong. I don't want you to say you were not treated fairly. So I'll call you at midnight tonight to see how you're doing. OK?

KEVIN: (*Astounded*) You will?

THERAPIST: Yes, at midnight and at four in the morning, too. I know you're going to have a rough night. I'm still skeptical, but I want to make sure you're all right. I can help talk you through some of this. If you make it through the night, I'll call you three times tomorrow. And we'll continue this schedule throughout the seventy-two hours. If you relapse, as I expect you will, it's good-bye. Find another patsy.

Ordinarily I space my calls every three hours. I modified this with Kevin because I wanted to let him hurt as much as would be tolerable. I was mindful that Kevin was being motivated largely by pain.

KEVIN: (*Even more astounded*) I think that will really help.

THERAPIST: One more thing before you go. Do you have a friend who has never been addicted or who is recovering who could sit with you the next seventy-two hours?

KEVIN: (*After some reflection*) Yes, Elaine would do that for me. She is a Jesus freak and has been trying to convert me for two years. She would be delighted to see me sober up.

THERAPIST: Have her call me this evening, as I have certain instructions that will help her help you through this. OK?

Kevin agrees, and after carefully reviewing what is now a therapeutic contract, the session ends.

THE AFTERMATH

Kevin succeeded in remaining drug free throughout the seventy-two hours. I called him three times every night and three times every day. I would listen to Kevin describe his withdrawal and then relay to him what he might expect in the four hours before I called him again. This tends to take the edge off the terror, as the patient knows what to expect. At about the sixtieth hour I was able to tell Kevin that his withdrawal had crested and that he would begin to feel better bit by bit. Each time I called I also spoke with Elaine, whose own tension was building up as the hours progressed.

Four hours before the allotted time had transpired, Kevin called to make his appointment. I told him that he would not be given an appointment until the seventy-two hours had fully transpired without his having resorted to drugs or alcohol. Kevin became angry and called me unreasonable.

I retorted that I had already been around that track. He had made it through sixty-eight hours but was afraid he could not hold out any longer: he would get his appointment, do drugs, and then come to the appointment for which he was ineligible. He insisted I was unreasonable, cursed me, and hung up the phone.

However, he did call at the seventy-second hour, proudly announcing he was clean and sober, and claiming his second appointment. He was told to come right to the office. By this time I knew

Kevin would succeed, so to fully reward him I had saved some time so that I would be able to see him immediately.

At the second appointment I ate crow for a while, then began the paradoxical challenge that would prepare Kevin to go through a six-month outpatient program for which sobriety was the criterion for continuance and the goal for the rest of his life.

THERAPIST: You did real well, Kevin. I'm so proud of you that I'm delighted to be wrong about your ability to stay clean for seventy-two hours.

PATIENT: Now what? Do I get something to get me through the next three or four weeks?

THERAPIST: Kevin, I just knew you would not really be ready to go clean. See, already you're talking about getting script (prescription). I've seen it before. You got through the seventy-two hours dreaming about the pot of drugs at the end of that rainbow.

PATIENT: That's not fair. You're jumping to conclusions again.

THERAPIST: No, I've just been around this track too often. You're not ready.

PATIENT: I'm ready, damn you!

THERAPIST: To go into a program of abstinence for six months? Who are you kidding, me, yourself, or both of us?

PATIENT: I'm serious. Already I feel better in just seventy-two hours. I know it's time to go the mile—you know, clean up my life.

THERAPIST: Well, Kevin, I'm really going to sock it to you this time. If you go a week squeaky clean you get another appointment to get you started in the six-month program. If you can't go one week, you'll never make the six months.

Kevin agreed, called at the end of seven days, and was given his preliminary session in which the group structure, rules, and expectations were presented. He had been clean and sober over ten days by his third session and eagerly accepted all conditions for entering the group program.

Kevin graduated from the program—early in the course of which he had obtained a job—and remained in recovery. He understood relapse prevention and always made an appointment to come in whenever stress in his life was threatening his recovery. He participated in both Alcoholics Anonymous (AA) and Narcotics Anonymous (NA), and continued to talk with me within his own mind. Whenever he did not obtain an answer, he knew it was time to come and see me.

I first saw Kevin in 1967 and followed him during the more than three decades since, through his marriage, the birth and rearing to adulthood of his two sons and a daughter, and a successful career from which he is now retired.[1] We chose this case because it demonstrates the power and importance of the first session with a substance abuser. Kevin had conned eight psychotherapists prior to seeing me, and I was to have been the ninth.

Throughout the thirty years, I saw him whenever he needed to come in, and never once has he relapsed. Repeatedly Kevin marveled out loud how he was challenged to turn his whole life around in a session in which he had expected to deceive yet another therapist, which would have enabled him to continue his life of chemical dependency.

Note

1. For a fuller description of the subsequent, intermittent sessions with Kevin that followed his six-month group program, see Cummings, N. A. (1991). Brief, intermittent therapy throughout the life cycle. In C. S. Austad & W. H. Berman (Eds.), *Psychotherapy in managed care: The optimal use of time and resources* (pp. 35–45). Washington, DC: APA Books.

Suggested Readings

Bloom, F. E., Lazerson, A., & Hofstader, L. (1985). *Brain, mind and behavior.* New York: Freeman.

Brick, J., & Erickson, C. K. (1998). *Drugs, the brain, and behavior.* Binghamton, NY: Haworth Press.

Brown, S. (1995). *Treating alcoholism: A volume in current techniques.* San Francisco: Jossey-Bass.

Carlson, N. R. (1986). *Physiology of behavior* (3rd ed.). Boston: Allyn & Bacon.

Cummings, N. A. (1991). Inpatient versus outpatient treatment of substance abuse: Recent developments in the controversy. *Contemporary Family Therapy, 13,* 507–520.

Cummings, N. A., & Sayama, M. (1995). *Focused psychotherapy: A casebook of brief, intermittent psychotherapy throughout the life cycle.* New York: Brunner/Mazel.

Dobzhansky, T., Ayala, F. J., Stebbins, G. L., & Valentine, J. W. (1977). *Evolution.* New York: Freeman.

Goldberg, S. (1986). *Clinical neuroanatomy made ridiculously simple.* Miami: MedMaster.

Holum, J. R. (1983). *Elements of general and biological chemistry.* New York: Wiley.

White, R. K., & Wright, D. G. (1999). *Addiction intervention: Strategies to motivate treatment-seeking behavior.* Binghamton, NY: Haworth Press.

The Authors

Nicholas A. Cummings, Ph.D., Sc.D., is president of the Foundation for Behavioral Health, chairman of the Nicholas and Dorothy Cummings Foundation, Inc., and distinguished professor at the University of Nevada, Reno. He is a former president of the American Psychological Association. He is the founding president of the four campuses of the California School of Professional Psychology and chief psychologist (retired) for Kaiser Permanente, San Francisco. Cummings served as executive director of the Mental Research Institute in Palo Alto, California. He is the founding president of the National Academies of Practice, Washington, D.C. He also founded the American Managed Behavioral Healthcare Association and the National Council of Schools of Professional Psychology. After practicing for a number of years as a master's-level psychotherapist, he received his doctorate (1958) from Adelphi University, New York.

Janet L. Cummings, Psy.D., is president of the Nicholas and Dorothy Cummings Foundation, Inc., and a member of the clinical adjunct faculty at the University of Nevada, Reno. Formerly she was staff psychologist for American Biodyne (now Magellan Behavioral Care). Before becoming a psychologist, Cummings earned degrees in genetics and in linguistics. She received her doctorate (1992) from Wright State University School of Professional Psychology, Ohio.

Index

Death: from overdose, 105–106; from speedballing, 67
Deceit. *See* Denial; Lying, conning, manipulating
Delancy Street, 171
Delirium tremens, 96
Dementia, 71, 73–74, 96
Demerol, 57–58. *See also* Opiates
Denial: as cause of failure to diagnosis, 1–2, 17–18, 79; countering, by motivating patients, 115–117, 119–120, 147–170; cultural differences and, 16; disguised disclosures and, 128–130; expressions of, in first session, 128–131; family's, 19–23; of foodaholics, 76; the games of, 171–201; hitting bottom and, 148–151; mechanisms of, 17–18; in narcotic addiction, 58–59; obstinacy and, 151–152; perfectionism and, 198–201; power of, 100; as psychological phenomenon, 26; therapist's collusion in, 79, 148, 182–184, 226–242; ubiquitous nature of, 1–2, 45, 86–87, 143, 151. *See also* Lying, conning, manipulating
Denial, confronting, 4, 243–253; about blackouts, 167–170; by labeling of games, 171–201; by mobilizing rage, 163–167; by motivational strategies, 115–117, 119–120, 147–170; with paradoxical strategies, 152–170; therapists' reluctance in, 226–230; with threat of loss, 131–143, 152
Depressants. *See* Central nervous system depressants
Depression, 38; in alcohol users, 55–56; in amphetamine users, 48; in cocaine users, 46–47; self-medication of, 144–145; suicide risk in, 145; treatment of, 144–145
Der Stunken relationship, 204–205
Designer drugs, 34, 62–64; mechanisms and effects of, 63, 64; names of, 62; typical users of, 63, 64
Detoxification, drugless, 10–11, 113–115; duration of, 114; for heroin addiction, 114–115, 118; psychotherapist's role in, 114–115, 123. *See also* Substitution; Withdrawal
Detrich, C., 171
Dextroamphetamine, 48

Diabetes, 113, 177
Diagnosis of enabling versus sincere family members, 21–22
Diagnosis of substance abuse: casual asides and, 128–129; error rate in, 79–80; failure of, biases and, 15–25; failure of, countertransference and, 230–232; failure of, reasons for, 1–2; false-positive, 79–100; in first session, 79–100; importance of correct, 1–3; issues in, 127–131; presenting problems for, 33–76, 84–100; psychological misdiagnosis versus, 2, 33, 79; signposts for making, 87–100; trouble as indicator for, 84–100
Diagnostic scales, 128–131
Differentiation, failure of, 96–97
Dipsomania, 82
Disease model, 112, 113, 224, 239–240. *See also* Abstinence
Dissociative anesthetics, 64–65; typical users of, 65
Dolls, 51. *See also* Barbiturates
Dopamine (DA): amphetamines and, 47; cocaine and, 45; gamma-hydroxybutyrate and, 63; in older adults, 74
Doriden, 53
Double bind-paradox combination, 161–162
Downers, 49–60; amphetamines and, 48–49; depressant type of, 49–57; opiate type of, 49, 57–60; types of, 49
Driver's license: court-ordered therapy for restoration of, 139; suspension of, 88–89
Driving under the influence (DUI): denial in face of, 18, 159–160, 189; lack of charges, in benzodiazepine users, 50, 51; as presenting problem of alcoholics, 57; as sign of addiction, 87–88; social attitudes about, 223
Drop outs: hallucinogen use in, 60; inhalant use and, 66
Drug alerts, 68
Drug classes, 45–67; addiction to substitute drugs within, 39, 45, 107, 192–195; brain cell alterations and, 41–42; environmental influences on preference for, 38–40; importance of, 24; prevalence of abuse by, 27

game in, 186, 187; substitution
approach to, 107, 194; typical, 75;
woe-is-me game in, 175
Forgetfulness, 51
Frazzled nerves, as presenting problem, 1
Free clinics, 171
Freebasing, 45
Freud, S., 96
Friends, loss of, 91, 92

G

Gambling, compulsive, 44, 194, 209
Games, 170, 171–201; blame, 172,
179–180; defined, 172; feeling,
181–182; file card, 190–192; insight,
182–184; musical chairs, 192–195;
origins of, as therapeutic intervention, 171; perfectionism and,
198–201; rescue, 177–179; rubber
yardstick, 185–186; special person,
195–198; value of labeling, 171–172;
vending machine, 188–189; victim,
175–177; woe-is-me, 172–175
Games People Play (Berne), 171
Gamma-aminobutyric acid (GABA)
system, 49, 50, 51
Gamma-hydroxybutyrate (GHB), 63
Garcia, J., 61
Gasoline milk, 148–149
Gay men and lesbians, 80–81, 180
Gender: amphetamine use and, 47–48;
choice of drugs and, 45
Genetic factors, 35–36, 74, 113, 239,
240
Geropsychology, 71
Glutamate receptors, 64
Glutethimide (Doriden), 53
Grandiosity, 46, 47
Grass, 61. *See also* Marijuana
Grateful Dead, 61
Gratitude, 138
Group therapy, 113, 120–123; for bor-
derline patients, 145; for codepen-
dents, 219–220; duration of, 121;
frequency of, 121; games used in,
171–172, 175–176; group size in, 121,
122; individual therapy versus,
120–121; intensive (IOP), 119–120,
122–123; prerequisites for, 123;
requirements for, 121–122, 123; typical, described, 121–123

Guilt feelings, of family members who
are not enablers, 22

H

H, 57. *See also* Heroin
Hair pulling, 49, 95
Hallucinations, in amphetamine users,
95–96
Hallucinogens (psychedelic drugs), 9,
57, 60–62; types and names of, 60;
typical users of, 60–61, 145
Health insurance status, 27
Hendrix, J., 105
Heroin, 57, 58–60; dilution of, 28;
names for, 57; overdose of, 28,
105–106; stimulants combined with,
58; synthetic, 62, 63; withdrawal
from, 59, 60, 114–115, 118
Heroin addiction/addicts, 57, 58–60;
alcohol abuse by, 56–57; as dealers,
28; demographics of, 58; drugless
detoxification of, 114–115, 118;
methadone treatment of, 107–108;
prenatal, 37, 38; presentation of,
58–60; prevalence of, 27, 58; term of,
198; tolerance stages of, 104–106;
Valium use by, 51, 59
Heroin chic, 58
Higher power, 138, 151, 225
Hitting bottom, 100, 148–151; motivat-
ing patients who haven't, 115–117,
120, 147–170; relative definition of,
148–150
Holier-than-thou attitude, 201
Homesickness, 56
Hophead, as first-order word, 198
Horse, 57. *See also* Heroin
Hospitalization. *See* Inpatient treatment
Housewife addicts, 51–52, 60, 213–214
Housewife's stress syndrome, 214
Humanistic therapy, 93
Humility, 225
Humor, 4, 11, 229, 230
Husbands, as enablers, 204, 207–208

I

Idaho, 62
Immigrants, alcohol use and, 54–55
Impaired physicians, 30–31, 213
Impaired psychotherapists, 213,
237–239

DATE DUE

OCT 0 1 2003		
OCT 01 2004		
APR 1 8 2006		
JUN 0 2 2006		
JUN 0 2 2006		
GAYLORD		PRINTED IN U.S.A